Positive Alternatives Exclusion

The problem of school exclusion is one of the major educational issues of our time, responsible for the loss of hundreds and thousands of school days every year, with the numbers of children and young people barred from participation in our schools increasing annually.

This book looks at what schools can do to build more harmonious communities and engage students – particularly those at risk of exclusion – more productively in all areas of school life. It describes the Positive Alternatives to School Exclusion Project, a partnership research study, based at the School of Education, University of Cambridge. This was a multi-phase (primary, secondary, FE) empirical study of the thinking underlying what schools and colleges were currently doing to foster inclusion, and to reduce and prevent exclusion.

The book provides detailed case studies of the approaches and strategies being adopted in a variety of different frameworks, drawn from the case studies, which can be used by practitioners working in other settings to support their own reflection and development work. Particular importance is placed, throughout the book, on valuing the domain of personal experience in the life of the school community. This theme is explored in detail, drawing on the case study material, suggesting ways in which it might become a priority focus of further development work in schools.

Paul Cooper, Mary Jane Drummond, Susan Hart, Jane Lovey and **Colleen McLaughlin** are all members of staff at the School of Education, University of Cambridge.

Positive Alternatives to Exclusion

Paul Cooper,
Mary Jane Drummond,
Susan Hart, Jane Lovey
and Colleen McLaughlin

London and New York

First published 2000 by RoutledgeFalmer
11 New Fetter Lane, London EC4P 4EE

Simultaneously published in the USA and Canada
by RoutledgeFalmer
29 West 35th Street, New York, NY 10001

RoutledgeFalmer is an imprint of the Taylor & Francis Group

Typeset in Garamond by
Curran Publishing Services Ltd
Printed and bound in Great Britain by
TJ International Ltd, Padstow, Cornwall

British Library Cataloguing in Publication Data
A catalogue record for this book is available from the British Library

Library of Congress Cataloging in Publication Data
Positive alternatives to exclusion/Paul Cooper . . . [et al.] .
240 pp. 13.8 x 21.6 mm
Includes bibliographical references and index.
1. Mainstreaming in education–Great Britain–Case studies. 2. Inclusive
    education–Great Britain–Case studies. I. Cooper, Paul, 1955–
LC1203.G7 P68 2000
371.9'046—dc21   00-028197

ISBN 0–415–19758–9

Contents

Illustrations

Figures

Tables

Boxes

Acknowledgements

This book is the product of a collaborative process that took place over nearly three years. To name all of the people who gave time and energy to this process would require a document that would double the length of the book. What must be said, however, is that without the generous investment of time, energy and enthusiasm of many people this book and the research project on which it is based would never have materialised. In particular we would like to thank the staff and students of the five schools and the FE college that were the focus of the research. First we would like to thank all of these people for inviting us into their institutions and for making us feel so welcome. We would also like to thank the many adults and students who gave up their time to fill in questionnaires, participate in interviews and engage in other research activities. Without their patience and candour there would be no research study. Special thanks are also due to those staff and students who were our research collaborators, and who engaged with us in data gathering and analysis, and in disseminating findings. Their hard work and insight gave enormous depth and richness to the project, and their good humour and enthusiasm not only sustained the work through difficult times, but also made participation a genuine pleasure. Their willingness to take on the substantial work involved in the project, in addition to their already massive workloads, was nothing short of heroic.

A second group of people we would like to thank includes colleagues at the Cambridge University School of Education who gave time and thought to the project, particularly in its early stages, and helped formulate both the principles on which the project was founded and its methodology. Their contributions were significant in many ways, and we will always be grateful to them. Added to this group are colleagues from other institutions, particularly those who contributed to two events, a seminar and a conference, at which conceptual aspects of the research were explored and developed.

Another indispensable group of people is made up of the secretarial and support staff at the School of Education. The complexities of ensuring efficient communication between members of a huge research team, spread across seven different institutions, are enormous. Pauline Mason fulfilled this role with expertise, style and good humour. We would also like to thank the many secretarial staff, both at the School of Education and in the research institutions, for their hard work in transcribing taped interviews and in dealing with all the other important clerical work on which research projects depend. In particular we would like to thank Christine Goad at the School of Education for making such an excellent job of the enormous task of preparing the final manuscript.

Finally, we wish to thank the School of Education's research and development fund committee for providing us with the financial support to carry out the project.

We sincerely hope that all of the many people who in one way or another gave support to the project feel that this book is an outcome worthy of their effort. And it is to them that the book is respectfully dedicated.

Research Team

Bruce Andrews
Mike Chapman
Anthony Clearly
Marion Dadds
Lesley Dee
Nicola Edwards
Alison Embley
Jay Fowler
Di Fuller
Fiona Giles
Karen Grimes
Kevin Healy
Elizabeth Holland
Bridget Howard
Alison Jones
Anna Kendall
Sarah Lindridge
Ralph McCluskey
Ray Peate
Martyn Rouse
Chris Searle

Raphaella Sichel
Bob Sproson
Susanne Stewart
Diane Thompson
James Thompson
Philip Tompkins
Audrey Wainer
Andy Watts
Simon Wheeler
Barrie Whelpton
Philip Younghusband

Writing Team

Paul Cooper
Mary Jane Drummond
Susan Hart
Jane Lovey
Colleen McLaughlin
Di Fuller
Simon Wheeler

1   Introducing the Positive Alternatives to School Exclusion Project

Neil's story

I used to live in a town about twenty miles from here. When I lived there I went to the local grammar school. Then I had to move. So I decided to come to this school. It was getting to be too much: getting up early in the morning to travel all that way. In fact sometimes I didn't bother going to school. Sometimes my mum knew that I weren't going to school; sometimes I just didn't go. That's what led to them throwing me out of school.

Well, to be honest, I had some problems at home first of all, and I ran away from home. And I weren't going to school. So I was just bunking off, basically. I was just going around places. I used to take my clothes with me, when I was at home that was. I'd just go round to my mates, you know. Then my mum got a phone call from the school saying that I wasn't attending school. They said that even when I was attending I was usually late, and that because of this they weren't gonna put up with it no more. So they chucked me out! I didn't get called into the school. My mum had a phone call from the head master saying that they were throwing me out. She also had a letter from the school, saying what had happened, and why they were throwing me out.

At first my mum weren't happy about it. But then, a day or two afterwards, she said I can stay with my sister for a little while, till I'd sorted it out. Then my mother made me go and live with my sister in a different town.

Before I got accepted here, I was out of school for about two and a half months. With my record I thought I might not get accepted by another school. And I wondered: what will it be like if I don't get accepted anywhere? I thought: I'll be leaving school soon to get a job. It's time things got sorted out.

Well, to cut a long story short, I went back to my mum's. After I'd stayed there a while she phoned up this school, and the social services did as well. After that I came down here to have a look round and speak to Mr Williams [the head master]. At that time Mrs Jones was the head of year, and she was ill so she weren't here. So every time my mum got in contact with the school, they told her that they didn't know if I was accepted yet, because Mrs Jones wasn't there to talk about it! So I came down here again and the head master said: 'when will you be able to start school?' And I said: 'as soon as possible!' I think this was a Thursday. Then he said: 'will you be able to start on Monday?' So I did!

I like quite a lot of things in this school. I know a lot of people. I get on all right with the work and the teachers. It's all right. Here the teachers sort of let you go at your own pace, but sort of push you as well. They help you a lot. At the grammar school it was a lot of pushing. Teachers were really hard on you. They were pushing you to do more work than you was capable of doing. And when I said: 'I don't know whether I'm capable of doing the work that you've set me, because it's too hard,' the teachers took it as a bad attitude towards them. If you say that here [at the current school] they don't take it as a bad attitude; they are more understanding.

This is the story of how Neil came to be a pupil at one of the schools that participated in the research project described in this book, told in Neil's own words. Although the interview took place in January 1997, it is a story that could have been related at almost any time in the history of compulsory schooling. At the time of writing, however, this kind of story is more common than ever before.

It is the story of a young person struggling to survive in circumstances that almost everyone would recognise as stressful and many would experience as downright hostile. Neil has unspecified 'problems at home' that are severe enough to make him run away; he fails to attend school; his living circumstances change; the school eventually decides to 'chuck out' Neil, and leave him with the worrying prospect of not being able to complete his education at a time when he believes that success in school will have a major impact on his future life chances. Fortunately, the story appears to have to take a positive turn when he moves to a new school. Here he finds a school where he experiences a more supportive and positive style of teaching than he has previously; where he is accepted as a person as well as a pupil.

It would be easy to jump to many conclusions about the main sources of difficulty in Neil's life. This would not, however, be a very fruitful or constructive exercise. What is clear to us, as educationists, is that Neil's experience of life outside school has not always placed him in a position that has made it easy for him to engage in positive ways with schooling. This is in spite of the fact that he claims to see positive value and purpose in achieving success at school. It is impossible to avoid seeing images of isolation, directionlessness and powerlessness embedded, in the personal dimension of this story, with those of callousness and rejection in the account of the 'grammar school'. Here is a vulnerable young person, struggling with enormous personal difficulties who is unceremoniously discarded by his school: a fact he learns via his mother, a third party. This event only serves to add a further negative dimension to his story. To his historic and current personal 'problems' are added fears and anxieties for the future. The potential that schooling might have had to offer a positive future is snatched away. Interestingly, his reaction is not to blame the school, but to recognise the difficulties that his poor record will create when he tries to find a new school.

There is much to learn from Neil's story about the negative human consequences of exclusion as well the many and varied possibilities that exist in schools for enhancing the lives of students. The research project that we report here, though, was also motivated by a broader concern. We were moved by a sense of the inequity of a maintained system of education which is excluding increasing numbers of those who are statutorily entitled to its benefits. The proud principles of the 1988 Education Reform Act, defining the purposes of education in terms of the spiritual, moral, cultural, mental and physical development of all students, are betrayed by the practice of exclusion. Furthermore, the UK is a signatory to the UN Convention on the Rights of the Child (1989), which unequivocally asserts every child's right to education.

It is not just the excluded who may suffer in the process. It is worth considering what is being learned by an excluded student's peers, when the exclusion takes effect, and the offending member of their society is removed. What might young children and teenagers conclude, when they see that a person of their own age, who, for whatever reason, does not conform to the required norms of behaviour, simply vanishes from their midst? What might they be learning about the capacity of a society – their society – to act in just and righteous ways towards every one of its members? In our construction of the problem of exclusion, issues of social justice are central.

The origins of the research

When the research project which this book is based upon was set up in 1996 there was also growing concern nationwide about the dramatic rise in the incidence of permanent exclusion from school in the first half of the 1990s (Parsons, 1999; DFEE, 1997; Stirling, 1992). Cases of individual students, including some of primary age, had begun to hit the headlines with increasing frequency. The teachers' views were represented mainly through the vociferous demands of some teachers' unions that local authorities protect their members from unruly pupils by making provision for them outside mainstream schools. In the absence of alternative views, this particular union perspective appeared to speak for the profession as a whole.

Yet, because of our own experience and our daily contact with teachers and other educators, we were confident that there were many who did not see exclusion as an acceptable solution to the problems posed by the most challenging students; we knew that there were many educators who were already, in their everyday professional lives, continually trying to break down barriers and find ways of engaging disaffected students more productively in school life. We were inspired by the example of Earl Marshal School in Sheffield where the then head teacher, Chris Searle, was actively promoting a policy of non-exclusion.

Our idea was to make contact with such people and to explore with them what it was possible to do from inside the school to help reverse the current trend towards increased exclusion. We hoped to draw on their understanding, and their insight into creative possibilities for the development of existing practice, to begin to map out alternative ways of responding to challenging behaviour in schools, other than seeking to remove an ever-growing number of students.

As we discuss in more detail later in the chapter, most previous research had concentrated on the phenomenon of rising exclusion itself: its causes, costs and consequences, and the gender, social and ethnic composition of excluded groups. Some studies had begun to draw attention to factors within schools' organisation and practices which appeared to make a difference to pupils' behaviour and to their willingness to engage positively in school life. From this body of work, it was possible to draw out implications for positive action that might be taken in schools to help reverse the trend. As far as we were aware, however, there was no research which focused on what schools were already doing to create conditions which would engage all students – especially those most vulnerable to exclusion – more productively in all areas of school life.

This was the focus of the 'Positive Alternatives to Exclusion' (PASE) project, which was carried out in 1996–7. Our aim was to explore how teachers in schools where there was a commitment to working to reduce and prevent exclusion were setting about the task. Our starting assumption was that, whatever the nature of the constraints within which teachers and schools operate, there is significant scope for positive action and intervention within every institution. By exploring and documenting the possibilities pursued by specific schools in specific contexts, we hoped to be able to create some more generalised insights and understandings about the task of building positive alternatives to exclusion that would support the development of work in other schools. From our own previous experience, research and reading, we anticipated that the most powerful approaches were likely to be those where improvements in behaviour came about as a by-product of development work in schools designed to enhance the quality of school experience for all pupils.

This book tells the story of the research and what we learnt from teachers and students about the task of building positive alternatives to exclusion. In this chapter, we provide some more detailed background to the research, including its relationship to other recent work in the field. We then explain more fully the research questions that guided the study, the principles that underpinned it and the methodology employed. In particular, we explain our commitment to working in partnership with the teachers in our case study schools, and how this translated into practice in terms of how the research was negotiated and conducted in each setting. Finally, we provide a brief overview of the structure of the book as a whole.

The problem of exclusion from school

To summarise, then, the starting point for our study was concern over the human cost of school exclusion, and a recognition of the urgent need to reverse this process. At the heart of this concern was our awareness of the damage that exclusion does to children and young people. This concern is coupled with a recognition that exclusionary practices effectively debar students from their moral entitlement to mainstream educational services.

Between 1991 and 1996 the annual rate of pupils being permanently excluded from state schools in England increased by approximately 400 per cent, with the 1997/8 figure standing at 13,041 (Parsons, 1999). Although the majority of these pupils were from the secondary age range (84 per cent), the greatest rate of increase over this period was found to be in the primary sector: 1,796 pupils of primary age and 10,639 pupils of secondary age were permanently excluded from mainstream schools, and a further 605 excluded from special schools (ibid.).

Where a school placement is not currently secured, LEAs are by law required to provide 'education otherwise than at school'. In practice though this can mean a child as young as six remaining at home, provided with only two sessions a week, of one and a half hours each, from the LEA's home tuition service. Parsons describes his own involvement in one such case, as a school governor. He felt himself forced to resign, after failing to persuade colleagues that it was 'morally unacceptable for a school with a community-wide responsibility to exclude a child, particularly one so young'. His perceptions of the boy and the provision subsequently made for him at home, following exclusion, were as follows:

> He is small, confused, obviously troubled, and a great strain for his mother. He is also interested, wants to please and values a structured and predictable activity. He continues to receive weekly counselling and is now on Ritalin. At the start of the Autumn term when he became a Year 2 pupil, he remained at home with very little happening that will lead to 'reintegration back into mainstream school'. In the spring term of 1999, LS was continuing on three hours of home tuition.
>
> (Parsons, 1999, p. 177)

In another case (Hayden, 1997b), a mother reports the impact of permanent exclusion on her seven year old son:

> He was rejected from two schools. . . He felt nobody wanted him or liked him. . . He was here all day. He wouldn't dress, he wouldn't wash, he wouldn't eat. He was just like sitting on the chair watching the telly all the time.

The head teacher who had reluctantly made the decision to exclude this boy recognised that exclusion would compound his difficulties:

> I agonized for a whole day before I did it. . . . I knew, knowing all of the situation Chris was in, that I was doing exactly the same as everybody else had done to him in school and elsewhere. We wanted him to be happy at school and be with all of us. I felt let down by the support I was getting. . . . It shouldn't have happened. The poor little devil had been doing so well. I felt so badly . . . but what alternatives did I have?
>
> (Hayden, 1997b, p. xi)

In addition to official temporary exclusions, Stirling (1992) identifies a range of 'unofficial' forms of exclusion by which schools persuade both parents and the students themselves to collude in their exclusion. Stirling found, in a study of one local authority, that when such 'imaginative' unofficial forms of exclusion were taken into account, exclusion rates were fifteen times higher among children in local authority care than among the general population.

The alarm inspired by this trend is intensified when we consider the fact that it is those children who are particularly vulnerable who are most likely to be excluded. School exclusion needs to be understood in the broader context of social exclusion which always victimises the most vulnerable members of society.

For example, Hayden found, among a group of 265 children excluded from three English education authorities, a high number of children experiencing a combination of personal, family and schooling difficulties (Hayden, 1997a). These problems included personal difficulties in the form of few or no friends, low self-esteem, and behavioural difficulties. Their families were more likely to have experienced difficulties in the form of relationship problems, social services involvement, violence or abuse among family members, criminality, and family trauma, such as illness or bereavement. These children were also more likely than most to experience educational underachievement, and to have attended schools experiencing staffing problems, recent budget cuts, inadequate behaviour management policies, unsuitable school accommodation and problems of communication and record keeping in relation to the excluded child's learning difficulties and needs.

These findings suggest that prior to being excluded, students are often already experiencing a set of difficulties that alone would tend to put them in the category of children at risk of further personal and social problems, such as adult criminality, physical and mental ill health and poverty (for example, Parsons, 1999; Blau and Gullotta, 1996; Rutter and Smith, 1995; Farrington, 1990; Rutter and Giller, 1983). Thus children who are excluded from school often have the burden of interrupted schooling added to their existing difficulties and unfavourable life-prognosis. These insights form the basis of the acknowledgement that exclusion may often be a symptom of unmet pupil need, which appeared in a recent UK government policy document (DFEE, 1997: *Excellence for All*). For many students, while the schooling they receive may sometimes be far less than ideal, exclusion from it, at the very least, adds calculated insult to already significant injury.

The most common reasons given to justify formal exclusion are anti-social and unruly behaviour (Stirling, 1992). It tends to be boys rather than girls who are excluded, with boys accounting for 93 per cent of primary exclusions, 81 per cent of secondary exclusions and 88 per cent of exclusions from special schools (Parsons, 1999). Furthermore, there is evidence to suggest that the practice of exclusion discriminates against some students, particularly boys from African-Caribbean backgrounds (Parsons, 1999; Hayden, 1997a; Bourne *et al*. 1994). This social patterning suggests strongly that rising exclusion needs to be understood as a socially produced phenomenon requiring a complex social and political analysis in order to penetrate its underlying causes.

In particular, it is important to take account of the impact of changes in education policy and legislation over the last decade on patterns of integration and exclusion. Many commentators appear to agree that the pattern of rising exclusion is directly related to the introduction of a market system of education, through various changes incorporated in the 1988 Education Reform Act. The introduction of a National Curriculum, a national system of assessment, local management of schools, league tables, parental choice, the opportunity to opt out of LEA control and introduce a greater element of selection of pupil intakes have combined to create a 'new value context' (Ball, 1993, p. 108) which significantly affects how teachers and other educators construe their responsibilities with respect to troubled pupils and challenging behaviour, and the range of 'appropriate' responses that they feel able and willing to consider. With schools constantly under pressure to improve their examination and SATS results, there is a temptation to direct resources and human effort into those areas which are most likely to enhance achievement, as measured in these terms. As Hayden (1997b) notes in her review of the impact of education policy,

> The introduction of published league tables of examination results and other indicators of performance in schools has created a climate less likely to be sympathetic to children not only producing no positive contribution to these indicators, but who may also prevent others from doing so.
>
> (Hayden, 1997b, p. 8)

The reduced tolerance of pupils with troubling or challenging behaviour evidenced in the current context is, according to Stirling, more than just an unfortunate side effect of this new education policy:

> In the operation of market forces, disparity is what drives competition; we have to have losers in order to sustain the winners.

Rather than promoting equality of opportunities through education, inequality is a necessary driving force within a competitive system. Consequently, I consider the resulting disadvantaged group identified as 'Pupils with Problems' as an integral and necessary feature of a competitive education system.

(Stirling, 1996, p. 61)

While a persuasive case has certainly been made regarding the link between education policy and rising rates of exclusion over the past decade, variations in exclusion rates – nationwide and within particular LEAs (Parsons 1999; Kinder *et al.* 1999a/b) – suggest that nevertheless there is scope to resist the pressures that are leading to increased inclusion. While we do not deny the importance of the wider social and political factors we have outlined above, our project was set up in the belief that it still remains possible for teachers and other educators to take positive action to reverse the unacceptable trend towards exclusion. It was also our belief, based on previous experience and research, that the kinds of development work in schools directed towards this goal would also be of benefit to the wider student group who are unlikely ever to find themselves at risk of exclusion.

From exclusion to inclusion

Although the starting point for our research was a concern about rising exclusion, in fact what we really set about investigating in the Positive Alternatives to Exclusion project, was the process of inclusion. In the educational context, the absence of formal exclusion does not automatically imply the presence of inclusion. Exclusion from school is the active process of barring or shutting out the pupil from the activities that take place within the premises. Inclusion, on the other hand, involves the shaping of the school environment as well as the development of students' images of themselves (and others' images of them) in ways that lead to all students' active, willing and constructive engagement in the life of the school (Booth and Ainscow, 1998). For some students this process of inclusion will also involve the dismantling or reshaping of work already done by the exclusionary process.

In making our focus inclusion as opposed to exclusion, we were also concerned to acknowledge the plight of those students in schools who are neither formally excluded, nor seen as behaving in ways which might put them at risk of exclusion. This group of students has been described by James Pye as the 'invisible children' who are 'forgotten', 'lost' and 'abandoned' in what Pye terms 'Nomansland' (Pye, 1988).

These students are indeed physically present in classrooms, but they are disengaged, both intellectually and emotionally, from the educational process. These students are not intentionally barred from the educational process; theirs is a passive form of exclusion, which is defined by the failure of the inclusion process. If we think of excluded students as having had their invitations to learn withdrawn, we can think of these 'invisible' students as never really having had anything more than a half-hearted invitation in the first place. Where the excluded pupil's relationship with the teacher is often characterised by conflict, the 'invisible' student's relationship is, at worst, characterised by indifference, or, at best, characterised by a benign collusion: neither 'bothers' the other.

Benefits for all students

For us then, the process of inclusion is of paramount concern, because it represents both a positive response to exclusion, as well as a framework for embracing the needs and interests of all students. The research described in this book started from the assumption that while schools and teachers cannot alone overcome all the social, emotional and behavioural difficulties that most students will, at some time experience, the conditions for learning that students encounter in school will always play a crucial role in promoting (or inhibiting) their active and positive engagement in the social and academic life of the community.

Statistics collected by the UK children's mental health charity Young Minds (1999) has indicated that, at the very least, 10 per cent of school-aged children in England experience, in clinical terms, a range of serious emotional and behavioural problems, such as conduct disorder, anxiety problems and other specific conditions including autistic spectrum disorders and obsessive compulsive disorder. We might add to this a consideration of Attention Deficit/Hyperactivity Disorder, which describes a constellation of severely socially and educationally debilitating attentional and behavioural problems, the prevalence rates for which vary internationally between 1 per cent and 6 per cent of school aged children (Tannock, 1998).

It is instructive to take the Young Minds 10 per cent prevalence rate as encapsulating all of these problems and difficulties, and then compare this with the aggregate percentages of school students (Table 1.1) who are formally excluded from school (>0.1 per cent); those who attend Pupil Referral Units (PRUs) (<0.1 per cent), and those who attend special schools of all types (1 per cent). The clear implication of this comparison is that, in England, the overwhelming majority (well over 80

Table 1.1 Exclusion and emotional and behavioral difficulties in English schools

---

Currently it is estimated that:

> 10% of children (936,000) experience EBDs[1]
> 1% of children (93,500) attend special schools[2]
> <0.1% of children (7,700) attend Pupil Referral Units[2]
> >0.1% of children (13,000) are excluded from school over a year[2]

Therefore, the most conservative estimate is that >80% of children classified as experiencing EBDs are in mainstream schools.

Sources:
1   Young Minds (1999)
2   DfEE Stats Dept.

per cent) of school aged children experiencing a wide range of emotional and behavioural difficulties are enrolled in mainstream schools.

However the term 'emotional and behavioural difficulties', as it is used by Young Minds, is best understood as referring to extreme and persistent manifestations of emotional and behavioural problems, which are commonly experienced, albeit to moderate or mild degrees, at different times by most people. The extent to which any school contributes to the exacerbation or alleviation of these problems at their most serious is, therefore, likely to have significant implications for all the students in the school.

The new policy context

As acknowledged earlier, government policy plays a highly significant role in facilitating and constraining the work of teachers in schools. In the period since our research was carried out, a change of government has brought about changes in social and educational policy. This now reflects an overt commitment to inclusion, while paradoxically leaving in place many of the mechanisms of the former market forces policy which, as already noted, many commentators have argued is directly implicated in the dramatic rise in exclusion rates.

The 1997 Education Act highlights some of the important responsibilities of local education authorities, schools and teachers, for meeting the needs of children and young people who exhibit disruptive behaviour. This theme is more fully developed in the Green Paper on special needs education (DFEE, 1997), which offers unambiguous support for the concept of inclusive education for children with special educational needs, and emphasises the relationship between disruption, exclusion and unmet social, emotional and educational needs.

Unfortunately, these relatively positive measures were accompanied by less welcome developments, which included the extension of the maximum period of fixed term exclusion from fifteen to forty-five days. This change, combined with measures relating to the use of physical restraint, after-school detention and the introduction of home-school contracts, appears to sit uncomfortably with the vocabulary of inclusion, co-operation and support evident in the official presentation of government education policy, and prominent in other policy initiatives.

Another major initiative is the government's policy on social inclusion. In a recent consultation document the Minister for School Standards, Estelle Morris, expressed the government's commitment to reducing the number of pupils who are not attending school due to exclusion or truancy (DFEE, 1999). An important aspect of this document, which it shares with the Green Paper, is the emphasis on 'the skills and professionalism of teachers and school staff' (ibid. p. 5). These documents are built, in part at least, on the belief that it is the day to day management of schools, and the thinking and actions of staff in these schools which contribute most significantly to the experience of students. It is an exploration of these factors, they suggest, that is the most promising source of insights into why some schools perform considerably better than others with similar student intakes.

The documents also recognise, however, the need for supportive and enabling structures around and between schools, which are provided through policy and strategic planning at national and local government levels. Developments at government level include modifications to the National Curriculum for students aged between fourteen and nineteen to allow for broader and more vocationally oriented study, as well as the setting up of a National Advisory Group on Personal, Social and Health Education.

In addition to these initiatives the government has provided funds to support LEA and school level development work in relation to disaffection, truancy and exclusion. It has also given a small amount of financial support to educational research aimed at the identification of good practice in relation to social inclusion (for example, Daniels *et al* 1999). This last development represents a particularly welcome departure from the previous government's open hostility towards educational and other forms of social research. We can only hope that this development heralds a genuine commitment to an evidence based approach to policy development.

Principles underlying our own research

While welcoming such centrally-funded research initiatives, our own approach was somewhat different from the policy-oriented research commissioned by the DFEE. To clarify these differences, we will examine briefly the research carried out by Daniels *et al.* (1999) referred to earlier. Their approach was to examine practices in schools which had been rated highly by OFSTED (that is achieving a grade one or two) and perceived by them to be particularly effective in their management of children with emotional and behavioural difficulties. The intention of the research was to identify school and teacher characteristics that might be associated with effectiveness. The study provides useful insights that will be of practical value to schools and teachers keen to develop their structures and practices (Table 1.2).

Nevertheless, there is also a degree of familiarity and predictability about the five key characteristics of effective schools identified in this

Table 1.2: Practices in schools rated highly by OFSTED

- *Leadership:* heads and senior management teams in these schools provided effective leadership, particularly in their communication of appropriate values, preferred ethos and aspirations for the school as a whole.

- *Sharing Values:* this usually took the form of a core of staff working co-operatively with one another and pupils to ensure the active participation of all students in school affairs. A further characteristic related to staff willingness to critically reflect on their performance and to make changes on the basis of this reflection.

- *Behaviour Policy and Practice:* this entailed the provision of a common behaviour policy for all pupils and staff, which was consistently monitored and in which there was consistency between approaches to dealing with all pupils.

- *Understanding EBD:* this involved a key member of staff who understood the nature of emotional and behavioural difficulties, and were able to distinguish these from routine misbehaviour.

- *Teaching Skills and the Curriculum:* this involved the necessity of including opportunities for children to learn from their own actions, through active involvement in learning tasks and the need for an appropriately challenging curriculum. These are, of course, essential components of the educational programme for all pupils.

Source: based on Daniels *et al.* (1999)

study. This is perhaps an inevitable consequence of the approach to the research adopted. There is an element of circularity built into a study of institutional process which takes, as a starting point, a set of judgements (OFSTED reports) based on the premise that particular school processes (that is management approach, policy provision, quality of pedagogy, organisational ethos) have a significant effect on student outcomes. This problem is compounded by the fact that the research methods used in the study rely heavily on the perceptions of staff in the schools studied, with only limited corroborative data or evidence of the perceptions of other school participants, such as students.

We draw attention to these methodological features of the study in order to identify the ways in which our own research differs, not to imply that the study is without value. Our own research began with a much more open-ended agenda. We thought it unlikely that the answer to our central question 'What can schools do to create conditions which preclude the need for exclusion?' would simply take the form of a list of tried-and-tested strategies, although there is, of course, much that teachers can learn by hearing about the range of strategies being developed in other contexts. Strategies which 'work' in one context cannot simply be imported into another school context, because what makes strategies effective in one context is bound up with the key features of that specific context, including a particular alignment of inclusionary and exclusionary pressures (Booth, 1996) and practitioners' particular understandings, values and ways of construing the problem and its associated task.

Our assumption was that the solution lay in a 'particular orientation towards problems', including a belief in the school's power to make a positive difference to pupil behaviour, a willingness to listen and learn from the perspectives of others – especially including the pupils themselves – and a commitment to taking whatever action possible to enhance the quality of pupils' engagement with all aspects of school life.

This commitment, moreover, presupposes a belief that all students have the capacity to become willing, active and positive participants in school processes. This capacity, however, is rarely realised automatically. It has to be purposely nurtured by the school environment, otherwise it may remain dormant, or may sometimes be masked by attitudes and behaviours which actively deny the existence of the students' powers to engage and learn.

We therefore sought to work with teachers and other educators who shared these commitments and, in their everyday professional lives, were working to reduce and prevent exclusion. We made no prejudgements about the nature or quality of the work that they had already done or were currently doing. Rather than trying to identify characteristics of the most 'effective' schools, or specify models of practice for other schools to emulate (as in the case of the policy-oriented research referred to above), we were concerned with studying how, in those schools where there was a professed commitment to finding positive alternatives to exclusion, teachers construed the issues and set about the task. For this reason, we designed the research to focus on teachers' thinking: the knowledge, under-standing and reasoning influencing their judgement in deciding what strategies to pursue, in evaluating the outcomes of action taken and in deciding what further directions to pursue. We also made it a condition of the research that participating schools should be committed to listening to and learning from all participants, including and especially the students themselves.

The principle of partnership

From a methodological point of view, a further important principle guiding the research was that we should work in partnership with teachers and other educators in schools. For many years now there has been debate about the relationships which have traditionally prevailed between those who teach and those who carry out research into educa-tion. It has been argued that the traditional social relations of research, where researchers come in from outside to study the work of teachers and schools as 'objects' of their research, are unhelpful and even exploitative (for example Oliver, 1990).

Teachers and other educators have traditionally had little opportu-nity to influence the research agenda, to set the research questions, to contribute to designing and carrying out the investigation, and to analysing and writing up the findings. The outside researchers have generally controlled the process from start to finish, and their voice has been the privileged one in reporting what was found. This may at least in part explain why research 'on' the work of teachers and other educa-tors in schools has frequently had little impact, either on those who participated directly, or on those who might be expected to make use of the findings in developing their own practice.

In determining to work in partnership with participating schools and other institutions, we were hoping to create a more equal and reciprocal relationship, which would actively involve our colleagues in the schools at every stage of the research process. The whole rationale for the project was to learn from the practical experience of professionals who shared our values and commitments. We wanted our research to take the form of an exploration of what staff and students actually did and thought on a day to day basis; in the course of this exploration we wanted our partners to engage in an analytic and developmental process, which would enable them to improve their practice in promoting positive alternatives to exclusion. In this way we hoped that the research process would make a practical contribution to addressing the problems associated with exclusion. It seemed that a partnership approach was the only type of relationship that would be consonant with these aims.

Methodological issues

In practice, what this meant was that, while the broad focus of the research had already been determined by the university research group, the specific focus within each institution was defined by staff in each school in consultation with the university researchers. Once the precise focus for the research in each setting was agreed, the school staff and university researchers worked collaboratively: data collection methods and the division of responsibilities for data collection and analysis were similarly negotiated in each setting.

A focus on mainstream provision

We wanted the study to cover both primary and secondary phases, and to include schools in a range of different urban and rural locations in order to ensure diverse settings and intakes. Given our particular interest in what was happening in mainstream contexts, we chose not to include Pupil Referral Units (PRUs) or special schools, though it did seem appropriate to include a further education (FE) college which made provision for students at Key Stage 4 who were at risk of exclusion from their mainstream schools.

We realised that the FE college might be construed as an exclusionary rather than an inclusive option, but felt that there are important distinctions to be made between the use of FE provision, and the PRU/special school options. Perhaps the single most important distinction is that while PRUs and special schools are primarily settings for individuals who are deemed to require education outside the mainstream, this is not the case with FE colleges. Further education colleges are, to all intents and purposes a form of mainstream provision, open to all, that do not carry the (deserved or undeserved) stigma attaching to PRUs and special schools. Furthermore, it is possible that by attending a FE college during

Key Stage 4, some students may accrue benefits which will serve them in good stead when they make the formal transition to FE at the end of their compulsory period of schooling.

Having said this, given our commitment to the idea that inclusion is a process, rather than a state, it might have been appropriate for us to have included other forms of provision in our study (such as PRUs and special schools), where the staff in these settings were committed to promoting mainstream inclusion.

Current exclusion record

Although we were clear that staff in our case study schools would need to share our commitment to positive alternatives to exclusion, we did not make the complete absence of exclusions a necessary condition for participation in the project. We had to recognise that in practice, there may be circumstances in which a student's interests are best served by exclusion. For example, when interactions between an individual student and some teachers are persistently marked by open conflict that is severely damaging to the student, and when there is little or no prospect of improvement over the short or medium term, exclusion may come to be seen as the only realistic option.

There is of course a potential danger in such a view, since it could be argued that so long as the option of exclusion remains there will always be occasions for its practice. Nevertheless, working to reduce and present exclusion is a long-term development process. We reluctantly concluded that it is possible for staff groups, on the one hand, to express a genuine and active commitment to finding positive alternatives to exclusion, while still, on occasions, resorting to exclusion.

Recruiting participants

We felt that it was essential that our research partners should volunteer to participate in the research. Since we were looking – first and foremost – for participants who shared similar values and commitments to those underlying the project, the most effective approach seemed to be to hold a conference in which we would highlight the need for our study, provide an account of our proposed methodology and invite volunteers to participate.

A conference attended by more than eighty people was held in Cambridge in May 1996. From the volunteers who came forward, following the conference, and from other contacts in the region, six institutions were recruited:

- Anne Fine primary school, a small inner city Voluntary Aided school, in cramped Victorian buildings, with about 200 children on roll, and a mixed intake.
- Virginia Woolf High School, an 11–16 urban comprehensive school, with 950 students on roll. The catchment area suffers from economic and social deprivation, and unemployment is higher than the national average.
- T. S. Eliot High School, an 11–18 comprehensive school on the edge of a city, with over 2,000 students and a large sixth form.
- Ogden Nash, a Voluntary Aided Roman Catholic upper school, with 380 pupils on roll, set in the middle of a local authority housing estate on the edge of a light industrial area.
- William Shakespeare upper school, a mixed comprehensive with 280 students on roll, in a busy town in the Greater London area. The roll is falling and the school is seen by some parents as less attractive than its main rival in the town. The catchment area is one of the most deprived served by this LEA.
- Rudyard Kipling College, a further education college in a small city in a shire county, which offers a pilot college programme for a group of Year 11 students, working in partnership with the local education authority Student Support Service.

The institutions recruited were wide-ranging in respect of their type and size; location (in terms of urban, suburban and rural); the socio-economic characteristics of their intake, and the performance characteristics indicated by OFSTED reports and league table positions. It was regrettable, however, that only one of the volunteering institutions (Anne Fine primary school) could be said to be representative in terms of the presence of students from ethnic minority backgrounds. Given the over-representation of students from certain ethnic minorities in formal exclusion figures we see this as a significant limitation of our study.

Preserving anonymity

There is inevitably a tension between fully acknowledging the contribution of our research partners, without whom the study would not have been possible, and preserving the anonymity of the schools and the individuals involved in them. Pseudonyms have been chosen by each of the institutions involved, and these names have been used in all sharing of information both among the participating institutions and with the wider educational community.

Focus on the day-to-day thinking of participants

Given that our intention was to illuminate the processes through which staff in schools promoted positive alternatives to school exclusion, the question was where do such processes reside? Were they to be found in formal policy documents, or through an analysis of management structures and strategies? Could such processes be physically observed, in the patterns of social interaction and individual behaviours of staff and students? Would it be appropriate to look at each of the institutional worlds we would encounter through the eyes and thinking of the students and staff who participated in these settings on a daily basis?

Ultimately, we would find a place for all of these strategies, but it was the day to day thinking of the participants that, from the outset, was our central focus. It was through this channel that other aspects of institutional life (such as management structures and school policies) would be opened up for exploration. Our reasons for adopting this approach are based on the assumption that human institutions tend to be idiosyncratic in character. No two schools are exactly alike, though they may appear to share common characteristics. Different schools may adopt identical formal patterns of organisation (management structure or student grouping policy for example), but the ways in which these organisational patterns impinge on the daily behaviour and experience of individuals in the institutions may differ enormously. These differences constitute the informal culture (or ethos) of the institution, which is a product of interactions between the formal organisational structures of the setting and the personal characteristics of individual participants. These interactions are, furthermore, embedded in a wide range of influences external to the institution, including the family backgrounds of staff and students, the communities served by the institution, and, in turn, the broader national and international political contexts.

By focusing our research on the day to day thinking of staff and students about what they do and why they do it, we would be able to gain access to everyday reality as it is perceived by different participants. This approach would enable us to learn about the processes involved in creating positive alternatives to exclusion, as we examined how the everyday thinking of staff and students engages with the obstacles and the opportunities that they perceive in their current situations. It was the ways in which positive alternatives are generated, as much as the alternatives themselves, that interested us.

To summarise, the aims of the research were as follows:

• To develop our understanding of the ways in which teaching staff, students and, where possible, parents and communities, construe the issues surrounding school exclusion, including its nature, causes and effects.

- To develop models of inquiry, analysis and reflection that promote effective practice in the handling of behavioural problems in educational settings and the prevention of exclusion.
- To develop our understanding of the ways in which educational institutions can help to prevent student exclusion and at the same time promote positive student engagement with the school community.

Structure of the book

The rest of this book is devoted to an account of the research that was carried out in each of the six settings. An entire chapter is devoted to five of the case studies, and one school is covered over two chapters. It will be seen that each case study generated a distinctive set of issues.

Chapter 2, on Anne Fine primary school, is the first of our case studies. A central theme in this chapter is the tension between the staff group's determination to create a safe, predictable environment in which their pupils can feel secure and, on the other hand, their desire to foster the pupils' capacities to be self-determining. Extracts from interviews with a range of pupils are used to generate insights into how the staff's policies and practices impacted on their daily lives in classrooms, corridors and playgrounds.

Chapters 3 and 4 give an account of Virginia Woolf High School. Chapter 3 focuses on what was being done in the school that was directly intended to support students, by enhancing features of school experience in ways which would hopefully impact positively on learning and behaviour. It looks in detail at two initiatives: a personal tutoring scheme and an initiative designed to support excluded students on re-entry. A substantial part of this chapter was written by a member of the school staff who participated in the study. Chapter 4 focuses on what was also learnt about the needs of teachers, in the task of building positive alternatives to exclusion. One important theme is the importance of dialogue: the need to create conditions where people, both staff and students, feel listened to and supported, if they are to be able to respond positively to learning opportunities.

Chapter 5 deals with T. S. Eliot comprehensive school. At the heart of this case study is the staff group's commitment to implementing their Positive Discipline for Learning programme. Here we find the staff of this large multi-site school wrestling with the challenges of developing a whole school approach to problem behaviour, based on shared understandings among staff and students and directed towards positive engagement with the curriculum.

Chapter 6 describes Ogden Nash upper school. Though similar in size and type to William Shakespeare, Ogden Nash represents in many respects a more socially advantaged educational setting. This chapter charts the development in staff thinking about the nature of the problems that leads to exclusion for some students. This development is marked by the shift from a preoccupation with policy and structure to a concern with the individual biographies of students.

Chapter 7 deals with William Shakespeare upper school, a small urban school, serving a fairly disadvantaged area. In this chapter we see staff and students grappling with severe difficulties on a number of fronts, not the least of which is the threat to their survival as a school posed by their publicly more highly esteemed neighbour. To these external pressures are added what the staff see as their disproportionately large share of students with problems of various kinds. The theme of this chapter is the school's efforts to develop approaches to preventing and dealing with difficulties that are compatible with a person-centred ethos.

Chapter 8 gives an account of Rudyard Kipling Further Education College's provision for disaffected Key Stage 4 students. This case study focuses on the importance of autonomy and freedom for students, and how these factors can contribute to the development of positive alternatives to school exclusion through their impact on students' conceptions of self.

The remainder of the book is devoted to three chapters in which a number of issues and common themes drawn from across the six case studies are dealt with in depth. Chapter 9 presents a number of different frameworks for understanding positive alternatives to school exclusion that can be extrapolated from the case studies. Chapter 10 focuses on the central issue to emerge from the study: the importance of personal experience in generating positive alternatives to school exclusion, and in understanding the effectiveness of these approaches.

Chapter 11 is a critical account of the research process as a whole, drawing on the perceptions of some of our partners in the case study schools, as well as on the reflections of the university team. The book concludes with a brief consideration of how the research reported here could be developed in the future, in which we reiterate our commitment to making research work in practice.

2 Anne Fine Primary School

'respectful, enjoyful and appropriate' according to one of its pupils.

Introduction

Anne Fine is a Voluntary Aided primary school in a central London borough. There are 197 pupils on roll, housed in two early Victorian buildings, described in the school's OFSTED report (June 1996) as 'distinguished but cramped . . . not an ideal educational environment.' The two buildings are separated from each other and from the playground and parish church by side roads, which have to be crossed by pupils many times during the school day. The three infant classes, for example, cross one road to go to assembly, to dinner, to hymn practice and PE sessions in the Hall, and two roads to go to the playground. The seven classrooms are small and feel crowded to an observer, especially in Years 5 and 6. The intake is mixed, and around 40 per cent of the pupils travel in from another borough, making, according to OFSTED 'a fairly typical inner city mixture.'

There are some pupils from professional families, as well as a proportion from 'less advantaged groups' housed in local authority housing nearby; the free school meal entitlement is around 21 per cent, slightly above the national average. Of the pupils, 27.4 per cent are from minority ethnic backgrounds, predominantly Caribbean or African (national average 10 per cent). There is a high level of pupil mobility and the OFSTED report notes that in the summer of 1996 only eight of the current Year 6 class of twenty-two pupils had attended the school since their admission to the reception class.

A senior inspector in the local authority suggested Anne Fine primary school as a possible site for the Positive Alternatives to Exclusion project, because of the developmental work the staff had been doing on their behaviour policy, including their approach to bullying. The OFSTED report also commented favourably on these aspects of the school's work:

> the spiritual, moral, cultural and social development of the children is one of the school's strengths. . . . Relationships between children and adults are very good, and where tensions do arise between groups of children, these are being addressed by emphasising the value placed on social harmony and respect for others, and through the strategies adopted to reduce bullying behaviour.
>
> (OFSTED Report, June 1996)

After two preliminary visits to the school, and meetings between the researcher, the head teacher and the staff group, the school joined the project in January 1997. Over the year that followed the researcher carried out tape-recorded interviews with six members of the teaching staff, including the head teacher, and twelve small group interviews with pupils from each of the year groups except the reception class (Year 1 to Year 6). The researcher also documented non-participant observations made in the dinner hall, at assemblies and in classrooms. During the spring and summer terms of 1997, the head teacher was conducting a parallel investigation, associated with her participation in a long in-service course for head teachers provided by the local education authority. As part of her work for this, the head teacher carried out a survey of pupils' views on their school experience, with an explicit emphasis on aspects of effective teaching and learning. Every child in the school contributed to structured discussion groups and completed pupil questionnaires. During the same period, there were other continuing initiatives in the school, including the work of play leaders during the dinner-time break, the use of outreach workers in supporting individual pupils, and the staff's developmental work on the PSHE curriculum, led by the senior member of staff with responsibility for this area. The researcher was fully briefed about these initiatives, and some issues associated with them did arise in the interviews with both staff and pupils. However, these initiatives are not discussed in this chapter, though it was clear that they were making worthwhile contributions to the overall approach to behaviour.

The final interviews with senior staff took place in January 1998. Looking back over the school's year-long involvement with the project, the head teacher reflected on their reasons for taking part:

Head teacher: We'd reached a point in our lives . . . we've got our good teachers here. We know how to deal (we think) with our special needs children; we've got a good curriculum in place, our planning has been complimented by OFSTED. We are now digging really deep. And yet another way of enhancing the curriculum and a child's life in school is to look at behaviour, at attitudes, at personal development, because I think that all adds to enriching the curriculum.

In all the researcher's discussions with the head teacher, formal and informal, over the year, these themes were significant. 'We're here for teaching and learning' were words often on her lips; she was unashamedly willing to repeat herself to get the point across.

Head teacher: You know that's why I do that big thing on Mondays in Assembly. It sets off our week 'Why are you here? And why are your teachers here?'

The ritual the head teacher refers to here was, by this time, well known to the researcher, both through first hand observation and through the references made to it in staff and pupil interviews. Every Monday morning the head teacher goes through a familiar and friendly routine, asking the assembled school 'and I want every hand to go up: why are you here?' The routine answer, from any one in the ranks of cheerfully hand-waving pupils is: 'To work and to learn.' The supplementary question: 'And why are your teachers here?' is also duly answered: 'to teach us'. The head teacher's comment on this part of the routine is interesting:

Head teacher: It does affirm for them, [the staff group] no matter how bad they might be feeling, or however grotty the weekend was, we value you being here because you have come to do an important job.

The value of teaching, the centrality of learning, the indivisibility of school achievement and positive behaviour, the concept of a curriculum that fosters both intellectual excellence and continuous personal development: these are the key notes of the philosophy that runs through everyday life at Anne Fine primary school.

The behaviour policy: paper and practice

The whole staff group were involved in drawing up the behaviour policy, an extremely positive document, emphasising rewards rather than sanctions, and the quality of relationships rather than rules and regulations. The policy is based, as it sets out at the start

> on a quiet yet firm insistence on high standards of behaviour at all times, drawing its strength from community of purpose, consistent practice and constant vigilance.

There are sections on role-models, rights and responsibilities, these last set out in parallel columns for school staff and parents/guardians. There is a section on bullying and how it will be treated, which includes a detailed and outspoken paper defining bullying behaviour. It is striking for its vivid and explicit use of language. For example, bullying behaviour as defined here includes, as one would expect, intimidation, threatening remarks, excluding people; and also

- Sniggering or eyeballing if someone else is in trouble.
- Playing lurgy games.
- Putting notes in people's trays.
- Making people lend you things or swap things.
- Giving excuses 'it was just a joke' or 'I was only playing' when someone complains about your behaviour.

These definitions, reeking of the rough underworld of classrooms and playgrounds, are impressive in their recognition of the pupils' capacity to suffer, and the responsibility of the school community to prevent that suffering. The document also lists other forms of unacceptable behaviour at considerable length; again there is a marked sensitivity to children's feelings, both physical and emotional.

In our school it is unacceptable to:

- push or shove on the stairs
- armlock
- headlock
- whip people with clothes or bags
- lift people up
- prevent people from going to the toilet . . . (selected items from a list of twenty)

These prohibitions may seem minute ('We are rather pernickety', said the head teacher), but the pain they are designed to prevent is authentic enough. The pupils' voice is audible here; there is more to being bullied than being subject to highly visible and violent assaults on the person. The bullying policy is attentive to the detail of pupils' experiences; it recognises the triviality and meanness of the acts of the bully. What is more, as both staff and pupils were prepared to assert, it has made a difference to the quality of people's lives.

The behaviour policy also reviews a range of rewards and privileges, including the head teacher's 'Special Mentions' book, a notebook in which, every week, staff members record the names of children whose achievement or behaviour is worthy of positive recognition. The names and citations are publicly announced in assembly, and the chosen pupils are also commended in the school's weekly newsletter to parents. There is a parallel system of 'Behaviour books', or 'bad books', as some of the younger pupils call them. There is one such book in each classroom, to be used by the class teacher or any other member of staff, and books are also available in the two playgrounds and the dinner hall. These are collected by the head teacher every week and monitored for issues that may need further action – an interview with parents, perhaps, or a discussion between class teacher(s) and head teacher, sometimes involving the pupil(s) concerned. The researcher was given access to all these forms of documentation, rich and revealing sources of evidence.

In the analysis that follows, a brief review of the school's achievements, as seen by pupils, staff and researcher, leads into four sections in which a selection of the huge mass of interview and observation data is re-examined. This process reveals some of the themes that can be discerned below the surface of every day events, some individual stories, and some more general issues that, it is hoped, will contribute to a fuller understanding of how the behaviour policy at Anne Fine primary school impacted on the lives of those who work and learn there. The concluding section of the chapter raises some questions about the educational value of life in schools, and draws on a variety of texts to suggest the most effective ways in which children can be supported in one crucial dimension of their education, their learning to act as members of a harmonious and caring community.

A review of achievements: the views of children and teachers

The pupil interviews were conducted in small groups of two or three, tape recorded and transcribed. The children were selected by the head teacher, in consultation with the class teachers and the researcher, to give a variety of points of view and to represent the mixed intake of the school. A short list of discussion points was shown to the children at the start of the interview, and was left on the table throughout the session so that they could track their progress through the schedule. At the close of the interview the children were asked if there were other questions or issues they would like to raise. The interviews lasted approximately half an hour, and were relaxed and friendly experiences. The children, even the youngest, appeared to understand that the researcher was genuinely interested in their points of view, and to recognise how the conventions of television and radio interviews were being adapted for the purposes of the project.

Children from every year group were able to articulate their understanding and appreciation of different aspects of the school's positive approach to behaviour. The most public practices stimulated the most frequent comments, which were largely favourable, with a few dissenting voices, mainly from the older children. For example, every group of children had comments to make about the Behaviour books. A typically positive endorsement came from a Year 5 pupil:

Pupil: I think they are very good because when people have a problem they do go to the teacher and everything and they put it in the book . . . and they kind of say 'come on now, apologise,' and when they do it is sort of fine and they have made up and it doesn't happen again, does it?

Two Year 4 pupils saw things much the same way:

Pupil: The Behaviour book's good. Because if we never had one, there'll be still bullying, and our school'd be not that good. . .

Pupil: The Bullying book [*sic*] keeps you in control and all that 'cos you know you are going to get in the Behaviour book if you do something really naughty.

Another Year 5 pupil was confident that the Behaviour books were having an effect:

Pupil: It is really good because of the bullying, because in case some people were getting bullied, they put the Bully book, and it was really good because some people could maybe open up a bit more about it. They thought, what *can* they do? But now they can do quite a lot about it.

But not everyone was so sanguine. The Year 6 children were noticeably more cautious in their evaluations.

Int.:   Suppose you didn't have the Behaviour books? Do you think the behaviour would get better or worse?

R: Worse.

E: It is improving. But not as improving as everybody thought it would, I don't think.

Pupil: [Behaviour books] I don't think it really works. It hasn't made that much of a change, except for like, three people. . .

Int.:   Well, if it changes three people, that's a change worth making, isn't it?

Pupil: Yeah but like there are millions of others, like twenty other people who haven't changed.

Int.:   Are you saying it's the same people who always get their names in the book?

Pupil: No, not all the time, they get away with it.

On the other hand, one seven year old (Year 2) reported his satisfaction with the system

Pupil: If we didn't have a Behaviour book, it would be just bad behaviour all the time . . .we wouldn't be able to work properly. . . Before the Behaviour book came, I kept on having bad dreams.

The Special Mentions book was appreciated by many. Typical comments included:

Pupil: That is very good. It makes people feel better about themselves as well for doing something very good, and it actually gets mentioned.

Pupil: I think it's a good idea that they put it on the newsletter now.

Pupil: Yes, they can be proud of it. Well, I think most people would like to be and so would their parents.

Again, it was the Year 6 pupils who were prepared to identify the shortcomings of the system

Pupil: I don't think that works, because if you try and do something really hard, the teacher never sees . . .

Pupil: Sometimes the teacher doesn't see . . .

Pupil: [Some pupils] show off like, because they're in the book . . .

Pupil: I'm *never* in the book, so I feel bad.

Pupil: They're like D. 'I've been in the book about eighteen times.' [imitates D's voice]

Int.: That must make him popular!

(All): No! [laughter] Completely the opposite!

Other pupils saw a little further than the systems of rewards and punishments. Two Year 4 pupils were asked who they would nominate, if there were to be a 'Special Mentions book for teachers.'

A: I would write our teacher, Miss S, because she can be funny and she helps us a lot.

L: I think all the teachers because they give us their time and everything. If it wasn't for them, we wouldn't be here. Would we know all this stuff?

A: No.

L: Exactly. That is a very good question. . .

Int.: So you would put teachers in because of the time they give you . . . ?

A: Because if it wasn't for them, we wouldn't be here and we wouldn't know this stuff what we just told you. . . . The thing is sometimes people like K, people who work in the office, who get a lot of effort into it, like the newsletter and everything, they don't really get a special mention, so I think they should. They do deserve one.

In another group, a Year 4 pupil summed up on behalf of her peers: 'The school is a good school because it's very strict and it's a peaceful school.'

The teachers also had many positive comments to make about their whole-school approach, though without any smugness or complacency. They were equally clear that there were weaknesses, and work that needed developing. One common theme was clarity; the importance of shared expectations for teaching staff, for children, for parents, for ancillary staff:

Staff: One of the really good things has been that in all of the work that we have done as a staff, we have become much, much clearer, much clearer in our own expectations and in our expectations of the children. I also think the children are so much clearer about what's going on.

Staff: The people at lunchtime, they know now, that if something goes wrong, that it's going to be recorded and therefore it will be remembered, it's there in black and white and they know that something will be done about it. They know we've got a clear procedure. And it helps the parents as well. As far as evidence goes, there you go, in black and white in our Behaviour books, and it's really helped them, as well, *understand*.

Staff: That's the one thing that's stood out to me, that people are a lot, lot clearer. Everybody is. It has really been good in terms of having evidence of children's behaviour, and talking to parents and talking amongst staff and looking for patterns of children's behaviour and it has been very good. I feel that when I write something down it has got some purpose and it is going somewhere.

This sense of purpose, combined with the security of written evidence, gave one member of staff exactly the support she needed for this aspect of her work:

Staff: I would say that [the Behaviour books] have been fantastically useful in identifying patterns in behaviour, in providing evidence, in providing a tool to be able to work with children and parents together.

But there is always more to be done.

Staff: There are things we can do, I'm sure. Because nothing ever stands still, you can always improve . . . I'd never say we'd got it *right*. I don't think you can ever say that . . .

Staff: Sometimes I think it's because we're so rushed we don't have time to sit back and think about it. . . it's having the time.

And as the staff interviews progressed (some lasted over an hour), some teachers found themselves having second thoughts, as they took the 'time to sit back and think about it.' The themes of clarity, consistency and purpose all came in for some serious and sincere re-examination:

Staff: I think there aren't enough times for the non-teaching staff to be really clear about what we have been talking about – as clear as the teaching staff – and also having strategies to deal with the problem.

Staff: I think the Special Mention and student of the week awards carry a certain amount of confusion for some children. . . Now what I've got to remember to do is make it very clear to all the pupils that we recognise achievement in pupils who don't always appear to be good models, because I can see the looks on some faces and I know they go home and say 'Why's he getting a mention for whatever?' because they've seen him behaving badly . . . and what I do say now and I qualify this, and say 'What we want to do is recognise when pupils have made a really big effort to change.'

Staff: If I'm being honest, I just wonder if we have the strict consistency about how we deal with what's written in the book. I think that's maybe the next stage, the next step.

Staff: Our special mentions, at the moment, they're good – they are good, and I think it's a really brilliant idea. *But* I don't think we're particularly sure about why we do it.

In spite of this evidence of a critical watchfulness in the teachers' evaluations, the overall message was clear: the work this staff group had done and were doing was having the desired effect:

Staff: What we are striving for here . . . it's the positive frame of mind, and the positive feeling that all that engenders, that I think helps you to learn and helps you to achieve.

At the close of the final interview with the head teacher, the researcher asked about the way forward for the school. The head teacher's reply emphasised that the developments and changes she aspired to would only be possible because of the work that had already been done.

Head teacher: (We have been able) to get so many structures embedded, and so many things are a given now; the glorious white file! [points to the fat staff handbook] It's all in there. This is what you do when you do so and so, this is who you go to to talk about this . . .

Int.:   It's like a bulwark against chaos, you've built a lot of the
                defences, you're 'building on the rock' sort of thing . . .
                [referring to the hymn sung at assembly that morning:
                'The wise man built his house upon a rock'].
Head teacher: Yes. [emphatically] *The foundations are in.*

The pupil survey data, collected in the previous Spring and Summer
terms, are useful corroborating evidence for the head teacher's certainty,
the rock-like character of her conviction about the strengths of the
school environment as a place where pupils could work and learn, safely
and successfully.

For example, the pupils were asked how they learn best: their
responses revealed a range of attitudes to learning including courage,
pride, perseverance and patience. 'What do teachers do to help you
learn?' was answered by some Year 1 pupils at the literal level: 'they
help you learn little things. Little things help you learn big things.'
Year 4 and Year 5 pupils' responses were more abstract and their
comments on good teachers included references to many moral qualities: charity, integrity, steadfastness ('She never lets you down'). Across
the school, children spoke of their desire for a happy teacher who smiles
a lot, an interesting comment, perhaps, on the joyful quality of the
virtuous human being. Some comments on the questionnaire were
crudely frank ('Behave at lunchtime and frist play is aporling') and
demonstrate that these pupils at least are brave enough to make their
dissatisfaction heard. In many other responses there is a theme of
struggle and persistence. For example: 'What do you think working
hard means?' 'Giving your whole self.' Similarly, a good teacher is one
who will 'push you into believing that you can do it'.

Evidence from other sources

The researcher's non-participant observations, made during regular
visits to the school (between November 1996 and January 1998) are
further evidence of the school's achievements. There are many examples
of children acting responsibly, contributing to the smooth running of
the school, joining in classroom routines of considerable complexity
and occasional severity, and safely crossing well-used roads in large
groups, sometimes as many as eight times in a day. In the Year 4, 5 and
6 classes, working in silence was regularly expected, and in the infant
classes there was an emphatic insistence on the need to listen atten-
tively during whole class teaching and discussion sessions. The
children's behaviour during assemblies and hymn practice was

exemplary, with lavish praise given by the head teacher for whole school efforts (such as their singing: 'Superb!') and for individuals who had distinguished themselves in some way ('I can't take my eyes off S today. S is a person, I hope he won't mind my saying it, who has worked so hard to improve his behaviour.' (S blushes, but nods approval.) 'Every time I look at him, I see him trying so hard.') After a later reference to children sitting well, ready to leave the hall for playtime ('that lucky row there, with S sitting in it'), a Year 2 girl spoke to the researcher in the playground with some pride, 'I was in S's row.'

At the end of term assembly ('not so much an assembly, more of a celebration' as the head teacher commented to the researcher) there was a large-scale distribution of printed certificates, presented by the caretaker to every child who had achieved consistently high standards of behaviour, as well as to all those who had 'worked very, very hard to improve,' in the head teacher's words. The atmosphere was excited, and the teachers, too, were touched. 'It's like the Oscars!' whispered one to the researcher. Here was public recognition on a grand scale of many small, private achievements, which had possibly gone unremarked until this termly ritual, since the weekly Special Mentions book was used by teachers and other staff more selectively, singling out particular children, week by week, for an enormous variety of notable behaviours.

Indeed, the diversity of children's thoughts, words and deeds that were identified as worthy of special mention was at first almost bewildering. In the half term September–October 1996, for example, before the researcher's first visit to the school in November, there were 242 separate entries in the Special Mentions book, naming 116 different children (number on roll = 197). A rough and ready classification of these into categories shows that comments were most frequently made about achievements in specific curriculum areas.

Each of these categories can be further subdivided, giving intriguing insights into aspects of the staff group's value system in action, and

Table 2.1 Number of special mentions, September–October 1996

Achievements/curriculum areas	242
Pupil behaviour	49
Pupil effort	40
Pupil improvement	12
Presentation of work	10
Achievement (other)	10

demonstrating how their priorities are communicated to the children, and to each other.

The mentions of individual pupils for their behaviour, for example, the second largest category, are heavily weighted towards listening, with ten individuals nominated for listening well, or for their good 'listening skills', and two whole class mentions. Concentration (six mentions) and good manners (six mentions) make up the bulk of the rest. These figures suggest that many of the behaviours being reinforced by these public acts of positive feedback are very much those of pupils, learning the conventions of their school community. As Mary Willes so dramatically concludes, in her observational study of children in their first year in school: 'finding out what the teacher wants and doing it, is the primary duty of the pupil.' (Willes, 1983, p. 138). From the evidence of the Special Mentions book, it seems that what the teachers at Anne Fine want their pupils to do is to achieve well across the curriculum, to listen, to make strenuous efforts, to improve, to overcome difficulties, to try hard, and to be enthusiastic.

But that is by no means the end of the story. There is also evidence of children being nominated for what the moral philosopher and educationalist David Carr describes as 'those homely and familiar excellences called the moral virtues – honesty, tolerance, fair mindedness, courage, persistence, consideration, patience and so forth.' (Carr, 1991, p. 269). In this sample half term, children were mentioned for their helpfulness, their kindness, loyalty and trustworthiness. At other times, children were singled out for their patience, courage and personal strength, virtues that appeared in the pupil survey data as well. Carr argues that the job of acquainting children with these moral virtues 'is the highest and most important task of education;' there is evidence that, at Anne Fine primary school, this task is indeed consciously present in the minds of the educators, even if it is not given the absolute priority that Carr claims for it.

There is corroborating evidence in the Behaviour books that learning in the moral domain is part of the children's everyday experience. In one of the infant classes in particular it was noticeable how a large proportion of the incidents recorded were major or minor breakdowns in child–child relationships: thumping, slapping, spitting, pushing, name calling and so on. These turbulent interactions were noted in some detail, and the teacher's account, more often than not, included the word 'because'. For example:

Teacher: Dan was extremely upset because S had said that his mother was going to complain to the school about Dan calling him stupid. Dan had then called S's mother stupid, which made S upset.

Teacher: W pushed down hard on N's head because 'She wasn't worrying about herself'.

Teacher: W told N to move 'otherwise I'll whack your bum off'. There was confusion between W and several others because they all claimed they were last in the line [the last person shuts the gate].

Again and again, the action taken is recorded as 'We talked about this . . .' or 'Class discussion about it . . .' As this teacher and her class of young children talk about their disagreements, their upsets, their hurts and grievances, they are examining the causality and reciprocity of relationship. Through small group and class discussion, they are both creating and studying a curriculum of harmonious human behaviour, in which the key concepts are respect, tolerance and mutual attachment. During the rest of the day, these children are working within the territory mapped out by the National Curriculum and its subject areas; but in these short sessions, in which relationships are repaired and harmony restored, they are doing a different kind of work, engrossed in a curriculum with the moral virtues at its core. Their curriculum at these times seems to come close to that defined by Derek Morrell, one of the founding fathers of the Schools Council, in a speech given in 1968:

> The curriculum, if it exists at all, is a structure erected on a base of reciprocal personal relationships. In curriculum we are concerned with human beings whose feelings and aspirations are far more real and immediately important to them than the cognitive development which is the educator's stock-in-trade.
>
> (quoted in Thornton, 1986)

Going deeper – making meaning

In the following sections, the focus shifts from the surface of events, the observable present tense of school and classroom events. A selection of data is re-examined in order to uncover the ways in which pupils and teachers make sense of their experiences, and to throw light on the internal, thinking work that these children and adults do, as they carry out the public acts of daily life.

One interesting source of data for this part of the investigation was disclosed during one of the teacher interviews, when the discussion turned to the equal opportunities work that had been the theme of a recent staff development initiative. Working together, the staff had constructed sets of questions for teachers to ask themselves. There were questions for the head teacher, another set for a class teacher, one set for a curriculum co-ordinator and so on. The teacher who had taken the lead in this work was aware that there was still scope for development, particularly with non-teaching staff such as the midday supervisors and administrative staff, who, she thought, needed the opportunity 'to sit down and work on the issues', just as the teaching staff had done. The sets of questions the teacher showed the researcher, still in draft, were impressive evidence of the staff's awareness of the need to *work* on their principles and priorities, to do the thinking, together, that would stitch the principle (of equal opportunities, in this instance) into the fabric of teachers' lives. For example, the class teacher's list included these questions:

- Do I give all children opportunities for recognition? [for example Special Mentions, student of the week and so on]
- Do I make provision for children who are less demanding?
- Do my teaching styles allow me to help children before they ask for help?

These questions, and others like them, suggest that this staff group were making conscious attempts to pull together different strands of their professional responsibilities. They were deliberately interweaving aspects of their pedagogy (helping children, in a supportive, scaffolding role) with their common principles (on equal opportunities), and with their agreed symbolic practices (such as the student nominations), strengthening each strand by speaking out loud to each other about their interconnectedness.

The head teacher's final interview also touches on this theme of making connections

Head teacher: I think it's important that I hang on to all the bits of my teaching and that they (the pupils) see me doing other things, in order that I don't become the behaviour lady, or the sorter-out of problems. I think that's down to me in the way I teach, and the way I present. I think it's important that the links are made, that I make links in my assemblies, that I make links when I do my classroom visits, that I make links when I'm on lunch duty and all those other things . . . so it's very much about our school life.

She was explicit about the need to connect the pupils' growing understanding of appropriate behaviour with the fundamental purposes of education. They may know (and can certainly recite) some of the attributes of 'the good pupil' (the theme of a recent assembly) but as the head teacher asked (herself? or the researcher?)

Head teacher: What does being well behaved *do for you?* That's the question, isn't it? It's one thing to be well-behaved, but what do you get out of it? There's got to be a *pay-off*, hasn't there?

She was not referring to certificates or other ephemeral, or symbolic, privileges.

Head teacher: It has to do with work – and achievement – and the joy of learning (slowly and deliberately). You've got to be obvious and up-front about it and keep making those connections.

This awareness of the need for teachers to be consciously 'making those connections' was apparent in another teacher interview. This senior member of staff was asked which aspect of the school's overall approach seemed to be most significant in terms of the principle of inclusiveness, and her discursive reply ended with the reflection 'I think it's *working* with the children really' [her emphasis]. In the discussion that followed, she described how she and the head teacher both set about this task of working with the children (working, not naming, praising, punishing or rewarding). 'Working' involved, in this teacher's construction, setting aside time and space for talking to children:

Teacher: giving them time, talking through their various problems with them, taking them seriously, being on your own with them. . . . Sometimes these children need a heck of a long time and I think that was something we were conscious of – that there are some children who do take an awful lot of our time . . . One tries to be fair but it can be quite hard when you know they need something special.

This teacher seems to be explicitly recognising some fundamental characteristics of children's learning, whether they are learning to be pupils, or learning the moral virtues, or learning with a curriculum focus: that learning is always, even within the public institution of the school, a personal and individual process, which sometimes needs personal and individual support. She seems to be accepting that slow learning (learning done slowly, not learning done by slow people) is every bit as worthwhile as other kinds, and that not all pupils need the same levels of support.

There is evidence that the children too, are aware of both the differences and the congruence between, as it were, the big ideas at the heart of their education, and some of the particular practices in which they are encoded. For example two seven year olds (Year 3) were asked when and how they learned about appropriate behaviour:

T: Sometimes Miss S tells us to come on the carpet and we have a little talk.
N: And she says, 'I'm dreadful of your behaviour, don't ever do that to me again.'
Int.:   So you learn about behaviour when you are on the carpet?
T, N: Yes.
Int.:   And anywhere else?
T, N: No!

Taken at face value, this exchange might suggest that as yet, these children see little connection between the lessons learned on the carpet and learning in other dimensions of their lives.

However when the same two pupils were asked what helped them to learn, one mentioned 'happiness – yeah, that helps us'. This comment suggests the beginning of a more profound understanding, an emerging appreciation of at least one attribute of effective learning: its relationship to the learners' well-being and internal state of mind (rather than their position on the carpet). In the conclusion to the interview, when asked to sum up their feelings about the school in just three words or phrases, these two pupils contributed, in turns:

T: School is very very good.
N: School is sometimes boring.
T: No, school is not always boring.
N: I said sometimes . . .
T: I said it's very very good for children.
N: School is good, school is boring.
T: And school is good for your eyes and ears.
N: No, school is good for your learning.

This is an impressive conclusion for seven year olds to have drawn;

in spite of occasional tedium, the message has been received, the connection made, the commitment – to school and learning – already, consciously, in place.

Similarly, a group of Year 4 children, speculating about what would happen to people who did not attend school, arrived – via a discussion of the crucial importance of getting a good job – at this conclusion:

M: And they need to learn to do things for when they were older.

A: And also if they didn't go to school, and they didn't want to learn, they would probably turn out as a robber, because they wouldn't know how to treat the world.

This is important learning, surely, being made explicit here by an eight year old: that in the little world of the neighbourhood primary school there is much to learn about that other great world, opening up in the children's future, including how it should be treated, and how it may treat its inhabitants.

'Working with the children,' emphasised the teacher quoted above; the children too, do the same kind of work, silently, individually, making meaning for themselves out of the hurly-burly of the school day. 'School is a funny place' said the head teacher to the assembled school one day, perhaps (and perhaps justifiably) anxious about the behaviour of the researcher writing copious notes throughout the twenty minute assembly routine. In a sense though, it is no funnier to children than any other place, just one more set of experiences from which they will construct working models, provisional and incomplete as they inevitably are, of how things work and hang together, what makes people tick, and lose their tempers, and what part children play in all of this.

Difference, divergence and individual children

Much of the work at Anne Fine seemed to owe its effectiveness to the energy that had been expended in achieving clarity and consensus, shared meanings, whole staff agreement and common approaches. For all that, any behaviour policy can only be put into practice in a series of individual encounters, unique constellations of events, where history never repeats itself and every achievement or transgression has to be evaluated afresh. Common approaches cannot create absolute convergence in the complexities of school and classroom life. There must always be attention to differences, to divergence, and to the individuals who make the difference.

The head teacher was emphatic in describing the emphasis of her work with individual pupils.

Head teacher: Something I will always include in any conversation in here [the head teacher's room] with an individual who has needed the carpet treatment, I say: 'I'm not talking about Daniel, I'm talking about some of the things that Daniel has done', and they are completely separate . . . It helps me in those situations, I don't know whether it helps Daniel, but it helps me to say 'I care about you very much as a human being and I want to do my best by you and I want this school to be somewhere that you want to be and to achieve in, but at the moment you doing things that are getting in the way of all that'. . . . I don't want Daniel to go out of here thinking I despise and detest him and I'd rather he wasn't in my school. I want him to know that I want him to be here, and I want him to have a good education while he is here, and I want to help him to show us more of all those wonderful qualities he has and the good side of him, which I can see all the time. And I talk about that.

The urgency and energy of the head teacher's voice in this passage are significant; they convey her absolute commitment to making sure that every pupil understands that the school rules and regulations drawn up in the interests of the harmonious community, are also essentially in the interests of individual pupils. 'This school is for *you*, Daniel', she seems to be saying, as well as for all the others. It may be a crowded public place, but it is also a place where each and every different individual can lead a purposeful, meaningful and rewarding life.

Other teacher interviews reinforced the importance of this theme. Staff members seemed to be reflecting out loud on some of their normally unspoken priorities – that the school should make human sense, to every unique individual, not just institutional good sense to the adults who enforce the school's code of conduct. One teacher spoke of a pupil who had experienced serious and long-term difficulties in meeting the standards of behaviour required by the school:

Teacher: I'm thinking about people like Tom, I'm thinking about how to deal with someone like him, and I don't think the way to go about it is to permanently . . . [she lists some of the sanctions applied in the past]. I think he gets enough. . . . I am actually trying to sit down and talk to him, friend to friend, because whatever is going on, I want the best for him at the end of the day. But that's a long process, to try and win him over, to let him know that I do care about him.

It is noticeable how the teacher here explicitly refers to Tom as a person, not as a student, pupil, child or kid. It is remarkable how she speaks of him as a friend, as someone she cares about, whose point of view she is interested in. Later in the same interview she speaks about a boy in a previous class who shouted all the time.

Teacher: And I asked him 'Why do you shout so much, why don't you just try and speak quieter?' and he said 'Well my Mum and Dad are always shouting at each other' and so he sees them shouting at each other and just to talk in normal conversations, well that's just not what they are used to, so it's quite a long process to try and explain to him that you don't need to – Gosh, why do I sound so negative about it?

In the next sentence she goes on:

Teacher: I know identifying role-models is all very good, and special mentions, but I just wonder what goes on in their heads when they hear about all these wonderful children being mentioned all the time . . . I am trying to think from their point of view as well.

This teacher is explicitly re-examining her acts as a teacher from the individual pupil's perspective; she is working from the premise that pupils' behaviour is likely to make sense to them, and that teachers will do well to try to participate in their pupils' acts of meaning-making.

The evidence for these individual acts can be found on every page of the transcribed pupil interviews, as they draw on their present experiences, and memories of their recent past, to illustrate the points they are making. The youngest children were not the only ones to be shamelessly anecdotal. For example, every year group had detailed stories to tell the interviewer of playground incidents that had left deep impressions, sometimes even physical scarring. But their playground issues were not identical with their teachers' concerns or those of the midday supervisors, judging from the adults' entries in the playground Behaviour books. For some children the most unacceptable aspect of playground behaviour was the adult veto on particular games (British Bulldog was mentioned more than once). One group of Year 6 children expressed a unanimous longing for slides, and one girl wistfully added, in a dreamy sing-song voice: 'in my nursery, we used to have swings . . . and seesaws'.

When the interviewer checked these sentiments out with other groups, there was universal approval. These children seemed to be staking out a claim to be offered children's experiences, at least in their time away from the classroom. And children's experiences do not necessarily figure in their teachers' plans for them. Two seven year old boys (Year 2) illustrate this point.

Int.: When you're in the playground, do you learn anything?
A: Yeah we do. We learn about nature. We learn about animals. We see lots of pigeons. – [warming to his theme] – I like the playground best, because I build little nests for the birds.

His close friend N joins in and they animatedly describe what they do, how they collect the sticks, how you have:

N: to forage to get the best places, you have to fight for them, to get the right places, so the Juniors and Year 1 don't get them . . . Sometimes people exclude you out of their games and you have to look for other sticks . . .

In response to questions about classroom learning, this young child frames his priorities differently.

N: I might be a naturalist when I grow up . . . My passion is to go back to [his country of origin] and help some people to help the wild life.

However in the playground, his passion is expressed in the secret world of birds and little nests that he shares with his closest friends. If there are no slides, at least there is space for the imagination. Is it a coincidence that two other children from the same class are also heavily into sticks?

Int.: What are the best things that happen in the playground?
A: We pretend that we're making cheese with the bark, because we scrape it with sticks, and then [detailed description of how to make cheese]. . . And then they steal all our sticks and our pieces of bark and then we have nothing left . . . and we mustn't react.

These children's play is not a trivial pursuit: they take it seriously enough. And clearly, they are still learning, even though they have temporarily left the classroom and its priorities far behind.

For all the emphasis on clarity and consistency in the staff's approach to behaviour, there was also evidence of their awareness and appreciation of the endless diversity within the community of children. There were occasions when it seemed as if an individual teacher came face to face with the newly-recognised individuality of a particular pupil. There is a small but revealing set of entries in the Special Mentions book, which can be interpreted as miniature memorials to some such moments. The teacher has seized an opportunity to reflect back to the pupil what seems to be happening to them both. Then, in the very public arena of the Monday morning whole school assembly, the pupil hears the teacher's personal interpretation spoken out loud, a shared reading of an intensely individual story.

For example, Miss H writes, of a child in her class 'a special mention to F who cheered up Miss H. It's lovely to know someone cares.'

Some other entries: 'to L, whose wide grin is a constant source of cheer to her teacher.' . . . 'to H, who has been feeling unwell, but still battled on and always managed to raise a smile.' . . . 'to S, for being so understanding when her model was accidentally destroyed. Without a fuss she started again and smiled away her disappointment.'

These comments suggest the possibility of classrooms where teachers and pupils take each other, and the differences between them, seriously, emotionally and intellectually. There is evidence of a developing reciprocity, of mutual benefit, in these flashes of emotional intelligence across the adult–child divide. On hearing that she cheered up Miss H, F will have had her attention drawn to her teacher's openness to caring and expressive acts. The disappointed S will have learned that her feelings were acknowledged and respected. The unwell child H will have heard that his teacher appreciated his struggle to 'raise a smile,' and may conclude that smiles are a viable and valued currency in classroom interaction.

There is no doubt that in this school, the work of inclusion, of understanding, of moral education, in David Carr's sense of the words, is a continuous process, an abiding discipline of both affect and cognition. The foundations are in, in the head teacher's phrase; the policies are publicly displayed, the adults have reached consensus, but the negotiation and construction of individual meaning is always work in progress.

The language of encounters

During their interviews, the children were given a variety of opportunities to talk about the teachers and other educators in the school. It was surprising (to the researcher) how many children referred to these adults' physical attributes in recording their appreciation and affection. 'She is kind to us and she has nice hair.' 'I never let go of her when I cuddle her.' 'She's lovely.' These were by no means singular contributions. At first it seemed sensible to dismiss these and other similar comments as irrelevant, immature, immaterial to the issues being investigated. Gradually though it became evident that these artless confessions of physical attraction could better be understood by considering them alongside other elements in the data.

The tape recorded interviews took place in a small room with doors at each end, on which 'Do Not Disturb' notices were posted to prevent interruptions. This enclosed setting, and the introductory explanations by the researcher of the interview process, seemed to engender a sense of security in the children. In every interview there were passages when the children seemed to be ready to abandon the formal discourse of the school, and to stray from the familiar question and answer routine of the classroom. Much of the time they did rely on predictable and well-rehearsed replies to questions they had heard often enough before, in classroom pep-talks and Monday morning assemblies. They all knew, by heart, for example, the conventional response to the head teacher's weekly question ('Why do you come to school?' 'To work and to learn.') Some of the time though, all of them took the plunge, however briefly, and dropped their guards. Then from their lips came tumbling stories which their teachers had almost certainly never heard, and child–child exchanges of breathtaking crudity (to the interviewer), causing hilarious mirth to the interviewees. It was as if the physical intimacy of the interview room, small, quiet and private, had triggered a disposition to recognise the intimacy of a variety of human relationships, and a capacity to venture beyond the formal and conventional, even during their brief encounters with the researcher and her tape-recorder.

This insight into the children's sense of the intimate has stimulated a re-reading of the tributes to their teachers' personal characteristics quoted at the head of this section, which no longer seem irrelevant or immature. Some of the time, the children seemed to represent the relationship between themselves and their teachers as distant, impersonal, arbitrary, unfair, even punitive. They also seemed to recognise though that this relationship can also be close, intimate, personal and loving. They see their teachers as human beings, like themselves, with feelings, who need cheering up, who can be bad-tempered, who can suffer and be consoled. One child told, with an eloquent look of distress, a story of bad behaviour that had taken place when the class teacher's baby was seriously ill. The children probably never forget that their teachers are always in authority over them, that they have the power to arbitrate in their disputes and make judgements about their behaviour. Their acceptance of the dominant status of their teachers and the other adults in the school does not however blot out a parallel understanding, a knowledge of the closeness and attraction of all human beings, one to another. An awareness of this closeness is, some of the time, caught up in the meanings that both children and teachers make.

Madeleine Grumet, curriculum theorist and feminist, writes challengingly of the relationship, in contemporary schooling, between pedagogy and patriarchy. She claims that 'most of our classrooms cannot sustain human relationships of sufficient intimacy to support the risks, the trust and the expression that learning requires.' (Grumet, 1988, p. 56). At Anne Fine primary school, in the piles of documentation amassed by the researcher, there is evidence of just such relationships, intimate, trusting and expressive.

During a discussion of the supporting role of the classroom assistants, and the work of one particular member of the team, Miss G, a nine year old girl interrupts the interviewer:

A: Also one day I was really ill and she was helping me and she was calming me down because I had a problem in my belly and I had to wee in a pot and give it to Miss G and she was helping me not to think about it and she took me for a little walk and it was nice.
Int.: And you haven't forgotten?
A: I can remember it like it was yesterday.

This candid, detailed memory is surely an example of the kind of human relationships that Grumet calls for in classrooms. The teachers, too, reveal their capacity to enter such relationships, and to express their awareness of what is going on within them. The following page from the Special Mentions book, for example, contains not just four fine portraits of individual children, glowing and fresh in line and colour, but also a miniature of the teacher herself, the person who notices these things and risks expression of them in the crowded assembly hall.

G, for a truly wonderful portrait of Gerald. I am sure he will treasure it always.

T, for his consistently good graphical ideas, he shows real talent in this area.

J, for his enthusiastic, and well remembered contributions to our discussions on the Crimean War. I like to see his hand waving!

K, for always completing her assignments on time, to a very high standard, and her constant effort, especially in Poetry. She has a real feel for words, and a poet's soul to go with them.

As she writes these words, this teacher has little in common with those teachers castigated by Grumet, who certify the 'system' (her inverted commas) and 'who repudiate the intimacy of nurture. . . in their work in education.' (op. cit., p. xvi). The language this teacher uses to delineate her pupils is far from that which dominates the discourse of schooling according to Grumet: 'language that celebrates system and denies doubt, that touts objectives and denies ambivalence, that confesses frustration but withholds love' (op. cit., p. 59).

There are certainly systems in place at Anne Fine. There are systems for crossing the road, for measuring and rewarding achievement, for escalating degrees of discipline, punishment and part-time exclusion (normally three days, for the gravest offences of deliberate violence). These systems are well-documented, out in the open, known and referred to throughout the school community. Three more special mentions will illustrate this point:

L, for being a reliable leader when the class crosses the road. She always remembers to wait with her toes behind the curb line. (Year 1)

C & A, for working hard to write more than one sentence in their writing and to remember full stops.

To three children who have had full marks in their spelling test and to six others who almost made full marks. (Year 2)

This is evidence of a shared attention to detail, of a commitment to clarity, in demands and expectations, of systems designed to be supportive of all.

There are systems for more extreme cases too. On the researcher's final visit to the school, there had been an explosive incident of violence the previous day, and the instigator had been suspended for three days. The head teacher was aware of the irony of the timing of this incident and referred to it more than once in the interview that took place that day, but, as she saw it, the system left her with little room for manoeuvre.

Head teacher: I hate doing it, but I've got an audience of 200 people. They'll be saying 'What *is* this school about?' . . . I know these three days are probably the worst thing for [child excluded] right now. But twenty-nine children saw and heard [the incident].

The offence triggered the system; the system (temporarily) excludes the child. But the system does not extinguish the human capacity for compassion, for doubt, for questioning, for tenderness. The head teacher brooded aloud:

Head teacher: I asked myself a thousand times yesterday, am I doing the right thing? Yes, I know I'm doing the right thing, according to our school behaviour policy, but all those question marks; all the time, they are looming in my mind. . . The worst bit is the dilemma. I feel so much for that child as an individual and I want *so desperately* to help her to overcome all the problems she has. I quite understand how she's become a victim, she was bullied mercilessly in her last school.

During the morning session, just before this interview, the head teacher had taken an infant assembly, where the theme was rules.

Head teacher: [to assembled children] What do we need to have to make our school a happy place? It begins with R?
Child: Role-models.
Head teacher: That's a brilliant answer [repeats question until child supplies the required word, rules].

She returned to the theme in the interview, emphasising the unwritten purposes of the system, the human dimension of the rule of law in the school.

Head teacher: That's why I've gone back to the rules thing in my assemblies this week. [as if she was addressing the pupils] We *have* to have these things, we *have* to ask you these things, because we know from our experience, you'll all be a lot happier, and feel far more secure and comfortable, and be able to get on with your learning.

The school system calls for rules, and obedience to rules. But the human beings who constitute the community of the school can do more. In their encounters with one another they can do as Grumet suggests, and prioritise the intimacy of the relationships between those that the rules were written to protect.

Conclusion

In *The Sane Society* (1956) Erich Fromm gloomily argues that contemporary society is far from sane, and that it will, if allowed to continue in the way it is going, end in robotism, alienation and destruction – insanity and inhumanity at large. The alternative, the healthy, sane society, can only be achieved by redefining the relationship between human beings and the societies they construct for themselves and each other. The focus of our attention should not be the adjustment of the individual to his or her society; our critical questioning should explore whether society is well-adjusted to the needs of its members. Is society, as we know it, fit for human beings? Does it further their healthy development, or inhibit it? Is it a good enough place to exercise our humanity in?

Questions such as these, suitably scaled down, can clearly be directed at particular institutions within society, not least to schools. So, adapting Fromm's formula, we could ask, not whether individual pupils are well-adjusted to the norms and cultures of the schools they find themselves in, but whether schools in general, or individual schools in particular, are well-adjusted to the needs of their pupils. How much do they contribute to their educational health and well-being? To their development as human beings? To the exercise of their growing human powers?

'You know I'm going to ask you this,' says the head teacher of Anne Fine, to the assembled pupils, every Monday morning: 'Why are you here?' As they answer in unison: 'To work and to learn,' another question suggests itself: is the school a fit place for this enterprise? Will these pupils, here and now, today and tomorrow, work and learn, in ways that contribute to their humanity, to their capacity to live fulfilling, worthwhile lives? Clearly, the answer is yes. The evidence is rich, solid, convincing. This school is a secure place; there is working and learning in every corner. 'You have to be strict about it,' said one teacher,

> the small secret little things. . . I want them to *know* I will come down on it. They have to feel *safe* in the classroom. They feel, 'Yeah, she's in charge, she won't let it happen' . . . I want them to know that I'm the teacher. I *am* the teacher.

The researcher invited her to continue, to identify the key concepts within this view of the teacher's role: 'With me it's *fair*, above how individuals feel about me. And *safety* for the people who need me.'

Within this safety, then, children work and learn. The citations in the Special Mentions book, discussed earlier, illustrate the qualities of work and the varieties of learning that are valued at Anne Fine. At the head teacher's assemblies too, the messages are underlined. Developing a school-wide theme on friendship, the head teacher asked for contributions to her concluding sentences: 'a very important part of our work in this school. Part of our work in this school, is to do what?'

Pupil: Making people happy.
Head teacher: Good girl. Making people happy is an important part of our work in this school.

There is agreement then at Anne Fine, about what the school is for, and about why the teachers and pupils are there. There are still questions worth asking though about the division of labour between them. The radical thinker and progressive educator, Edmond Holmes, has challenging views on this topic, which are relevant here. In an essay written in 1913, not long after he had retired from his post as Chief Inspector for Elementary Schools, Holmes reiterates his central criticism of the elementary system as he knew it (most eloquently and fully argued in the 1911 book *What Is and What Might Be*). The core of the problem, according to Holmes, is our unwillingness to accept the principle of self-education, to acknowledge that children's learning must be done by children, that adults, however well-intentioned, cannot do it for them.

> From morning to evening, from day to day, from year to year, [education] does, or tries to do for [the child] most of the things which he ought to do for himself – his reasoning, his thinking, his imagining, his admiring, his sympathising, his willing, his purposing, his planning, his solving of problems, his mastering of difficulties, his controlling his passions and impulses, his bearing himself aright in this dealings with others. . . . It will allow him to do nothing for himself which it can do or even pretend to do for him; and it thus develops into an elaborate system for paralysing activity.
>
> (Fisher, 1913, p. xxiii)

These angry accusations, penned in passion so many years ago, still have the power to make us pause and reflect. Are his criticisms still meaningful? Do we, today, intervene, interfere, interrupt the learning that pupils would more effectively do for themselves without us? Is there a possibility that the frameworks we design to support learning, in their attention to detail, their pursuit of clarity, are, in practice, over-designed? Could support be experienced as constraint?

In the final interview with the head teacher of Anne Fine, the researcher picked up on a reference to an attitude of 'zero tolerance' being expressed in the Behaviour books, and her comment 'We're getting terribly pernickety'.

Int: because some of the stuff in the Behaviour books, it is little.

Head teacher: It's little. But we also know from our experience that little can get very big if it's not addressed . . . I think if you bother about the little tiny things and the detail, you never get those big explosive unpleasant things.

Indeed, the incidence of 'those big explosive unpleasant things' was very low. As the pages of the Behaviour books demonstrate, and the researcher's observation notes confirm, 'the little tiny things and the detail' were constantly being reinforced, normally with an emphasis on the positive. One entry in the Special Mentions book singles out a pupil for 'Always working and sitting quietly.' But there was also a more negative side to the process. The teachers themselves were well aware of the pressure they put on the children in this respect. For example, lining children up in order to cross the roads and to move them around the cramped buildings was a source of frustration to both teachers and their pupils. As one teacher observed:

Teacher: They just resent being told all the time to line up, and you know, the older they get the more they hate it.

And another:

Teacher: I just sort of feel they're terribly repressed – and yet it works – it works in many ways.

A third teacher echoes this note of regret:

Teacher: Just getting out of the building to the playground is a major operation and I don't really like it in some ways. . . With four classes trying to get out in a confined area, you feel as if you are on their backs the whole time. You know, line up, stand straight, walk to this door, walk to that door. It is quite unnatural. But I do appreciate that if you didn't do that it would be all hell.

These comments and others like them seem to be suggesting that, some of the time at least, the need to enforce obedience may be at odds with other more truly educational purposes. If the pupils were not so frequently invited to obey their teacher's detailed instructions, could they be doing other, more important, and ultimately more rewarding work? Erich Fromm seems to offer some encouragement for this possibility. It is one of the functions of society, he argues, to 'shape the energies' of its members in such a way that their behaviour is a matter of '*wanting to act as they have to act*' (Fromm, 1956, p. 79, his italics). Goethe says very much the same thing: 'Duty is when one loves that which one commands oneself to do.' (quoted in Nobel, 1991, p. 127). And a contemporary moralist, J. Gilligan, echoes the key concept of love: 'only when people are doing what they want to do, rather than what they should do, can they act out of love rather than out of fear.' (Gilligan, 1976, p. 145).

There are educational implications to be drawn from these very different writers, arriving at this one simple conclusion by their various routes; one is that when education is predicated on obedience, opportunities are lost for other kinds of learning, which cannot be done to order. The principle of active learning, of what Holmes calls self-education, must be maintained, if the school is to function as a proper setting for children, active learners every one. Holmes' contempt for passive learning, 'learning by swallowing', expressed at length in his 1911 book, is a useful reminder that not all kinds of learning are equally desirable. In active learning, children's energies are channelled into their desire to understand, to make sense of the world and the people in it; Susan Isaacs calls it 'this thirst for understanding . . . a veritable passion' (Isaacs, 1932, p. 113).

Jane Roland Martin, an eminent curriculum theorist and feminist, makes the same distinction between active and passive learning, but in different terms. She contrasts education for spectatorship, in which pupils are not required to bring their intelligence to bear on living, in which they are taught to be unthinking observers of the world, with education for participation. In schools that are properly matched to their needs, argues Martin, children will be learning to live in the world, not just to know about it, to take part in it, not to suffer disconnection from it. And in such schools, the curriculum will be constructed around care, concern, connection and nurturance. The virtue of caring Martin defines, most eloquently, as lying between the excess of indulgence and the deficiency of coldness (Martin, 1992, p. 110). Here Martin's analysis is directly applicable to some of the processes documented at Anne Fine. In one memorable lesson the researcher observed groups of Year 5 pupils rewriting the Beatitudes, using real people whom they knew well, members of their intimate families for the most part, to exemplify the New Testament text. In that classroom, that morning, the pupils were experiencing a curriculum that purposely connected learning and living. They were truly active learners, being given opportunities to exercise their own powers of care, concern, connectedness. The classroom was more than a safe place, more than a quiet and controlled environment. It was a place, for all that they were sitting quietly, where the pupils were autonomous and exploratory, rather than simply obedient and rule-bound. The challenge for teachers and children, not just at Anne Fine, but everywhere that children and teachers work and learn together, is to maximise the times and places when the lived curriculum is thoroughly congruent with the school's aspirations, with children's deepest needs, with their developing human powers.

3 Virginia Woolf High School (1)

Introduction

Virginia Woolf High School is an 11–16 urban mixed comprehensive school. At the time of the research, there were approximately 950 students aged 11–16 on roll. Thirty-one per cent of these were eligible for free school meals, and there were 275 pupils on the special needs register, of whom forty-six had statements. The great majority of the intake is from local authority housing.

Unemployment in the area is higher than the national average. Over recent years several of the traditional local light manufacturing industries, who used to employ from our catchment area, have closed down. It is not unusual to look in the local newspaper and read about ex-pupils appearing in the Magistrate and Crown Courts. Incidents such as joy-riding, drug abuse and sales, vandalism and violence are not uncommon; we also have significant numbers of children who live with domestic violence or who are young carers.

This is not to say that we are what may be labelled as a 'rough inner city school' with its stereotypical problems. We have a proportion of students who have genuinely high aspirations – a proportion which is slowly increasing – though the magic five GCSEs at grades A to C are attained by only about 25–30 per cent of children, placing us near the bottom of the LEA league table. Nevertheless our catchment can be seen as suffering from economic and social deprivation.

When I received the first flyer about the research, I was a temporary member of the school's senior management team, running a GEST funded project intended to support vulnerable and disaffected students. Known as 'Personal Tutoring', this was a scheme of individual support whereby volunteer members of staff used a mix of counselling and mentoring skills to attempt to help students remain integrated and successful within the school's structures, expectations and demands.

There were also a number of other initiatives underway in the school that were relevant to the themes of the research. I was keen for the school to be involved in order to give us an opportunity to review and evaluate what we were currently doing. Networking with other schools would enable us to exchange ideas, discuss strategies and learn from one another.

With the head's agreement, a small steering group was set up. In negotiation with members of the research team from Cambridge, it was agreed that the research would be principally concerned with exploring the perceptions of staff and students of the various initiatives that we were currently working on. Volunteers were invited to be actively involved in researching each initiative, and seven members of staff joined the research team. All staff were invited to express their views through a questionnaire. Members of the university team were asked to research the 'Personal Tutor' scheme and to carry out case studies of two selected pupils deemed to be at risk of exclusion.

The various initiatives that were selected for examination were of two kinds. On the one hand there were initiatives – like the Personal Tutoring scheme – which aimed to have an immediate impact, by offering additional support to individuals who were considered to be particularly vulnerable or at risk of exclusion. On the other hand, there were initiatives designed to develop and enhance of features of existing practice in school for the benefit of *all* pupils (for example developing the PSE curriculum, introducing Circle Time in Year 7, provision for developing literacy). Their contribution to the task of reducing and preventing exclusion would be a more indirect and long-term one: attempting to create a stable, secure and positive environment which would in turn make it more likely that students would engage productively in school life.

Over the nine months of our involvement in the project, differences of perspective amongst staff became such an important feature of the process that it would not be true to reality to present the findings of the research as if these reflected a common, collective understanding. In this chapter, I offer a personal account of the new insights that emerged with respect to the various initiatives that were currently under way. The analysis focuses in more depth and detail on the strategies for individual support, because these were the areas of work that I was most directly involved in.

In the following chapter, the Cambridge researchers explain how the emerging differences of perspective also helped to highlight the importance of giving equal thought and attention to what could be done to address the needs of teachers, alongside what we were doing for students, if we were to make further progress in developing positive alternatives to exclusion.

The Personal Tutor scheme

At the time of the research, there were ten members of staff acting as 'Personal Tutors'. Each worked with about six students. The Personal Tutors were an extra layer of support, not replacements for those within the existing pastoral system. The funding made it possible for them to spend time with their tutees, either meeting frequently for one-to-one work or providing support in the classroom.

Initially staff were asked to volunteer to become Personal Tutors (PTs). The main criteria I used for approaching staff and sounding them out as potential PTs were that they had a high level of self-esteem and emotional literacy themselves. They also needed to be resilient and committed to giving of themselves. This included a commitment towards being trained, in their own time, and supporting others in the team. I also felt that while I may have been seen as manager of the scheme, it was vital that I had a number of students to whom I could act as Personal Tutor myself.

I was fortunate that one Personal Tutor was already trained as a counsellor. She was able to act as a guiding light and support to the rest of us, especially when we felt out of our depth. However, it soon became clear that we needed formal supervision from an active professional and I found a local GP's counsellor who acted as supervisor and trainer for us all. I employed her to meet with us at least twice a term. She taught us how to support one another, keep things in proportion and to off-load within the team. She also helped Personal Tutors develop counselling skills. Because of the nature of the work we were doing it was essential that we became mutually supportive in a deep and totally non-judgmental way. It would have been easy for PTs to feel isolated and overwhelmed.

Students were, at first, identified by heads of year for possible inclusion on the scheme. There were no criteria set in tablets of stone; indeed there were many and various reasons why children were taken onto the project. Fundamental to whether or not they would be offered the chance of having a PT – and it was their choice – was whether or not they showed a commitment. If they failed to turn up to sessions they were warned; if those warnings had no effect then they were dropped from the project. We always had a 'waiting list' of children. One of my roles as manager was to protect PTs from themselves. As they were conscientious and very caring staff there were times when they wanted to take on more vulnerable children and I had to direct them not to.

As we became more expert in this work it seemed to become easier to identify those who would benefit from having a PT, even if their names were not put forward. This was especially true for pupils who were going through some sort of short-term crisis, either in school or at home.

The project was originally set up with the intention of helping reduce exclusions, so those at risk of exclusion were the first to be identified. However, as time went on and PT skills levels increased, we took on students who, for a number of reasons, were 'opting out' of working in school or showed signs of personal (but usually disguised) distress. We also had dozens of children who wanted to either self-refer or refer friends. Some had to be turned away. Not an easy thing to do, but it was an essential part of my management role.

Amongst those whom we worked with, there were children who were suicidal, who were bullied or were bullies, who had eating disorders, who took drugs and who exhibited self-destructive behaviours. There were some who had suffered bereavements, who had problems with sexuality, who lived with alcoholics in the family, who were habitually involved in petty crime and who were aggressive. I worked in liaison with social services, the police, local GPs, the school nurse and the Family Psychiatry unit. We knew our limitations and the professional boundaries; there were times when I had to reassure Personal Tutors that they had done all they could: just being there for the child was sometimes enough.

Personal Tutors saw their selected pupils once a week at least, for a lesson or longer. Records were kept of meetings and individuals were discussed, anonymously, at shared mini case conference meetings. This was a chance for tutors to discuss among ourselves possible ways forward with these children. And a chance to off-load. Sometimes we asked our supervisor to attend these meetings. We tried to share strategies and be as creative as we could within the limits we had of working in a school. Sometimes children were supported in particular lessons by their Tutor who would sit alongside them in the classroom; sometimes parents were invited in to a joint meeting; sometimes a talk and/or advice session sufficed; sometimes we used art therapy. Whatever we tried, the children always knew we were there for them, and would actively listen to them. In spite of some initial concerns, the fact that this was a different relationship to the usual teacher–pupil one, was not as great a problem as feared we had. Children were able to understand when a particular adult was being a 'teacher' and when a Personal Tutor.

In-depth individual interviews were carried out by a Cambridge researcher with three staff and six pupils who were currently involved in the scheme. The aim was to find out from staff what they saw as the aims of the work, how they felt it contributed to reducing and preventing exclusion, what skills they needed, and what training and support they received. Students were asked what they understood the Personal Tutoring scheme to be for, how it helped them, and how it was different from other sorts of help they received. Interviews were tape recorded and later transcribed; direct quotes are verbatim extracts from the tape transcripts.

There were many issues on which all three students agreed. For example, they commented on the importance of having someone who would listen to them, and knowing that what they said was respected and treated in confidence. The regularity of meetings, and knowing that the Personal Tutor was always there for them, were also crucial. The students wanted someone in whom they could confide and who would trust them, and give them a chance

> It's a really good idea I think for children like, well, me, that need help. To talk to someone. Not every child can bottle it up.

> There's someone you can talk to about anything and it's all confidential.

Problems at home, feelings of frustration and anger, difficulties with friendships and the way teachers treated the students, were all brought to PT sessions. There were also concerns expressed about coping with the work in class, and homework. The fact that there was an adult who cared about them and showed non-judgemental commitment towards them as individuals, freely giving time and energy and showing belief in them, was valued a great deal.

> She just like understands how I feel . . . and she'll say something, like, that'll mean something.

The students felt cared for, supported and attended to. It was different from the other sorts of help available in school because:

> You get their whole attention, don't you, and you get them to yourself . . . because like they don't have to deal with anything else.

For one student, this seemed to be the only opportunity to speak with an adult who understood:

> In some way my mum wouldn't understand about my behaviour in school, but Ms X do.

The opportunity to express feelings and frustrations in a 'safe' way and a secure environment was also recognised as important.

Being able to talk to her about it (has helped me to change) –
Getting it out of my system 'cos usually I keep it all bottled up
inside and I don't say nothing, but when I am with Miss I can tell
her everything that happened and then it's out in the open.

We talk about the people in my class. How the people wind me up
and all that. It helps me control my temper and not tell lies like I
always do.

The students commented positively on some of the specific strategies
introduced by Personal Tutors.

We write tasks for the next week. We write them down and I put
it in my pencil case and I can just look at it and then I'll know.

I wrote up a list of things that were good about me . . . yes it was
helpful. Yes, because whenever you feel like that you can sort of say
it in your head.

Asked about the part that they felt the scheme had played in
preventing exclusion, the students were convinced that, without
access to, and work with, the Personal Tutor, they would not still be
in school.

I'd have been really, really bad. I could have been suspended.

I don't think I'd be as happy in school. I don't think I'd actually
come some days if I didn't have a Personal Tutor.

I would have been kicked out of school straight away.

The students' perception of the vital part played by the scheme in
helping to prevent exclusion was echoed in the interviews with the
Personal Tutors. One tutor commented:

I feel it is important, it is very important. It does at least give the
child a voice, it gives the chance for the child to have time to reflect
over a number of areas around the schools, and problems they're
having in their own lives.

The tutors described the aims of the work in terms of building
students' self-esteem and helping the students deal with a variety of

issues including curriculum difficulties, bereavement, sexuality, rejection by parents, emotional and physical neglect and promoting emotional literacy. Although there were some differences, in their comments, in the relative emphasis placed on coping with school and coping with personal issues, all saw themselves as trying to help students to become independent and to learn how to take responsibility for themselves, their behaviour and its consequences.

> So the personal goal is for them to be strong enough to have their own morality, and own guidelines within themselves, saying yes to certain things and no to other things, and not being swayed maybe by the family or by the peer situation; to know inside themselves that this is me, and I can say yes to this, and I can say no to that, and be strong within themselves, and feel good about themselves, and achieve success.

Tutors felt that their work was generally valued by other staff, but there were concerns.

> I get sort of worried because there's always been the feeling that it might be a tacked-on bit; it's got to become more integral.

They found the sessions with individual students very demanding. The kinds of demands made are illustrated in one comment about the skills and personal qualities tutors need in order to fulfil this role.

> They need to be able, certainly, to listen beyond roles, words . . . to be able to question their own feelings; to be brave enough sometimes to put aside the rules of the school; to be able to hold the confidentiality of the student and to be able to hold the feelings and actually carry on with life.

Consequently, support from other Personal Tutors was important, as was the opportunity for outside supervision twice a term. The outside supervision 'really made a difference' in situations where tutors felt a lack of confidence about how best to tackle a situation. Having somebody say 'You're doing an OK job' was also important.

At times they found themselves feeling blameworthy and responsible for the misbehaviour of their students but were developing the capacity to stand back:

> There's an area where you really just have to trust and not take on

the whole total responsibility for the child. Some sort of trust that things are going to be OK.

Support for excluded pupils on re-entry

A further form of support that was available for individuals was a monitoring system for students returning from fixed-term exclusion. For some time, I had been concerned that when excluded students returned, there was maybe an interview with a senior member of staff, and sometimes with parent(s), and then they would be plunged straight back in to sink or swim. I felt that they were more likely to reintegrate success-fully, and avoid problems escalating into further exclusions, if some sort of system of support was in place to assist their re-entry.

Since I was still officially managing the GEST funded project, I had a few extra free periods; also, I did not have a tutor group and this meant that I was more often available to monitor individual children at key times of the day. I decided, in liaison with a head of year, to redesign our existing behaviour report cards in order to use them as a tool for my own monitoring. Like many secondary schools, we had a system where identified individuals carried a card with them from lesson to lesson for teachers to sign and write comments on, in order to keep a track of behaviour over a given period of time. My aim was to make them target-specific – thus allowing staff to recognise and reinforce the positive in their comments and interactions with individual students. I also wanted to remove the space for teacher comments as some staff used this space to sound off about a child or incident involving the child. This could aggravate a situation.

The students were invited to decide, with my guidance, what their behaviour targets would be. These were made clear on the card. Staff were asked to put a 'one' in the space for their lesson if the target was completely met, a 'two' if partially met and 'three' if not met at all. It was important to allow students to set only a few (maybe three or four) targets and at least one of them to be a target which I believed would allow the teachers to assign a 'one'. There was no point in reinforcing failure.

The intention behind what I was doing was to help the students survive and be successful. I met the students, individually, at the start of the day, before registration. I could then carry out basic checks with them, such as whether they had a pen, books, their completed homework. If necessary I would lend them a pen or provide them with paper. If they did not have text books then we discussed how they could avoid confrontation with a member of staff who would be understandably displeased.

I also met the students at break-time, lunchtime and after school. In this way I was able to monitor, through the report card, what had happened in a relatively short time and try to nip potential problems in the bud. I knew from experience that, without some sort of intervention, problems were often carried from one lesson to another and gradually each small incident could escalate into something serious.

If it looked as if a student was hooked into a downward spiral of this kind, I could offer the chance of flexibility. It was sometimes appropriate to suggest that individuals came to me, rather than went to their usual lesson, and worked in my teaching room, or alone. I would then see the relevant member of staff, gather in some work, explain the situation and take responsibility for that student. At other times the student and I could discuss possible tactics for a potentially difficult lesson: I would try to give them choices about effective strategies and set up a win-win situation between them and their teacher.

As I became more familiar with the students' perceptions of how they experienced their week I became more able to anticipate where the tensions might arise. Parallel with this, the students were becoming aware of my understanding. This made it easier for all of us. I knew I could say to a student, 'If it gets too difficult in XXX you can come to me'. The very fact that they had a 'bolt-hole' was often enough, though there were a few times when there were as many as two or three seated at the back of the classroom while I taught another class.

One of the university researchers examined the impact and effectiveness of the monitoring strategy described above as part of a case study of two Year 10 pupils who, at the start of the year, were considered to be at risk of exclusion. The report card had been highlighted by staff, students and parents as one strategy that did seem to make a positive difference to students' behaviour in lessons. As part of this enquiry, I was asked to keep an audio diary of what happened each day in my work with individuals over a period of several weeks. Three students who had experience of individual monitoring were also interviewed, in order to explore their perceptions of what was helpful in enabling them to get on better in school and avoid further trouble.

What emerged from this part of the study was that it was not just the report card that was important for the students, but also the sustained personal support being offered via a range of strategies. The report card itself was considered to be helpful, but there were reservations:

It makes me feel like everyone's watching over me all the time.

The fact that there were targets brought its own pressures:

Sometimes I can go up to the targets and sometimes I can't.

For one student, it was very important to have written proof that targets had been met:

They keep telling me I can do it, but if it's written down I know I can!

There were many parallels here with what students said was important about the Personal Tutoring scheme. Students valued the contact with someone who they knew cared about how they were getting on, whom they knew was there if needed, and who could be trusted to take action on their behalf if it seemed likely to help. Just having a brief contact and conversation could make all the difference.

He helps me out if things are going wrong, he'll talk to me and say be good.

We talk about breathing (part of the anger-management strategies) and what's been happening around school lately and how I've been getting on.

The anger-management strategies I had taught them included breathing exercises, self-awareness of their physical state, 'cognitive restructuring' or self-talk (whereby they tried to interpret what was going on in a way which would be less personally offensive to them) and visualisation. While finding these helpful, the students' accounts of their experience suggested that there were times when they just could not stop themselves doing things which would get them into trouble. They felt reassured that they had the option to get up and leave, with the teacher's permission, in order to cool off elsewhere.

I'd just flip . . . smash a window or something.

I was about to retaliate but I didn't (because I knew I could leave the room).

If I've been naughty or I'm in a mood . . . I go to . . . Mr. (Y) . . . and he sits me down and talks to me and then at the end of the lesson sends me back up to the teacher. It calms me down.

One student felt that the legitimacy of the strategy was not accepted by all staff. Requests to leave the room were sometimes refused. This could then provoke a situation where the student would get sent out anyway.

I was certainly aware, in my day to day contacts with staff, that there were considerable differences in terms of their perception of the value, overall, of this form of support for students. Some were pleased to know that the students were getting support; others were concerned that it was rewarding students for misbehaviour; others felt that it was an intrusion into their own discipline and practices. I always tried to negotiate with staff and keep them informed but sometimes I would only hear of incidents involving the students I was monitoring by accident. I often only got the students' perceptions of what had happened and had to spend time seeking out staff to hear their version. By the time I had gathered what I considered to be enough of the 'facts' it sometimes meant that the moment to respond effectively had passed.

The Cambridge researchers confirmed that considerable differences of perspective were indeed emerging in staff responses to interviews and questionnaires, not just with respect to the 'individual monitoring' strategy, but with respect to the various initiatives overall. In order to set these views in context, I shall summarise five other areas of development work currently going on in the school. Brief details of the research carried out in each area and key findings are given in Table 3.1.

Other initiatives

First, there was a new PSHE programme devised to meet what staff perceived as the specific needs of students at Virginia Woolf. The previous programme had leaned heavily on commercially produced resources and had little cohesion. It was intended that the new work would emphasise a skills-based approach, and that all staff should be involved in planning the identified modules. This would give the sense of ownership and commitment which had seemed to be missing. Furthermore it would also allow not only content to be discussed among staff, but teaching methods.

Because previous PSHE work had been worksheet heavy, it had tended to alienate students, especially those with poor literacy levels. It was also seen by staff as being rather dull. The new programme meant that more creative ways of delivering PSHE could be considered. Time was set aside for a variety of types of oral work, such as discussion and role play, and outside speakers were booked. Worksheets were revamped where necessary. A timetable for delivery of modules was formalised, allowing staff with particular interests and skills to deliver particular units of work,

Table 3.1 Virginia Woolf High School

Initiative	Data sources	Key findings
PSHE	Interviews with 15 students (by teachers)	• importance of tutor group and tutor as teaching unit • valued lesson content • made links with other curriculum learning • actively used outside classroom
	Questionnaire for whole staff (24 returns, n =61)	• valued teaching own tutor group • content meaningful to students personally • can enhance social skills/ self esteem
Circle Time	Interviews with 18 students (by teachers)	• valued chance to talk about problems • helped with relationships and with learning • sometimes uncomfortable
	Whole staff questionnaire	• positively viewed by staff, particularly those with direct experience of approach
Role of form tutor	Form tutor logs and interviews (8 staff, by teachers)	• highlighted different perceptions of role • admin. could hinder other aspects of role • tension between disciplinary role and building positive relationships • desire to do more to support learning
	Parent questionnaires (40 Year 9) 100% returns	• majority saw FT as first point of contact for information or concerns
	Pupil interviews (by teachers) (2 per year group)	• valued stability and security provided by FT • valued extra efforts made by FT (e.g. attending matches) • key concept 'trust'
Literacy Working Group	Readability survey of texts	• texts age appropriate but many children have reading age below chronological age
	Survey of key language/ literacy skills	• interesting common patterns emerged which could provide basis for discussion/development work (e.g. discrepancy between value placed on pupils listening to teacher and to one another)

	Survey of reading levels of excluded pupils	• association confirmed between low reading levels and pupils excluded, but some exceptions
GNVQ project-based course	Interviews with 12 students	• liked active learning, working at own pace
	Interviews with 6 parents	• felt children enjoyed subject, keen for younger ones to take course
	Interviews with 6 staff	• differing views about impact of course on motivation/behaviour; • highlighted demands on students as well as importance of short-term goals, opportunity for visits, for different type of relationship with teachers
Personal tutoring	Interviews with (3) Personal Tutors (by university researcher)	• being a Personal Tutor was frustrating and demanding, but highly rewarding
	Interview with project manager (by university researcher)	• importance for students of feeling genuinely listened to by an adult in school.
	Interviews with 6 students in the scheme (by university researcher)	• importance of ongoing range of support strategies for students • belief among students that being part of the project helped them avoid exclusion • newly acquired anger-management strategies deemed effective
Re-entry from* fixed term exclusion	Audio diary Interview with project manager Interview with (3) students Staff questionnaire	• importance of frequent and regular monitoring to pre-empt possible problems • creative solutions possible but skilful negotiation required • concerns from some staff about resources devoted to "the undeserving"
	Parents interview?	• the importance of reducing pressures on students, balanced with building students' inner resources.

---

*The bullet points in this section summarise findings for all the data sources although most Form Tutors taught most modules. The whole course was, and continues to be, regularly evaluated at pastoral team meetings and each year team makes recommendations for fine-tuning so that succeeding teams, who will teach the modules later, benefit from their experience.

Much emphasis was placed on the need to develop student self-esteem. As Form Tutors teach their groups for two lessons a week – for both tutorial time and PSHE – and as National Records of Achievement are firmly established and seen as having real value and currency among our students, there is scope for development and progression through work on self-esteem right through from Year 7 to 11.

Circle Time

Closely linked to the new PSHE programme was an initiative to introduce Circle Time in Year 7 classes. It has since progressed up the school. Circle Time is a way to encourage self-responsibility, self-control and emotional literacy. Although Circle Time is often practised more in the primary sector I saw no reason why it should not be useful at secondary level in our repertoire of strategies for enhancing self-esteem and emotional literacy. I introduced Circle Time in Year 7 in September 1996 where it was run by Form Tutors once or twice a week during tutorial time.

At their first session of Circle Time the students make up their own rules: the process empowers the group and its members are more likely to conform to them. Rules are based on truth, trust, responsibility, active listening, no 'put-downs', kindliness and support. They are negotiated, agreed, written down, and then displayed in the Form Room. The role of the teacher is that of guide, being non-judgmental throughout, and setting the tone for future work.

Circle Time tends to last between fifteen and thirty-five minutes. Sometimes the teacher can set the agenda, sometimes the students, sometimes an agenda arises naturally from circumstances or an incident involving one of the class. To help the process of Circle Time, an object, such as a scarf, shell or paperweight (my Year 10 Tutor Group chose a teddy bear belonging to one of their peers who left the school), is passed around the circle. Rather like the assembly in William Golding's novel *Lord of the Flies* (1954), where holding the conch signifies permission to talk and be listened to, the routine, imposed by the teacher, is that only the student (or teacher) holding the object may speak.

Because Circle Time gives a sense of security, identity, belonging, purpose and competence, sensitive issues can, eventually, be brought into the open. These issues might include bullying, dealing with bereavement

– or endings in general – relationships, the hopes and fears of the children, what makes them sad or happy or angry and how to deal with peer pressure. All these issues help encourage discussion about feelings and how to work with them: for many of our students emotional literacy is a new idea. The culture of the catchment area mitigates against talking about feelings. It is often described as a 'macho' culture. Consequently, some boys find this aspect of the work especially difficult. Giving validity to the expression of feelings through a forum such as Circle Time can enhance self-esteem, provide security, and demonstrate publicly that feelings are a natural part of being human.

The role of the Form Tutor

We were also in the early stages of reviewing and developing the role of the Form Tutor, due to be given priority in the School Development Plan the following academic year. Members of the research team felt that this was an important area to include in our work because Form Tutors can make a crucial contribution to reducing and preventing exclusion. In order to investigate how Form Tutors saw their role, eight of them were asked to keep a log of their activities, using a suggested proforma. They were then interviewed by colleagues on the research team to explore how they felt about how they were spending their time, and what seemed to help or hinder them from doing what they felt they ought to be doing in practice. By analysing this data, together with the views of parents and a small number of students selected randomly across year groups, it was hoped that ideas and questions would emerge that could become a focus for future development.

Work on literacy

A Literacy Working Group had recently been set up to explore ways of enhancing pupils' literacy development. This group carried out a survey of the readability of texts used in different subject areas, in order to see whether texts currently in use were accessible, given our data on pupils' reading levels. The reading test scores of pupils who had been the subject of temporary exclusions were also examined. The views of subject departments were sought regarding the essential and desirable language and literacy skills for successful engagement with the content of particular subject areas, and the most common difficulties that students were found to experience. It was hoped that a synthesis of these various sources of information would help to define some areas for further development work.

GNVQ

Another area that became a focus of interest during the course of the research was a project-based GNVQ course. Staff involved were keen to emphasise that it was not an alternative, low-level course for struggling or disaffected learners. What it offered, in theory, was an alternative (yet also demanding) style of learning, which might have more appeal for some students because there was considerable scope for developing projects in line with their own interests. While looking at attendance patterns in Year 10, one of the university team suggested that there might be a link between improved attendance and participation in the GNVQ course. She carried out interviews with selected staff, students and parents in order to see if their perceptions supported this hypothesis.

Accumulating evidence of the perceptions of staff, students and (in some cases) parents in relation to these various initiatives and developments provided encouraging confirmation that they were, in general, being well received (Table 3.1). Staff questionnaires also confirmed that their contribution – potential and actual – to the task of reducing and preventing exclusion was recognised by the wider staff group. The kinds of links made by staff are illustrated in the following comments taken from the questionnaire responses:

- (PSHE) Highlights issues related to personal value and well-being, two issues which drastically affect behaviour.
- (Circle Time) Gives students the opportunity to express their concerns and fears in a safe environment. Hopefully over time this may allow pupils to voice their difficulties before it is too late.
- (Role of Form Tutor) Very often hidden; but first route for many students and parents. Invaluable resource.
- (Literacy Working Group) Greater involvement across the curriculum. Less children 'switched off' by areas of difficulty, which can lead to disruptive behaviour.
- (GNVQ course) This should be an ideal way of contributing. The smaller groups and personal and individual nature of the work, and how it should be monitored, would help in providing motivation, regular feedback and a more mutual understanding of acceptable behaviour and attitude, and because of close monitoring, a better staff–student relationship.

Tension between intermediate and long-term goals

While many staff clearly recognised the potential of these various initiatives, it was also evident from the questionnaires, and from interviews with staff relating to the individual case studies, that many teachers were looking for more direct and immediate support than was represented by the sum of the various initiatives. The pressures and stresses which they faced on a day to day basis were very considerable. An approach which emphasised the long-term view left many people feeling unsupported in the immediate and short-term.

There were teachers who questioned whether it was in fact in anyone's interests, once things had reached a certain point, to pull out all the stops in order to prevent exclusion. Was all the human resource and effort, for instance, that was being expended in the individual monitoring scheme simply 'delaying the inevitable' (as one member of staff put it)? My own view was that unless something was done to support excluded pupils on re-entry, the kinds of problems that they would experience would be all too likely to provoke reactions that would lead to further exclusion. But did it depend upon maintaining indefinitely such intensive input, or was it (as I intended) a genuinely developmental strategy, in the sense of building up students' ability to manage independently and so become progressively re-engaged in school life?

Since one of the principles underpinning the research was commitment to give serious and equal consideration to the views of all those consulted, it was decided to take a closer look at the workings of the individual monitoring scheme in the light of these questions. Did the individual monitoring strategy indeed add up to more than an exercise in containment and damage limitation? On what grounds could it be claimed to be genuinely preventative? One interpretation of the nature of the support provided by the strategy – and grounded in the evidence – was proposed by the university researcher who had taken responsibility for this part of the project.

Scaffolding to support positive change

Re-examining the detailed audio diaries, and students' accounts of the strategies that they found most helpful, what came across most strongly was the enormous complexity of the demands made upon students during the course of a school day. These tended to become visible only when students failed to negotiate them successfully.

All students have to learn to manage the emotionally charged task of building relationships with their peers in their immediate class group and in the whole school. They have to negotiate their relationships with a dozen or more teachers, each of whom has different idiosyncracies, expectations, rules and routines. They have to cope with the demands of the formal curriculum, and, at the same time, negotiate their place and status as learners in terms of the accepted norms of success and failure both in and outside school. They have to cope with the insecurities of their developing adolescent identities: working out who they are and who they want to become, in school and outside. And they have to manage all of this and more in relation to other pressures, responsibilities and competing interests from their lives outside school which vie for attention: factors which, for youngsters, have a higher priority than the expectations of their teachers.

Students' accounts of their experiences helped to illustrate why these tasks can be harder for some students than for others. It may be because the pressures on them are greater; or it may be that, for a variety of reasons, they have fewer inner resources to draw on to help them cope. One such pressure can be created by unsatisfying peer relationships, when students see themselves as disliked or rejected by their class-mates. One student claimed that he was continually picked on by members of his peer group who saw him as 'weak'. He welcomed being sent to isolation (a disciplinary sanction which required students to work on their own away from their normal lessons) because 'you can get away from your class friends that really really bug you'.

Both staff and students, in interview, acknowledged the added pressures that come from having a reputation for trouble. This tends to make the student more visible to teachers, with the result that minor misdemeanours get picked up on when they may tend to go unnoticed when committed by others.

> The teachers are on the look out all the time, and so they see me do things that other people do but they don't get into trouble.

Tensions arise because it can feel to the student that teachers are 'going on and on' at them 'for every little thing', even though teachers are not intentionally being inconsistent in their responses to students. According to one student, having a reputation could also mean that, when he was in dispute with other students who were not usually in trouble, teachers were not so ready to believe his side of the story.

Teachers' perceptions of students' ability can also create pressures, since teachers may make more allowances for students whom they perceive as struggling. As one student noted:

> Every time something goes wrong or I mess about or something, they go 'Come on, you're an intelligent person, you can do the work' and everything. But most of the time the reason I'm messing about is because I can't.

When a student is perceived as 'less able', teachers may be more ready to see difficult behaviour as a symptom of difficulty with learning. But if a student is perceived as 'bright', teachers are more likely to interpret difficulties as a failure of attention or effort on the part of the student. When students so perceived seek help with work which they genuinely do not understand, their requests may be denied and there may be a breakdown in the teacher–student relationship.

Once these pressures are recognised, it is easier to appreciate why the task of simply getting through the day without trouble can seem to be so enormously daunting for some students at risk of exclusion; and why so many attempts at a fresh start – so poignantly recorded in their school files – soon broke down. No matter how much students may genuinely desire to change their ways, they will be unable to sustain the effort as long as the pressures they encounter in school outweigh the resources that they can call on in coping with them. Something has to change in the current balance of pressures and resources in order to make it possible for students to cope with the pressures more successfully. Action needs to be taken either to bring about a significant reduction in the pressures experienced by the student such that he or she can cope with their existing resources; or provide students with opportunities to develop and strengthen their inner resources so that they are better able to cope successfully with the pressures they encounter.

This analysis provided a new way of thinking about the function of the various different strategies that were being used as part of the individual monitoring scheme (and described on pp. 60 to 62). On closer inspection, some could be seen to be more concerned with reducing pressures on a short or longer-term basis; others with building students' inner resources so that they become able to cope more effectively on their own. Some, in different ways, fulfilled both functions.

It could be argued, then, that these strategies, far from merely 'delaying the inevitable', are genuinely preventative, because they help to create the conditions that make it more likely that students who desire change and improvement can be successful in achieving them. The strategies provide a scaffolding for students' own efforts: not doing it all for them, but creating conditions in which those who cannot as yet manage it alone can – with help – gain the confidence and skill to manage independently in the long term.

Building positive alternatives to exclusion

This analysis of the functions of the individual monitoring scheme can also be applied to the other initiatives that the school was developing

Table 3.2 Reducing pressures and building inner resources

Reducing pressures	Building inner resources
Providing bolt hole	Anger-management strategies
Checking equpment	Reminder of strategies they have and can use
Removing from lessons strategically	Encouragement
Talking through problems arising	Talking problems through to reach new understanding of self and others
Moving to another group	Attention to personal needs
Teacher-monitor negotiating with staff on behalf of student	Conveying a sense that what happens to the student really matters to someone

in an effort to prevent and reduce exclusion. Each can be seen as contributing in different ways to either or both of these enabling functions. For example, the Personal Tutoring Scheme was clearly concerned with helping to develop students' inner resources so that they were better able to cope with the various pressures encountered in school. The introduction of Circle Time in Year 7 was helping both to reduce pressures on students by enhancing peer group relationships and to build students' inner resources, by creating time for addressing personal needs and problems, and building confidence and self-esteem through the valuing of each individual's contribution.

Revisiting the various initiatives in this way raised the possibility that there might be other enabling functions reflected in current development work or in the ideas proposed by staff, students or parents as possible areas for future development. A third function was indeed identified, which was concerned with extending the range of opportunities provided within the regular curriculum for students to experience satisfaction and a sense of personal stake, or belonging. It was a source of considerable concern to some teachers, for example, and particularly some of those who were also Personal Tutors, that school seemed to have so little to offer some students by way of intrinsic, personal reward. In the words of one teacher, there was a need to 'give them a buzz about actually being here'.

Making the curriculum more personally meaningful and directly relevant to students was an important part of what the new PSHE curriculum sought to do. Circle Time, it was hoped, would give students a sense of having a genuine voice, of being accepted, known, valued and integrated within the school community. Comments of both staff and students suggested a need to review and extend the opportunities more generally available for personal acknowledgement and satisfaction within the curriculum as a whole.

Thus, one way of understanding the work going on in the school to prevent and reduce exclusion is in terms of three kinds of supportive change that together might be able to make a genuine difference to students' ability and willingness to engage productively in school life. To summarise, they are strategies or initiatives designed to:

- reduce pressures, so that success in coping becomes more likely
- build inner resources so that students have a larger repertoire upon which to draw enabling them to manage the pressures on them more successfully
- extend opportunities for feeling a sense of personal satisfaction and belonging.

This three-dimensional view of what might be involved in building positive alternatives to exclusion constitutes a new perspective on the various different initiatives examined in this chapter, showing what they have in common and how each might be seen as contributing to a coherent and positive strategy.

It also provides grounds for optimism in a way that teachers may find helpful when situations may appear to have reached deadlock. It shows that there is always scope for positive change, if we can alter the current balance between pressures, resources and opportunities in ways that are enabling for students. It also identifies the kinds of changes that it may be most fruitful to pursue, in finding positive ways forward: in work with individuals, within the curriculum and within the school as a whole. These ways benefit not only those at risk of exclusion. A supportive, healthy, caring ethos put into action, combined with a relevant curriculum taught in ways which truly engage the students, will surely be of benefit to all.

In this chapter, I have described how the project helped to generate a new perspective on the different kinds of innovative work going on in the school, and how these were collectively contributing to the task of reducing and preventing exclusion. However, this was by no means the whole story. What also emerged through the research was a heightened awareness of the need to give equally careful thought to the needs of teachers, and to the part that addressing their needs might play in the task of building positive alternatives to exclusion. We take up this important, complementary set of concerns in the next chapter.

4 Virginia Woolf High School (2)

DYNAMICS OF INCLUSION AND EXCLUSION: WHAT MAKES A DIFFERENCE?

Introduction

This second part of the story is written from the perspective of the university researchers, who were outsiders to the school. The research was a joint project on which we worked together but our position was not the same as the teachers', and this different perspective was acknowledged and built on. Nevertheless, ours was not an easy position of comfortable detachment. We had given an undertaking at the outset that we, and the research group as a whole, would be committed to understanding the issues, by taking account of everyone's point of view. We were also concerned with the positive: what people considered that the school was successfully doing or might further do to prevent or reduce exclusion. In this chapter, we describe how our commitment to fulfilling these undertakings became a critical driving force in our response to and analysis of the data, and in the form in which we chose to present our key findings to staff.

In the first two parts of the chapter, we describe how we gradually came to see that the key messages emerging about the importance of students' emotional state in the dynamics of inclusion and exclusion could also be applied to teachers. We explore the connections between students' emotional experiences and those of teachers, and show how we became aware of the necessity of addressing teachers' needs as a pre-requisite for further progress.

We also became aware of the complexity of the task of feeding back a summary of the research findings to staff in a supportive way, which would positively contribute to their development work. In the third part of the chapter, we describe how our efforts to fulfil this responsibility led us to analyse and represent our findings in the form of a set of dilemmas that could be used to support constructive dialogue amongst staff.

In our discussion, we draw on the data that we were given responsibility for collecting:

- in-depth interviews with six students and three staff who were part of the Personal Tutoring Scheme
- case studies of two students who were seen as 'at risk' of exclusion
- the audio diaries of the project co-ordinator
- interviews with twelve teachers who were involved with the case study students or who were involved in the Personal Tutoring Scheme
- a questionnaire given to the whole school staff and completed towards the end of the year of the research in the school.

Emotion and learning – the students' experiences

In our individual interviews with students, we tried to probe their perceptions of what led them to behave in ways that the staff found difficult, what made a difference to how they behaved and what strategies used by particular teachers they found positively helpful. What emerged most forcefully was their sense of the importance of their emotional state. These students described a sense of being full of feeling, of having things bottled up. For example, one said:

> Just like I have to be bad and that I have to take it out on the teachers sometimes and I do and I get detentions.

There was sometimes an accompanying expression of powerlessness. They talked of not being able to stop themselves from doing what they knew would get them in to trouble.

> It's really weird . . . like you know what you're doing but you can't stop and it just gets worse and worse.

No matter how much they desired and determined to turn over a new leaf and 'be good', sometimes something seemed to happen that made them flare up. Even when they knew that any further misbehaviour would have the direst of consequences, they would sometimes 'just flip' and lose control of their behaviour.

Being able to release this emotion by talking to their Personal Tutor provided an important safety valve.

> Getting it out of my system 'cos usually I keep it all bottled up inside and I don't say nothing but when I am with Miss I can tell her everything that happened and then it's out in the open.

This build-up of pressure was fuelled by day to day experiences which reinforced feelings of isolation, of not belonging. Ironically, it was the very issue of exclusion which these students identified as causing them difficulty. They talked of feeling excluded from the processes of the school and the classroom. They talked of being bullied, being singled out, being unable to complete the work or being identified as being different on the basis of family reputations.

> Well I had an older brother and he had a bad name so they maybe think I've got a bad name because they think I am like him so they think she's going to be bad like him, so they treat me different and that.

One student talked of wanting to be noticed but not wanting to be treated as different:

> I feel like she treats me different to the rest of the class.

For her, 'bad behaviour' comes

> when the teacher don't take any notice of them and they think they don't care and so I might as well carry on being bad.

Conversely, teachers who were respectful of individuals in their relationships were seen as helping the student to learn,

> He's friendly. He's not sarcastic either. And he's helpful, you see, he knows what he's talking about.

They also discussed the sense of difference that arises from being seen as stupid or unable to participate in learning in the classroom,

> Like, you get embarrassed if you sit there and say put your hand up and oh, I've got that wrong. You get embarrassed when that happens.

The size of groups was important to the students. Whole class formats presented challenges for many that smaller, more interactive learning groupings did not.

As we can see from these comments, it is the social and personal worlds of the classroom and the school that preoccupy many of the students; in a sense, this is their primary curriculum. The students' sense of personal or social exclusion becomes a significant force in their behaviour. Their comments echo the findings of previous research which suggested that teachers can reduce the degree to which they accentuate difference (Watkins and Wagner, 1987, p. 41).

What helped?

The interviews with the three students who were receiving personal tutoring showed that this experience made a real difference to how they felt about school, because it reduced the sense of emotional isolation and gave them a sense of being cared for. In her challenging account of the concept of care in education, the philosopher Nel Noddings has argued that:

> The desire to be cared for is almost certainly a universal human need. Not everyone wants to be cuddled or fussed over. But everyone wants to be received, to elicit a response that is congruent with an underlying need or desire.
>
> (Noddings, 1992, p. 17)

The interviewees talked about how being listened to and understood reduced their sense of difference, and their anxiety.

> We talk about whatever's worrying me, we talk about everything. It's good to have someone to speak to if you've got problems and if you need help with homework and things, it's handy. Sometimes people need someone to speak to.

Another student said, 'The teachers believing me is the most important sort of help I could have.' This student described how this relationship made her feel cared for and how it affected her. Her words seem to convey a sense of solidarity.

> That's the good thing about it, because I know that she's always checking up on me. That tells me that she's actually trying to help me, so I should pay her back in some way.

> Cos I think I've got to prove to her that I can be good and prove it to her and my Mum.

The students valued teachers' attempts to make sense of situations or help with strategies to deal with times of high emotion, conflict or being out of control.

This is not to argue for accepting the individual student's perspective as the only valid one, but to emphasise the value of accepting the individual's experience as a starting point for discussion, in which the teacher can act as a mediator, in the sense in which David Smail uses the term. He elucidates the relationship between 'annihilating anxiety' and lack of recognition. He argues that:

> The skill of the teacher is precisely in mediating the relation between the person and the world, in acting, that is, as go-between, seeking to satisfy the desire of the person to know the world by introducing to him or her what may in fact be known about it.
>
> (Smail, 1996, p. 76)

The students valued the opportunity for dialogue in the sense that it helped them to connect to someone and to make sense of their experiences. They also experienced what Noddings calls confirmation, a crucial component of caring:

> Confirmation is an act of affirming and encouraging the best in others.
>
> (Noddings, 1992, p. 25)

She goes on to detail three other elements of her construct of the ethic of care: modelling, practice and dialogue. She demonstrates that by modelling caring we show others how to care, whereas practice is 'the opportunity to gain skills in care-giving and more important, to develop the characteristic attitudes' (Noddings, 1992, p. 24). Our data show that the students valued all these elements.

Overall, then, the message from the students was that their behaviour was a direct reflection of their emotional state, which was itself a complex mix of sensations and influence:

- Feelings of belonging or isolation, inclusion or exclusion, difference from or identity with the group.
- Feelings of power and powerlessness.
- Feeling cared for, in a variety of ways.

Links with teachers' views

Questionnaire responses from twenty-four teachers indicated that their views of the kind of relationships that they wanted with their students were broadly in line with the kind of relationships that the students themselves identified as important. The teachers too were seeking friendly relationships based on mutual respect, without confrontation, expressing empathy and trust. Teachers wanted to create the conditions necessary for learning to take place. They wanted good relationships with and between students to allow for different forms of learning, for example, in pairs, in groups and as a whole class. They saw the ideal classroom as one in which all were involved, in which all students were motivated and working together in a harmonious way.

When asked to rate the initiatives being researched in terms of their contribution to the inclusion of students, most value was placed on those which helped individuals. Like the students, the teachers emphasised the importance of listening, developing coping strategies, understanding individuals and helping students to feel included. Also mentioned were classroom or learning based approaches, which focused on teaching and learning styles, the curriculum and student involvement.

However, many teachers also expressed frustration that the kind of relationship they ideally wanted to create with their students was difficult to achieve. Many felt that the problems they experienced in their classes were ones over which they had little power. They saw them as problems of senior management, the government, parents or the students themselves. The solution to these problems lay in the hands of others or in the removal of the students. Some teachers put forward the following solutions to the problem of pupil misbehaviour:

> Using the charisma of senior staff to convince students of the value of school and school work.

> Strong leadership and praise for staff.

> Put problem children into problem schools – government problem – they are not helping.

The staff who were interviewed about students at risk of exclusion also expressed this sense of powerlessness to influence and change the situation for the better. For some teachers, the feeling arose in part from previous unsuccessful experiences of trying to secure co-operation, to establish a better relationship, to encourage pupils to participate.

> I have tried absolutely everything I can think of: praise, positive reinforcement, encouragement, rewards, maybe the task is too

hard, but nothing has had any effect. If I try to give detention, X just laughs at me. I tried a report, but he didn't even look at it.

This sense of powerlessness was linked, for some teachers, to a perception that students were making a deliberate *choice* to disrupt lessons. Sympathy was at its lowest ebb when students were perceived as being wilfully disobedient, rude or obstructive. The assumption seemed to be that that if this was how the student was choosing to behave, nothing the teacher could do would make any difference unless the student made the choice – for him or herself – to behave differently.

X's reaction varies wildly from where she has done all the work you could possibly ask of and at other times when she has just sat there for two hours and done nothing, and all the cajoling and persuasion and polite talking in the world – and all the shouting – both have an equal effect and the result is zero unfortunately.

We were initially taken aback by the strength of feeling revealed in the data, and by some of the views expressed, which seemed to reflect values that were very different from those informing the project. Gradually, though, we began to see connections between the messages emerging from students and those being communicated by teachers.

Emotion and learning: the teachers' experiences

In many of the teacher responses there were signs of feelings of separateness and disconnectedness and these were accompanied by expressions of both high emotion and despondency. These teachers talked of feeling separate from the senior management or other teachers, from the government, from parents and from the students. The following two statements illustrate the strength of the teachers' feelings.

It would be nice if the respect I try to show them, they would reciprocate. Their attitude is always negative, aggressive and disruptive.

If only the students knew what the boundaries of acceptable behaviour are. It is far from acceptable and total lack of support from senior staff is perpetuating this problem.

As Andy Hargreaves (1998) has also noted, teaching is a highly emotional activity. It involves emotional understanding, and emotional labour; teachers' emotions are inseparable from their moral purposes and their ability to achieve those purposes. Hargreaves argues that teachers' emotions are rooted in and affect both their individualities and their relationships with other; these emotions are shaped by experiences of power and powerlessness, culture and context.

Certainly, such emotions were very visible in our data. The strength of feeling revealed in some of the questionnaire and interview responses was a considerable challenge to us until we realised that what the data were telling us was that, in the dynamics of inclusion and exclusion, the emotional state of teachers was just as important a factor as the emotional state of pupils, and indeed was subject to many of the same influences. We began to explore the possibility that the teachers' emotions mirror those expressed by the students, and that they are all related to the process of learning.

Teachers as learners

Isca Salzberger-Wittenberg, who has studied the emotional experience of learning and teaching, offers some explanations for the sense of helplessness that we had identified in some teacher responses. In writing about the experience of being a teacher she argues that 'infantile, dependent feelings easily come into play when one finds oneself in a learning situation.' (Salzberger-Wittenberg, 1996, p. 91). Not knowing what is happening, facing disorder and potential chaos, can lead to fear, particularly fear of failure. In the face of this fear, a desire for someone else to solve the problem and relieve the pressure is common.

> We need to be aware that the student/teacher relationship inevitably involves some degree of dependency and helplessness and hence evokes some of the more child-like hopes and fears within the learner.
>
> (Salzberger-Wittenberg, 1996, p. 97)

The teacher is forced into the position of learner when faced with 'difficult' behaviour from students; at this point the emotional dimension of learning can become unbearably uncomfortable. John Keats wrote about the capacity to bear 'uncertainties, mysteries, doubts' without 'irritable reaching after fact and reason' and called this 'negative capability' (Gittings, 1966). Some of the extracts from teacher interviews quoted above are expressions of just such irritability. Salzberger-Wittenberg (1996) argues that learning can only take place when we can bear anxiety long enough to try to make sense of what is going on. She argues that fear of failure and of criticism prevent teachers from seeking support from their colleagues; she suggests that one avenue to explore is how teachers can be helped to reflect, and to become learners about the emotional dynamics of the classroom.

Key themes

The juxtaposition of the accounts of students and teachers gradually illuminated the connections between them. Isca Salzberger-Wittenberg's account of the relationship between emotional states and learning seemed to sum up the key themes arising from these parts of our data.

> Our capacity to function intellectually is highly dependent on our emotional state. When we are preoccupied our minds are literally occupied with something and we have no space to pay attention, to take in and listen to anything else. When we are frightened we are more likely to make mistakes. When we feel inadequate we tend to give up rather than struggle to carry on with the task.
>
> (Salzberger-Wittenberg, 1996, p. 81)

The data reviewed here helped us to appreciate that this analysis applies to teachers as well as to students, indeed that teachers' experience mirrors that of the students. How teachers and students feel and behave in school, how ready they are to meet the challenges of learning, depends upon their emotional state, which, as we have seen, may include:

- feelings of belonging or isolation, inclusion or exclusion, and difference from or identity with the group
- feelings of power or powerlessness
- feeling cared for, valued and listened to or rejected and marginalised.

The recognition of parallels between teachers' and students' needs was a key element in our growing understanding. We suggest that there is a common dynamic for both teachers and students, incorporating similar elements. Teachers and students can react in similar ways to the fear of failure and to challenging situations that place them in the role of learner. They are all looking for acceptance, understanding and support. When teachers do not have these affirming experiences, they find it harder to face the challenges of classroom and school life, particularly difficult interactions with students, and so it is for the students.

On the other hand, if individuals – both teachers and students – regularly have experiences of being acknowledged and listened to, understood and cared for, they are more likely to be open to learning.

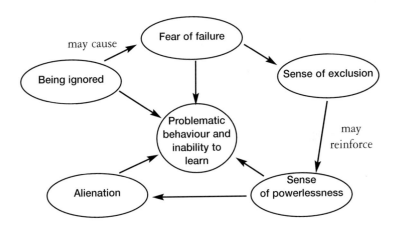

Figure 4.1: Exclusionary dynamic for teachers and students

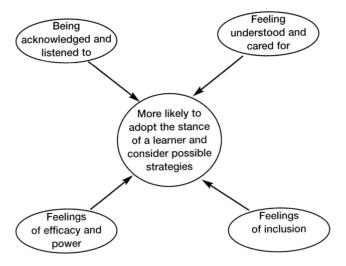

Figure 4.2: Inclusionary dynamic for teachers and students

Possibilities for intervention

In the task of building positive alternatives to exclusion then, we believe that taking steps to support and foster the emotional well-being of teachers is just as important as taking action to foster the emotional well-being of students in the task of building positive alternatives to exclusion. Indeed, our analysis suggests that addressing the needs of staff is a prerequisite for progress towards inclusion.

Once we have recognised these dynamics, we can use them to identify possibilities for intervention. People need not be locked forever in a defensive dynamic. If we understand how the dynamics operate and what makes a difference to people's responses, it may be possible to bring about a shift from a defensive to a more positive pattern; strategic action can be taken to enhance opportunities for staff, as well as students, to give voice to their thoughts, feelings and concerns, to receive care and support from others, and to have their needs and perspectives taken seriously.

These insights made us realise just how complex a task we faced in trying to feed back our findings to the whole staff group. Given the range of views and strength of feeling that had been encountered among staff, how could we fulfil our undertakings in a way that not only gave all the participants a sense that their voices had been heard, but also positively assisted the staff group to move forward in its work to prevent and reduce exclusion? Could we give feedback in a way that would be experienced by the teachers as empowering?

Towards constructive dialogue

Our case study data of individual students at risk of exclusion, and the support strategies used to prevent further exclusion, provided detailed insights into teachers' thinking that suggested a constructive way forward. While teachers frequently argued strongly for particular views and positions with respect to issues of behaviour and exclusion, their accounts also acknowledged the tensions and struggles inherent in these issues. They noted the pull of competing considerations and values which suggested different courses of action. For example, one teacher described the frustration she experienced in working with one individual who did not seem to respond to anything she tried.

> (X) probably has tremendous family problems but we don't know, we don't know this! . . . .and that still doesn't excuse the fact that one person will be allowed to disturb the whole class.

Her comments highlight the tension between her concern for the individual and her sense of responsibility for the rest of the class. Teachers also made reference to the compromises that they were forced to make in responding to challenging behaviour.

I've almost got to the stage where I let him get on with it, because that is time when I would be working with other pupils.

It was clear that the strategies they adopted were often felt to be far from ideal.

My fear is that with the amount of pupils in a class, if you don't give (x) aggravation he will just sit and it's easier not to aggravate him and leave him to do nothing.

The tensions, concerns and misgivings reflected in teachers' comments led to the idea of representing the differences of perspective reflected in staff interviews and questionnaires not as irreconcilably opposing positions but as different ways of resolving some common dilemmas of teaching.

This way of conceptualising the complexities of professional thinking and decision-making is not original. We drew on the work of Berlak and Berlak (1980), Winter (1982) and Pollard (1987) to help us to identify the dilemmas associated with teachers' responses to challenging or difficult behaviour. We searched back systematically through our data (staff interviews, questionnaires and audio diaries) in an attempt to identify a range of dilemmas and formulate them in terms that would be recognisable to all teachers.

Since our aim was to foster dialogue and avoid unhelpful polarisation of views amongst staff, the crucial task was to formulate the dilemmas in such a way that everyone could feel some sympathy with both poles of each dilemma. We wanted everyone to recognise that he or she shares to some extent the values represented at both poles, though each one might resolve the dilemma differently. The resulting framework would, we hoped, provide the common ground for the constructive dialogue that we were seeking.

The seven dilemmas that resulted from our analysis are shown in Box 4.3. We are not suggesting that this is a complete, or exhaustive, list, or that the values embodied in the poles of each dilemma are always, necessarily, in conflict. It is when teachers are facing the task of how to respond to challenging or disruptive behaviour that the two sets of values can emerge in the form of dilemmas. There is a pull between competing considerations; it seems impossible to satisfy those at opposite ends.

1. High expectations ◄──────────► **Relaxed, non-confrontational relationships**

On the one hand there is a need to maintain high expectations of work and behaviour that are continually communicated to students and reflected in the ethos of the school.

On the other hand, it is important to maintain a positive atmosphere. Continual correction of students for minor infractions of rules (relating to work or behaviour) creates bad feeling and can lead to confrontation which is best avoided.

2. Consistency, equality of treatment ◄──────────► **Differentiation of response**

On the one hand, students need to know what the rules are, what the consequences are of breaking them and to be confident that they will be applied with fairness and consistency by all teachers.

On the other hand, there needs to be flexibility in the application of rules and in responses to individuals, because it is not always fair to treat everyone the same.

3. Collective responsibility ◄──────────► **Individual needs**

On one hand, teachers have a responsibility to the whole class, and it is not fair to them if their lessons are continually interrupted by individual disruption or if the teacher's time is taken up with managing behaviour.

On the other hand, teachers have a responsibility to each individual child; it is part of schools' declared mission and teachers' professional expertise to seek to understand and respond to individual needs.

4. Need for correction ◄──────────► **Need for understanding**

On the one hand, students need to know what behaviour offends, and that if they do offend, there will be unpleasant consequences. This acts as an effective deterrent for many.

On the other hand, there are usually underlying reasons why students are behaving in ways that offend. Teachers have a responsibility to try

Box 4.1: Dilemmas of intervention (continued opposite)

to understand what is going on, and try to help alleviate difficulties or enable students to deal with them more acceptably.

5. **Student as independent** ◄─────► **Student as needy**
   moral agent **adolescent**

On the one hand, students need to be treated as rational people who are capable of making moral choices, and so are expected to accept responsibility for their behaviour.

On the other hand, students are in a period of their lives when things are in a turmoil; they are subject to many conflicting pressures and need sympathetic help and guidance when their behaviour suggests that they are not coping.

6. **Responsibility for staff** ◄─────► **Responsibility for**
   well-being **student well-being**

On the one hand, teaching is a highly stressful job and dealing with difficult students takes a huge toll on the physical and emotional resources of the staff. Teachers need to be protected from undue stress, if they are to be able to do their jobs well on behalf of all students.

On the other hand, students who present problems often have very difficult situations to deal with – often with little support – in their personal lives. School may be their only source of sympathy and stability in an uncaring and unstable world.

7. **Confidentiality** ◄─────► **Need to know**

On the one hand, it is important to maintain confidentiality with respect to sensitive information about students' personal circumstances and events in their lives outside school.

On the other hand, knowing about particularly stressful circumstances in students' lives outside school helps teachers to understand and respond sympathetically to behaviour that may be a reflection of personal difficulties.

Box 4.1: Dilemmas of intervention (continued)

To take an example, consider the dilemmas that a teacher might experience with respect to one student, Terry, on his return after a long period of absence including fixed-term exclusion. The teacher knows that he has missed key areas of work, and so will only be able to do the tasks set if she spends a great deal of her time with him. But she knows that this will be at the expense of time spent helping other children. How does she choose to share out her time? (Dilemma three.) Does she decide that, on this occasion, given the circumstances, the needs of the individual should prevail over the rights of the collective? Or does she decide that she cannot prioritise the needs of one individual over that of the collective (given, say, the imminence of examinations, her fear that he may resist her efforts to help, or the likelihood that Terry will absent himself for further long periods of time)?

Such dilemmas have the potential to promote constructive dialogue because they do not lend themselves to easy solutions. Given the complexity of considerations that teachers take into account in making such decisions, it seemed likely that teachers would recognise that they would resolve the dilemma differently for different classes, individuals and situations. We might, for example, have strict rules about lateness or times for handing in homework which we believe in applying with fairness and consistency. Yet all of us could no doubt think of occasions when we have made exceptions, taking account of individual circumstances (Dilemma two). Whatever the differences in teachers' values and perspectives, it is unlikely that any individual ever adopts a simple, blanket resolution for all eventualities.

Use of the dilemmas

We decided therefore to give our feedback to staff in the school through the medium of the dilemmas, which were then incorporated into the ongoing development work that the school was undertaking. The plan was that they would be used to help staff to acknowledge and discuss openly the tensions that they were likely to encounter on the ground during the implementation of their newly-agreed mission statement (Box 4.4). Staff had recently worked collectively to draw up a set of values and shared responsibilities towards pupils, staff, parents and the community. They were aware that the impact of this consensus would depend upon the extent to which staff found themselves able to embody these values in their practices, especially when confronted with challenging behaviour. We proposed that the dilemmas could be used to help raise awareness of the challenges and tensions that staff were likely to find themselves facing in their attempts to realise these responsibilities, to offer a shared language for discussing these tensions and how to resolve them in specific cases, and to help staff and management identify the support that may be needed in order to achieve the closest possible match between values and practice.

Our first responsibility is to the pupils at our school. We will help them to achieve the highest possible standards in their academic, personal and social development.

We will provide a broad and balanced curriculum which suits the needs of all our pupils and will maintain a calm, orderly environment enabling pupils to work and progress together. By using local and national data, we will ensure that our expectations of work are high, but realistic, and we will celebrate achievement in all its diverse forms. Care, support, encouragement and guidance will be provided for all pupils irrespective of gender, race, religion, ability or social background. We will foster good relationships within our school community, based on mutual respect and consideration for others.

Our second responsibility is to each other as members of staff, both teaching and non-teaching. We must work together in order to be effective and successful in educating pupils, and to gain fulfilment from our work.

Professional duties will be carried out efficiently at all times, making good use of the resources available to us. Working in teams, we will support and encourage each other to complete the necessary tasks, share our expertise and communicate effectively. Roles, responsibilities and lines of accountability will be accepted and we will show a willingness to listen openly to new ideas. Opportunities to further our professional development will be taken. All of our actions will be underpinned by the principles in which we believe: honesty, reliability, trustworthiness, courtesy and integrity.

Our third responsibility is to the parents of our pupils. They must feel confident that their children are in a safe, secure and stimulating environment and that we care about each child as an individual. We aim to work in partnership with parents to support their children's learning.

The school will make clear statements of policy and practice. We will listen and respond appropriately to the ideas and concerns which parents express. We will maintain regular contact though through the

Box 4.2 School statement of purpose and direction (continued overleaf)

logbook, meetings and annual reports, ensuring that parents are kept informed of their children's progress. We will seek to make parents feel part of the school community and encourage their involvement in all appropriate activities.

Our fourth responsibility is to members of the community. Local people must feel confident that we work within a clear moral framework and foster a sense of social responsibility amongst our pupils. We will develop the knowledge, skills and personal qualities commonly expected of young members of society.

We will keep abreast of local and national developments in education and other fields, ranging from the views of our neighbours to changes in statutory regulations. Links with the business community will be maintained in order to enhance our curriculum. We will make information on the school available and will publicise our achievements as widely as possible. We take great pride in our school and will actively promote its good reputation in the local community.

Box 4.2 School statement of purpose and direction (continued)

In summary then, we anticipated that the dilemmas would serve a positive, practical function, presenting some of the findings of the research in a way which created opportunities for different points of view to be legitimated and expressed. They contributed to the task of building the kind of climate where teachers would feel that they were acknowledged and listened to, understood and cared for, and so would be more emotionally able and willing to work together to create comparable conditions for students.

5   T. S. Eliot High School

Introduction

T. S. Eliot High School is a Year 8–13 school with 2,012 students and 127 staff. It has a large sixth form which attracts students from other schools, including some in the independent sector. It is situated on the edge of a city and a large number of the students are bussed in from neighbouring farming communities. However, it has a predominantly urban population, many students coming from high density housing areas. It is divided into three schools on adjoining sites. The Lower School accommodates mainly Year 8, the Middle School comprises mainly Years 9 and 10, and Year 11 and the sixth form make up the Upper School. The Upper School building is similar to an FE college, with common rooms, snack bars and posters advertising courses and colleges. The students are not required to wear school uniform (although a suitable form of dress is expected). The aim in the Upper School, according to a senior member of staff, is to create an adult atmosphere and a culture of learning which will assist students in gaining maturity and achieving better examination results.

Compared to other secondary schools, T. S. Eliot has well above the average number of Key Stage 4 pupils, that is the age group most vulnerable to exclusion (Castle and Parsons, 1997; Blyth and Milner, 1996). Yet when the school joined the project, only one boy had been permanently excluded during the previous two years (for unacceptably dangerous behaviour). Senior pastoral members of staff were proud of this record of non-exclusion. As one person commented, it suggested that 'we must be doing some things right'. Nevertheless, staff also had concerns about disaffection and disruptive behaviour, particularly in the current Year 10. They hoped that the project would provide an opportunity to endorse and build on existing good practice, while also identifying areas for further positive development with particular reference to their concerns about this group.

Positive discipline for learning

One important area of the school's development work over the previous two years had been the introduction of a 'Positive Discipline for Learning' (PDL) policy. This whole school initiative was developed on the basis of ideas derived from the work of the classroom management expert, Bill Rogers (1990). Its purpose was to establish a clear and consistent approach to discipline throughout this large split-site school, with its three separate staffrooms and (hitherto) three different sets of procedures for the use of rewards and sanctions.

A group of staff had attended a course run by Bill Rogers on PDL and a working party had been formed from members of departments throughout the whole school. Following consultations with the whole staff and departmental heads on issues of discipline, the working party produced a document for staff, summarising the overall approach to discipline which they proposed should be adopted on a whole school basis. The document included:

- clarification of pastoral team management structure and roles
- review of discipline, rules and consequences
- review of the referral system
- suggested classroom discipline plan
- introduction of a Time Out room
- proposals to improve communication across the site
- recommendations for the whole school duty system.

Central to Bill Rogers' approach are the principles that rights and responsibilities should be negotiated with pupils; that rules should be justified explicitly in relation to the maintenance of these rights and responsibilities; and that there should be clear consequences following from the infringement of agreed rules. These general principles were followed through in the PDL working group document. The aims of the behaviour policy and the rights of teachers and students, to be promoted through negotiated rules, rewards and sanctions, were set out as shown in Table 5.1.

Specific rules and their consequences – to be negotiated with students – were outlined in relation to six distinct aspects of discipline: Attendance, Punctuality, Attire, Class Behaviour, Treatment of Others and School Environment. Infringement of agreed rules, recorded through the use of 'yellow slips', would lead automatically to the operation of specific sanctions.

A further feature of the proposed policy document, also based on Bill

Table 5.1: Aims of behaviour policy and the rights of teachers and students

Aims	Rights
a) Pupils' self-control	a) To learn without interference
b) Pupils' self-motivation	b) To teach without disruption
c) Tolerance of and respect for the rights of others	c) To be heard and supported
	d) To be safe and feel safe
d) Fairness and honesty	e) To be treated with respect and dignity
e) A positive school ethos	
f) Higher self-esteem	

Rogers' approach, was the classroom discipline plan. The idea of a 'discipline plan' is to prepare in advance appropriate short-term and long-term measures to correct disruptive behaviour patterns, rather than relying on instant, on-the-spot reactions. It includes both preventative and corrective strategies, the latter being used to assist the teacher in dealing with incidents of unwanted behaviour in the least confrontational way possible, while still asserting the teacher's right to teach others without unwanted interruption (Box 5.1).

There were also some additional guidelines for teachers carrying out corrective action (Box 5.2).

Some of the items on this additional list echo parts of the guidance for preventative action (given on p. 94), in that they emphasise consistency, an encouraging atmosphere, the use of positive feedback, and respect for students. They are, seen in this light, a helpful expansion of the 'Rights of teachers and students' set out in the PDL document, offering teachers clear illustrations of what the recognition of those rights entails in practice. The guidelines seek to ensure continuity between preventative and corrective action. Any action taken in response to unacceptable behaviour is still essentially preventative, in that it seeks to maintain or restore positive relationships and avoid confrontation.

The PDL document also proposed taking up Bill Rogers' idea of making available a Time Out room where students could be sent when their behaviour could no longer be dealt with in accordance with the classroom discipline plan. In theory, this is not a punishment, but an opportunity for the pupil to work out a solution to the problem without wasting lesson time. The procedure for using the Time Out room was set out as shown in Box 5.3.

A series of departmental meetings was held, led by those who had been on the original training day. It was considered important that all staff should feel ownership of a policy that had been adapted to fit the

Preventative action

(to prevent or minimise unnecessary disruption)

- make your room aesthetically pleasing and functional
- prepare and use appropriate materials
- arrive on time
- plan interesting lessons
- cater and plan for mixed ability
- plan seating arrangement
- make clear the routines
- have clear, fair positive rules/make rules and consequences known
- plan the language you use when disciplining (neutral)
- plan to acknowledge and affirm positive behaviour

Corrective action

(how to respond when disruptive behaviour occurs)

In order from the least to the most intrusive, use:

- tactical ignoring
- simple, brief, polite directions
- rule reminder
- simple choice (for example 'put magazine in your bag or on my desk')
- casual or direct question (avoid 'why', for example, 'what should you be doing?')
- redirection
- make consequences clear (via choice)
- direct student to work elsewhere in room
- cool-off time (for example 'I can see you're upset, we'll talk later')
- interview with head of year to agree contract
- separation to nearby classroom, for example sixth form group
- subject detention (end of lesson, lunchtime, or after school)
- Time Out room (for dangerous behaviour, continual disruption or a safety issue).

Box 5.1: Preventative and corrective action

The teacher should strive to:

- minimise embarrassment and hostility (verbal and physical)
- use a respectful but assertive tone of voice
- affirm positive aspects of behaviour in lesson
- privately encourage positive behaviours
- avoid unnecessary argument
- give clear choices to maximise student responsibility
- be consistent in follow through
- make use of support systems through the yellow form or referral form.

Box 5.2: Additional guidelines for teachers carrying out preventative action

particular context of this school. Following a further training day for the whole staff, the working group's proposals were accepted, with the result that the approach had been in operation for a year at the point when the school became involved in the research.

Researching the whole-school behaviour policy

In initial discussions between the research team and senior pastoral staff, the implementation of this initiative was identified as an important area to focus upon. Some concerns were expressed about its effectiveness, and in particular about the use of the Time Out room. It had become clear that some departments were sending more students to the Time Out room than others. It was agreed to start by examining existing records on referrals, which provided evidence of patterns of referral, as well as staff and students' perceptions of the reasons for referral to the Time Out room. The analysis focused particularly on Year 10, as it was felt that there were more students vulnerable to exclusion in this year group.

Using the information gained from this analysis, one of the university researchers then carried out some lesson observation of Year 10 classes where there were pupils who were regular frequenters of the Time Out room. For ethical reasons, the research team agreed to avoid a focus on individual pupils. The purpose of the observations, and subsequent interviews with the teachers, was to gain insight into the operation of the PDL policy in the classroom, by exploring teachers' definitions and understandings of 'disruptive behaviour' and how these were linked to their classroom strategies, both preventative and correc-

Procedure

- Subject teacher completes a Time Out slip and sends the pupil with it to the Time Out room. Either then or at the end of the lesson, the teacher completes the referral form and sends it to the head of year.
- Duty teacher makes an entry in the Time Out register.
- Pupil completes a Time Out form (which will be passed to head of year).
- Behaviour plan discussed to decide steps the pupil intends to take to avoid repetition of the problem.
- Pupil to be interviewed by head of year within twenty-four to forty-eight hours to agree resolution and negotiate re-entry involving the teacher concerned with the original incident.
- Parents to be notified. If repetition of incident then parent interview needed.
- Persistent Time Outs will demand high level intervention, including behaviour modification strategies.

The room:

- must be accessible to the whole school
- must be comfortable but uninteresting
- pupils are readily observable and always supervised (back up from nearby teachers and staffroom)
- pupils are required to plan to improve behaviour (Time Out form)
- no student interaction
- emotionally neutral duty teacher
- rules and consequences to be displayed
- must be staffed during all lessons by senior pastoral members of staff (and other volunteers)
- will need a telephone and a copy of staff timetables
- must have a published timetable of duties.

Box 5.3: Procedure for using the Time Out room

tive, in terms of the policy document.

This study of teachers' perspectives was to have been accompanied by a similar examination of the understandings and perspectives of pupils who had been present at the lessons observed. Due to practical difficulties, however, it was not possible to complete this part of the research. The analysis therefore reflects just the range of views expressed by teachers, and this is acknowledged to be a limitation of the case study.

The university researcher carried out observations of fifteen lessons, one for each teacher who volunteered to be involved in the research. Lessons were followed up as soon as possible by an interview with the teacher. The interview focused on:

- staff perceptions of the PDL policy
- their understanding of the function of the Time Out room
- their understanding of the term 'disruptive'

The researcher also visited the Time Out room, in between these classroom observations and interviews, and observed what was happening there. One member of staff, observed while supervising in the Time Out room, was later interviewed.

Our analysis of these teachers' perceptions and practices is in no way intended to be read as an evaluation of the success of the PDL policy one year on. These teachers' views are not presented as being representative of the views of the staff group as a whole. What the analysis provides is insight into the complexities of implementing a whole-school behaviour policy: how individual teachers make sense of the new requirements and resolve the complex processes of assimilation and accommodation that the adoption of such a policy inevitably entails.

Staff perceptions of positive discipline for learning

The observation and interview data revealed that the PDL policy was being used, experienced and understood in different and sometimes contradictory ways by different members of staff. These different understandings and experiences shaped what they had to say about its value and impact, its strengths and limitations and its relationship to their own beliefs, values and practices.

Impact in the classroom

Those who were most positive about the behaviour policy were, in many cases, those who had been on the working party or who had worked closely with a colleague who had. Familiarity with Bill Rogers' ideas also made a difference. One teacher, when asked how the PDL policy affected her practice, answered:

I think it's a really good idea to try and be positive. I've read some of the Bill Rogers stuff on positive learning and I try to use it wherever I can, but there are some times when it's very hard to be positive.

As we have seen, the behaviour policy emphasises maintaining a non-confrontational stance and offering choices to students, especially those who find it difficult to keep the rules. For some staff, this approach merely reinforced what they already believed in and were doing already. For example, one teacher commented:

> One of the things I had taught to me was never put a child hard up against a wall with no way out . . . Always offer them choices even at the very last. Even if it's a case of you can breathe in or breathe out. But if you don't ever give them a choice, once they've lost face and are against the wall, there is nowhere to go, is there?

One teacher did not prepare a personal 'discipline plan', as the policy document suggests, but mentally identified certain members of her class who had difficulty concentrating throughout the lesson. She gave an example from the science class that had been observed:

> He works hard at the beginning, but to do that sort of lesson where you are working by yourself, an hour is all his concentration allows, so I would spend more time with him in the beginning because it would be a confrontation to try to get him to work at that level at the end.

Observation of another teacher who had been very involved in the PDL working party revealed that he was comfortable with allowing the students some time to settle in the room and chat before he quietly asserted his presence and expectation that they would start their work. Even though a group of boys seemed at one point to be trying to provoke a confrontation, he dealt with this calmly and humorously without confronting them or losing face.

This incident is a good example of how preventative and corrective action strategies can work together, helping to promote appropriate behaviour and defuse potential problems, while maintaining positive relationships. Other teachers also endorsed the positive, non-confrontational approach:

> Confrontation rarely works. For a start you have to win, and you never know if you are going to.

It's a lot better for teachers' sanity not to be confrontational . . .
you've got to remain calm. Getting excited and shouting at kids is
not going to help, it's not going to sort anything, it's only going
to make you more angry and more tense and the kids will pick on
it, and therefore it will get worse and worse and worse.

Two teachers pointed to positive effects that they felt the PDL policy
had had upon students' attitudes and responses in lessons. For one, this
was because children were clearer about the rules and consequences.

(Now) the whole thing is codified. Children know now much more
which actions are going to lead to reprimand and what is going to
happen. The worst thing for kids is not knowing in a situation
what particular actions are going to lead to if they do things, and
they get confused because they don't know what that's going to
engender.

For another, the clear linking of rules and consequences made disciplinary matters more straightforward, and helped to avoid confrontation.

Before then, especially if you had difficult students or not bringing
equipment or not in uniform, you would have to pick at them to
do something about it. Now you can disassociate the teaching from
the discipline so you don't have a conflict in the classroom. You
simply fill in the yellow form and post it. You reduce the
confrontation.

For both these teachers, the PDL policy had made a positive difference to the management of relationships and classroom interaction.
Yet, like the second of these two teachers, a number of those interviewed spoke of PDL in ways that focused on procedures associated
with the application of sanctions and with referral out of the classroom.
It was seen in terms of the issuing and following up of red and yellow
slips, connected with specific instances of unacceptable behaviour,
rather than as an ongoing process of negotiation between teachers and
students directed towards the development of a more harmonious
community.

One member of staff saw PDL uniquely in terms of the Time Out
strategy.

I do feel that the PDL is good, it is very good because it does enable
us to get rid of students. . . . . I think it was needed, I think we do

need something where if we have got a problem with a child, we can remove that child at that time.

This teacher's comment suggested that her understanding of PDL did not encompass the wider preventative and corrective strategies, and the principles underlying PDL in relation to which the function of the Time Out room needed to be understood. As we saw earlier, the Time Out room is mentioned in the policy document as the very last item on a list of thirteen possible strategies, ranging from 'the least to the most intrusive' in the classroom discipline plan.

Use of the Time Out room

There was general agreement about the importance of having a Time Out facility available but there were also differences of perception about what ought to be its aims and function:

> I'm not really sure about the Time Out room – I think it's really, really useful and certainly I've sent kids so that we can get on with the rest of the lesson, as well as to actually get rid of that child and to have it written down in his book, but what I don't understand about the Time Out room is that it's supposed to be a sort of positive thing: give the kid time, you know, a space, but I would say that most people use it as a punishment, which it is, because if you get three of them you get suspended, therefore it must be a punishment.

This teacher understood the rationale for the Time Out room as embodied in the PDL document, but also noticed an inherent tension between the intended positive emphasis and other features of the procedures associated with its use, as outlined in the policy document. Certainly, the guidelines provided in the policy document lend themselves to interpretations that would be consistent with both positive and punitive approaches.

This teacher's personal view was that Time Out ought to be seen and used as a punishment. He felt that there needed to be an element of punishment, as well as 'time to talk and think and all the rest of it.' His view was endorsed by other members of staff, who felt that if Time Out was seen as non-punitive, it would be exploited by students as a soft option to avoid work:

> Time Out as an idea is OK but it hasn't been thought through as it should be. Time out by some students is looked at as a freebie

'Hey, I can get out of this, I don't have to do my learning, I can just go and sit there and be quiet.'

One teacher, interviewed while he was supervising the Time Out room, also mentioned this as a concern that he had experienced himself. But working in the Time Out room had changed his view:

> I have been taught a lesson here because before I started doing this, I would have said that 80 per cent of children who were sent here would have used that method (work avoidance) and in fact my experience now tells me that's not the case.

Observation revealed that staff managing the Time Out room reflected these different views of the value and purpose of Time Out in the approaches they adopted with pupils referred there. Some staff performed their duty in an essentially consultative/therapeutic way, taking the opportunity to discuss students' feelings and problems in a non-judgmental and supportive way. Other staff performed the duty in a custodial, punitive way, using the time with students in the room to interrogate and instruct them on how they might mend their ways.

Although most of those who commented on Time Out felt that it was important to have such a facility available, there was also concern expressed that sending pupils to Time Out could be interpreted as a 'failure' on the part of the teacher:

> In the past some members of staff have felt that they had been criticised by a head of year because they have used the Time Out room and I don't think that should ever occur. I think it is there as support for us as much as anything else. . . there are times when you have a bad day and you send someone to the Time Out room when you would have perhaps dealt with it on another day. Perhaps you have to take account of teachers' swings and capabilities on certain days. We are not machines.

Among those interviewed, there were indeed some who expressed the view that teachers sometimes turned too swiftly to Time Out rather than using a range of classroom based strategies.

> I do think that there is a bit of a tendency for too much referring and too much bureaucracy. Most incidents that happen in the normal interchange in the classroom over a fifty-five minute period can be done by an instant reprimand *per se*. It doesn't require a bit

of paper, a document filling out that this or that has happened and feedback about the action that has been taken.

Another member of staff who was on the receiving end of the paperwork expressed a similar concern,

> It (Time Out) has some big disadvantages which I don't think we've actually begun to tackle yet. . . . It has led unquestionably as far as I'm concerned to a plethora of paperwork whistling around, and a feeling on my part . . . that what it's doing at the moment is relieving a lot of colleagues of what I would call the responsibility for classroom management.

Certainly there was evidence that responsibility for implementing the PDL policy had been taken up unevenly among those interviewed, and that some staff were selectively drawing on particular elements of the policy at the expense of others.

Theories of effective practice

The variety of teacher comment quoted in this chapter so far illustrates how much staff varied in their perceptions of the PDL policy. They differed in their assessments of its effectiveness, strengths and limitations. What staff valued and made active use of within the overall PDL approach, and the areas of concern that they pinpointed, varied according to whether they identified as salient features the underlying values and principles, or specific classroom strategies for the management of classroom interaction, or the more procedural elements, the application of rules, and the use of referral.

Staff interpretations and responses were also shaped by their personal values, experience and practices and the relationship that they saw between these and the PDL policy. In fact, it appeared from the interviews that the advent of PDL had – for these teachers at least – brought about little change in classroom practices and their interactions with students. It was as if the procedures of PDL were not related to the pedagogy of individual teachers. In some cases, this may have been because they felt that what PDL was advocating was just 'standard stuff', or that it reflected principles that they were already operating automatically in their classroom teaching. The overriding impression, however, was that teachers' practices remained bound up with and infused by their personal philosophies, understandings and with the styles of interaction which they had developed over years of teaching experience.

One teacher, for example, described in some detail how she enacted with individual children and with difficult classes her belief that the key to improvements in behaviour lies in building relationships with children. She described an approach based on patience, caring and sensitivity to individual needs which was somewhat different in its emphasis from the 'classroom discipline plan'.

> It takes a lot of time and a lot of patience, but I think after a while, if you have a little bit of a mother hen approach with these kids, you manage to establish some kind of relationship with them. I think I have managed to build up that kind of relationship with Sean . . . if you surround him with attention, with patience, because basically they need to be mothered . . . and if you manage to do that then you build up some kind of relationship and they start talking to you, they start confiding in you a little bit more, basically they start trusting you a little bit more. From the moment they start trusting you they stop being confrontational and they are better behaved.

The key concepts in this teacher's description of her practice: patience, attention and trust, are in no sense at odds with the concept of a 'positive school ethos', one of the PDL aims. Her account goes a long way further though in terms of the place of personal relationships in the classroom, rather than the strategic clarity and neutrality of the preventative and corrective action plans.

Another teacher described how she saw her central task in terms of building self-esteem (another of the aims of the PDL) through lots of positive strategies, in particular by encouraging pupils to see the link between taking pride in their work and taking pride in themselves:

> I do a little homily in front for the thought of the day and talk about them taking a pride in themselves, and they never usually make the connection between taking pride in their work and themselves.

She was very aware of the need to take account of the personal circumstances of students in determining how to respond to them, rather than strictly applying rules and consequences.

> I do in certain ways play it by ear but I try not to let the class see that. I kind of seem as if I'm black and white. 'You will do that or

else I will do this', but in reality, underneath the surface, you tend to deal differently with different kids.

This teacher too seems to be going 'beyond the letter' of the PDL policy, the better to implement its spirit. Whereas 'tolerance and respect for others' stand as aims in the policy, this teacher's priority is tolerance and respect for the differences between individuals, an attitude of trust and attention that echoes the sentiments of those teachers who emphasise the centrality of personal relationships.

Other teachers also talked about the need for flexibility in the application of rules and consequences. Although there were clear rules about uniform, equipment and eating in class, for example, one teacher considered that he was 'on a hiding to nothing' if he picked them up on every infringement of those rules. The task was 'knowing when it's important and when it isn't.'

> They know that they're not supposed to eat and drink and I certainly wouldn't allow it when they are doing practical work, and they know why not because it is dangerous. When they are doing practical work, I go round with a bin and say 'come on spit it out'. And by and large they will. But they'll be in there and having a drink and you have to ask is it really worthwhile at this point?

This awareness of the need for flexibility was bound up with recognition of the need to know pupils as individuals and to be accepting of differences. In one lesson, for example, a pupil was frequently observed shouting out. When asked about this after the lesson, the teacher replied 'Tracey shouts'. When pressed to say if this was acceptable behaviour in the teacher's judgement, she replied: 'She's not doing it for effect. That's the way Tracey is'. This approach enabled the teacher to handle the situation calmly, while nevertheless continuing to try to encourage Tracey to try out alternative ways of participating.

> I just keep griping away at it. 'For goodness sake, you don't need to shout, you can speak without shouting, what are you shouting for Tracey? You are going to give everybody a headache. If you've had a particularly bad day why are you shouting like that today?' And sometimes it makes a difference. She was quieter in that lesson than she is a lot of the time.

Another teacher drew on her knowledge of the circumstances

relating to an individual, in mitigation of his handling of the rude behaviour of one boy in the second lesson on a Monday morning.

> He is often upset after the weekend. He is supposed to go to his father but he often lets him down. He takes the anger out in class on Monday.

Flexibility and sensitivity to individual needs and differences seem to lie at the heart of these teachers' ways of responding to students; yet these qualities are not necessarily easy to reconcile with a pre-planned approach dependent upon clear, consistent and unambiguous strategies, as advocated in the classroom discipline plans.

Other conflicts of value were also identified by some teachers with respect to key aspects of the PDL policy, particularly the focus on avoiding confrontations, and offering face-saving choices. They saw this as undermining effective discipline and clearly wanted a system that was more punitive. As one teacher, who had previously taught in another school stated:

> I think this school is very liberal, and I don't think that the kind of liberal approach used here works with certain types of young people. . . I've observed the same pupils in my lessons and in other lessons and their behaviour is radically different and I think some teachers suffer from being too liberal . . . I would never tolerate that level of noise or abuse to me . . . I think kids are always probing where the weaknesses are and then they will try it on, it's their sort of coming of age thing.

Another member of staff accepted the positive approach but felt that it was important to confront unacceptable behaviour.

> one thing I am very intolerant of is people who argue back. I find that kind of truculence difficult in the room so I'm quite insistent with that certain formality to myself and to other members of the group. I don't like people being rude to the members of the group. . . . So in that respect I will make a confrontation situation, this is the line and you're not going to cross it, sort of thing. So in that respect perhaps I don't follow the policy to the letter.

As this teacher recognises, there is an inherent tension in the concepts of, on the one hand, teaching without disruption (when the teacher defines the criteria of disruption), and, on the other, pupils' self-control (when the pupils claim the right to argue their case and to be heard).

Teacher stress and attitudes to exclusion

From some of the teachers' comments, it was clear, too, that whatever their personal philosophies and beliefs, at times they struggled with feelings of failure and resentment about the demands which their role placed on them.

> Sometimes I feel depressed and I feel that I have failed because I haven't managed to get anything out of them. . . . sometimes I feel a lot of anger as well, I feel why should I have to put up with this crap, for crying out, I do my best with my job, I love those kids.

These feelings of ambivalence – the tug-of-war between commitment and self-preservation – were also reflected in teachers' comments about exclusion. For example, one teacher commented:

> I think sometimes it (this school) doesn't exclude at the cost of a lot of fatigue and tiredness of the teachers. I mean, the teachers have got to put up with a lot sometimes and cope with a lot and sometimes we feel it is a bit too much, but on the other hand the school has got a lot of qualities in the way that it caters for those kids. Most people in the school, I've found the teachers are caring, you know they do care a lot about those kids. They will avoid at all costs that they are excluded if that is at all possible.

Despite differences in personal philosophies and understandings of the behaviour policy, most staff interviewed were in favour of avoiding permanent exclusion. Exclusion was not seen as a solution to problems of challenging behaviour because, as one senior teacher said, 'If we do exclude six, there will be another six waiting down the aisles.'

Among other reasons mentioned by staff was the link between exclusion from school and social exclusion. As one teacher said:

> When you exclude you turn a school problem into a long term social problem.

Some staff thought that students excluded from T. S. Eliot might well be replaced by students excluded from other schools. They stated their preference for dealing with students they had known since early adolescence rather than those they would have to start with afresh in Year 10 or 11. These comments suggest a sympathetic willingness to build on relationships already established, and an awareness that knowledge of individuals can make a positive contribution to overall discipline.

When talking about student behaviour, and vulnerability to exclusion, several teachers referred to adolescence as a developmental phase. They referred to students who had given cause for great concern during Year 10 but had settled down in Year 11. There was plenty of anecdotal evidence to support the policy of moving students into the Upper School at Year 11, where it was felt that they benefited from the recognition of their physical and social development. They were rewarded by no longer having to wear school uniform and had the status of young men and women rather than children. It also meant that the importance of their work towards GCSE examinations was recognised.

In addition to staff attitude and commitment, there were several other features of the situation and of the school's approach that may have helped to contribute to its success in avoiding permanent exclusion. The stability of the staff group, which, on the whole, people only left for promotion elsewhere, may well have been a contributory factor. Also, the fact that all members of the senior management team had a teaching timetable, as well as making themselves responsible for 'high profile' duty in the areas where students gather in their free time, meant they were less remote from the students. Students seemed comfortable chatting to the head, and felt at ease to talk to any of the teachers on 'high profile' duty.

The pastoral head had been at the school for nearly twenty-five years and so had long-standing links with the families of current students. As well as keeping close to students through a substantial teaching timetable, she had a constant stream of students passing through her office during break times and dinner times. She also worked closely with social services and the probation service.

Although the development of a strong ethos of caring had been a characteristic of the school's work over a number of years, one senior member of staff felt that the PDL policy had been instrumental in encouraging positive attitudes among staff and a willingness to try again. He was clear that staff attitudes had changed in a number of significant ways:

> Staff are much more amenable to sitting down with me and discussing a particularly difficult pupil. Staff are much less likely

to say, 'I don't want him or her in my class ever again. You put him back in my class, I'm going to refuse to teach him.' I can't remember a member of staff saying that. . . . Staff I think are appreciative of the support that it is attempting to give.

Developing a whole-school policy

It is now a statutory requirement that all schools should have in place a whole-school behaviour policy setting out principles and procedures for maintaining high standards of discipline. Our study of teachers' perceptions of the value and impact of one such policy in one school reveals some of the challenges involved in moving from the formulation of a policy upon which all can in principle agree to the enactment of agreed principles and practices in the classroom.

Some of the difficulties of implementing a whole-school policy identified in this analysis of a sample of teachers' perceptions may reflect tensions inherent in the principles, procedures and practices outlined in the particular policy document. However, it may also be that such tensions are inherent in any attempt by schools to articulate a whole-school behaviour policy. Although at T S Eliot the implementation of the PDL policy involved consistent application of pre-established rules, most of those interviewed indicated that they still appraised and evaluated individual students' circumstances and used discretion in the application of rules according to their interpretation of the presenting behaviour.

We would argue that to acknowledge the existence of tensions in the implementation of a whole-school policy is not to imply that the initiative is floundering or was perhaps, in some respects, ill-conceived. Tensions between, on the one hand, the recognised demand for consistency and standardisation and, on the other hand, the will of staff to recognise and understand diverse individual needs are what will keep the policy alive and growing, developing and improving. No whole-school policy can be 'successfully' implemented on a once and for all basis. To be successful, initial principles and agreed practices need to be continually re-examined in the light of experience, stimulated by the staff's common commitment to understand and respond to the educational, emotional and social needs of their most vulnerable students.

6 Ogden Nash Upper School

Introduction

Ogden Nash, a Voluntary Aided Roman Catholic upper school, with 383 pupils on roll, is the third smallest of the four secondary schools in this study. Set in the midst of a local authority housing estate on the edge of a light industrial area, Ogden Nash School presents a number of superficial similarities to William Shakespeare School, the other upper school in our study. The school sites are physically similar, being surrounded by ample playing fields with teaching accommodation composed predominantly of single storey buildings which appear to have been built in the 1970s and 1980s. Unlike William Shakespeare, however, Ogden Nash is a denominational school. An immediate consequence of this is that the vast majority of the students come from outlying villages and towns in a largely rural county. Local children, by and large, attend the county upper school, which has more than double the student population of Ogden Nash and is literally next door.

Hidden difficulties

In contrast to William Shakespeare, Ogden Nash is a relatively high achieving school, scoring well above the national average in terms of GCSE results. Some staff at the school, however, are quick to point out that this owes much to the relatively favourable socio-economic circumstances of the pupils' home backgrounds. Unlike the head of William Shakespeare School, Ogden Nash's head teacher was not able to give the research team a detailed statistical account of the demographic and socio-economic characteristics of the student population. This in itself is perhaps indicative that social deprivation is not seen as a significant issue at Ogden Nash.

This is not to say the school is problem free. There is a sense in which the perceived relative prosperity of the surrounding area is seen to present its own set of difficulties:

> One of the challenges for us is that [the town where the school is located] is a very middle class area, all schools achieve good results and, therefore, staff feel under pressure to continually out-perform other schools in order to maintain numbers etc. While this is a perfectly good and valid challenge, we feel as a [senior management] team that some staff far too easily want a 'particular' student 'out'.
>
> (letter from deputy head to the university project team)

This view does not go entirely unopposed. Other staff refer to different challenges which they believe the particular student group they serve brings with it. In particular, there is a suggestion that the relative comfort and prosperity enjoyed by Ogden Nash students can lead to attitudes of complacency and even arrogance, which can in turn engender disruptive behaviour:

> I think classroom teachers [here] often have to suffer a little bit of rudeness, a little bit of lackadaisical behaviour and off-hand behaviour. . . If it was vice versa, [and] the staff spoke to the students like that, you would very quickly be picked up about it. I am not sure if it is to do with the policy of the school. This [geographical] area – the whole area seems pretty laid back. It's not a particularly bad area; so there's not a lot of social deprivation, and life's reasonably good. It's not a particularly affluent area all the time, but it's not too bad. You get the impression that people are fairly OK to sort of mosey along. And if you don't push them too hard, then they'll do things. Sometimes I think the students should do more, but I am sure that if you pushed them more you might get more bad behaviour as a response. So I don't know.

Juxtaposed in this way these quotations enable us to discern a common concern about difficulties in staff–pupil relations. Both portray the apparently positive aspects of their school and its intake as concealing a specific set of problems. On the other hand, there is disagreement about the fundamental sources of these problems. The deputy head attributes the cause of the problem to the attitude of certain staff. The other informant sees the sources of the problem as residing within the character of the student intake. The attitude of the second informant might be seen to confirm the view of the first. This does not mean, however, that there is a consensus about the nature of the problem; on the contrary, these two informants present conflicting attributions (Munton *et al.*, 1999) as to the cause of the problems.

While there is clearly not a consensus here, there is agreement that the school faces genuine problems. Over the course of the case study, interviews and meetings with school staff showed a deep concern, widely shared, about the problematic behaviour of a minority of students and the inadequacies of the school's response to it. The conflicts of attribution illustrated in the above example, however, were also reflected in the major findings of the study. A striking feature of this case study, in fact, is the way in which initial assumptions about the nature of problems and the possible avenues to solution changed in the light of these differences in perception being made explicit. This shift was a result of the processes of investigation and self analysis that were engaged with so wholeheartedly by the core team of staff in the school who undertook much of the research.

A major influence in this process of change was the fieldwork carried out in the school. A striking early finding from this study was the range of difference in perception between individuals and sub-groups in the school community of the nature of the issues identified by the school for study. In order to illustrate the nature and power of these differences the remainder of this chapter is structured as three, discrete sections.

The first of these deals with the way in which the main issues for research were generated, and thus reveals something of the distinctive perspective shared by members of the core team of school-based researchers. Although this group was appointed by a larger sub-group of the staff, and operated in good faith, with every intention of defining a research agenda that would serve the interests of the whole school, the agenda that emerged was in fact heavily influenced by the professional and personal interests of the members of this team. This is a good example of the manifold difficulties that are always involved in making claims about 'the school' as if it were a single, undifferentiated unit, rather than a composite of sub-units, each with its own set of preoccupations and issues.

The second section presents students' perceptions, which were sampled by a self-completed questionnaire. The questionnaire was designed on the basis of the core team's research agenda. Returns revealed unexpectedly diverse attitudes among students towards the school and its effectiveness in motivating them to achieve high standards in terms of both the formal curriculum and social behaviour.

It was of little surprise to the core team to find that a majority of students was relatively content with the school's motivational and support structures. However, the minority of students who found fault with different aspects of these structures, and the finding that some students appeared to be immune to their positive influence, were causes for concern.

In the third section we consider the perspectives of the teaching staff as a whole, the majority of whom were not members of the core team. Again, the data from this part of the investigation reveal a range of views which contrast and combine, in interesting ways, with the perspectives gained from the other two sources. Of particular interest is the way in which the teacher data help to shed light on some of the apparent conflicts between the perceptions of the core team and those of the students.

Determining the issues: core team perceptions

Initial discussions about the research at Ogden Nash were conducted between the university researchers and a large group of school staff, which included the head teacher, the deputy head, the year heads and several heads of department. This group discussed and showed general approval for the overall aims of the project. There was also consensus about the fact that Ogden Nash was a highly successful school for the vast majority of its pupils. However, while exclusion was not a major problem at the school, there was a general belief that a very small minority of pupils were at risk owing to behavioural problems in the face of which staff were generally ineffective.

Furthermore, there was concern about differences in apparent levels of motivation between year groups, for which staff had no consistent explanation. The current Year 11 was widely perceived by staff always to have been 'difficult', and was at this time conspicuous for the range and severity of behavioural problems presented by a small group of its pupils. This state of affairs was exacerbated by an apparent indifference towards the school's merit system that was pervasive throughout the students in this year group. While there was a high incidence of merit awards to other year groups, Year 11's performance was exceptionally low. There was speculation about the possible effects of the fact that this group had experienced a lack of continuity, compared to other groups, being the only year group not to have had the same team of class tutors from the beginning of their time at the school. It was suggested that the apparent motivational problems might have their roots in insecurities associated with this experience. A major aim of the study, therefore, was to generate systematic information that would help to shed light on what lay behind this year group's apparent difficulties.

On the basis of these concerns, and with an agreed commitment to the project, the large group then delegated the development and execution of the study to a smaller group (referred to throughout this chapter as 'the core team') which was to comprise the deputy head, a senior teacher and two heads of year. It was this group, along with two university based researchers, that defined the precise foci for the study.

Sharpening the focus

Identifying these concerns was a useful exercise, in that it helped members of the research team begin to make sense of the aims of the research in terms that were relevant to Ogden Nash School. Other measures were necessary, however, to establish a clear and practical starting point for the study. The best way to do this, it was decided, was by focusing on problems that arose spontaneously from circumstances surrounding at risk students and the school's efforts to deal with them. The most appropriate place to do this work was the pastoral team meeting, which was the forum where such issues were discussed, and where the decisions and recommendations that in effect constituted the school's response to such problems were normally made.

The intention was to enable the members of the core team to reflect on and analyse precisely what went on during these meetings. Key questions to be asked were:

- What were they trying to achieve in these meetings?
- What were they actually achieving?
- To what extent was what they were doing in these meetings contributing to the development of positive alternatives to school exclusion?
- What might they do to develop further the effectiveness of these meetings in promoting positive alternatives to school exclusion?

As at William Shakespeare School, in order to aid reflection, these meetings were audio-taped and transcribed. The transcriptions were then examined and discussed by the team at a subsequent meeting, with the above questions in mind.

This deceptively simple strategy was strikingly successful in enabling the core team to gain fresh perspectives on a procedure that was so familiar and well established that it was almost automatic. On examining the transcripts of a number of meetings the core team

114   Positive alternatives to exclusion

discovered that there was a range of significant problems that recurred repeatedly in different forms, but had tended to go largely unnoticed. These included conflicting perceptions of how important aspects of the school's pastoral system worked, and problems of communication both among the team, and between the team and other staff, in relation to information that might be important in understanding and responding to pupils' difficulties. There were seen to be inconsistencies in the ways in which different departments employed the formal referral system by which staff passed on concerns about individual pupils. The key realisation was that all these problems had a significant effect on difficulties which staff, including the pastoral team, had often attributed to individual pupils alone. As a result of this insight, the research team broadened the focus of their concerns, to consider the wider circumstances surrounding pupils who appeared to be experiencing or creating problems.

The issues that arose as requiring urgent attention were:

- the system of rewards and sanctions
- the system of communication between staff on pupil matters
- the system for keeping student records.

The core team wanted to know how students viewed the rewards and sanctions system, and what might be done to make it both more accessible and motivating. They also wanted to explore what appeared to be blockages in the exchange of important information about pupils. Their questions included: what were the sources of these blockages, and what might be done to overcome them? The issue of record keeping was related to the problem of communication and arose out of a recognition of the fact that a great deal of information about individual students was aired in the pastoral meetings (and at other times) but somehow never re-surfaced.

A powerful example of this concerned a girl who was exhibiting disruptive behaviour. Although the observable behavioural problems were well documented and widely known among staff, evidence supplied by the girl's mother, some of her peers and a teacher, that the girl might be suffering from an eating disorder, had not been recorded anywhere in writing. This case illustrated the possibility that whether or not pertinent information was available at an appropriate time was often a matter of serendipity, depending on the presence of a member of staff who happened to recall a specific piece of information as a result of having been party to a conversation. This was partly due to the fact that the recording of such information was not systematic. It was also noted that even when such significant information had been recorded it was not easily retrievable, being often embedded amid a plethora of information in bulky files.

The core team, in consultation with the university researchers, decided on two major approaches for addressing these issues:

- A questionnaire exploring students' perceptions of the nature, purposes and effects of the rewards and sanction systems to be completed, simultaneously, by every student in the school.
- A programme of teacher interviews which would explore perceptions of the school's approach to promoting positive pupil behaviour and engagement. The interviews were to be carried out by the university based researchers, as a measure to protect teachers' anonymity and the confidentiality of the interview process.

Students' perceptions: the student questionaire

The student questionnaire was divided into four main sections:

- Students' knowledge and understanding of the referral system.
- Students' knowledge and preferences in relation to available rewards and the system of monitoring cards.
- Students' perceptions of the importance of a range of factors in relation to their progress at school, including the role of different persons (teachers, other pupils and so on); the effects of the experience of success; opportunities to share concerns, and home–school links.
- Students' additional comments.

These questionnaires were administered simultaneously by Form Tutors and completed anonymously. Students were free to take the questionnaire away to complete in their own time, or not fill them in at all if they preferred.

The referral system

Questionnaires were returned by 320 students, 224 from Years 10 and 11 and 96 from Year 9. This represents 84 per cent of the school population of 383.

The questionnaires revealed that students in general had only a very limited understanding of the nature, purpose and workings of the system of referrals, merits and monitoring cards as they were construed by the core team.

Only 13 per cent (n=43) of all students recognised that referrals could be given for both good and bad behaviour, with the bulk of these (10 per cent of all respondents) coming from Year 10 and 11 students and only 3 per cent from Year 9 students. By contrast 64 per cent (n=204) of all respondents believed referrals to be concerned exclusively with disruptive or other rule breaking behaviour. There was a slightly higher rate of responses stating this negative view among Year 10 and 11 students (67 per cent; n=149), than Year 9 students (57 per cent; n=55). Approximately 6 per cent (n=18) of all students gave neutral replies which implied that referrals were designed to monitor students' effort and progress. Roughly the same percentages (14–18 per cent) of students in Years 9, 10 and 11 described referrals as 'bits of paper'. A few claimed no knowledge at all of the nature of referrals (4 per cent; n=13).

The description of referrals as simply 'bits of paper', when taken in conjunction with other, more overtly critical questionnaire data, might be interpreted to imply a degree of cynicism regarding the referral system. While a majority of respondents claimed that referrals served the purpose of regulating behaviour, and in a very small minority of cases (3 per cent; n=10), of enhancing academic achievement, a substantial minority of students (32 per cent; n=103) claimed to see referrals as serving either 'no purpose' (20 per cent; n=64) or some negative purpose (12 per cent; n=39). Negative purposes included leading to exclusion from school, and having a negative effect on pupils' self-esteem. It is interesting to note that these responses are equally distributed, in percentage terms, between students from Year 9 and those from Years 10 and 11, indicating that problems in the ways in which referrals are perceived are not limited to the problematic Year 11, but seem to be represented consistently across all year groups.

The clear impression created by these findings is that the referral system was only poorly understood by the vast majority of students, with the majority of students in all years surveyed seeing referrals as serving regulatory, rather than motivational purposes. A further conclusion was that 'at risk' students in Year 9 tended to have more negative attitudes than their peers. This was revealed by examining the returns of Year 9 students, whose 'EBH' scores (a measure of Effort, Behaviour and Homework completion rate) were required by the questionnaire. Students with scores indicating relatively poor levels of performance tended to reveal greater ignorance of or more negative attitudes towards the referral system than those with higher scores.

These findings indicate that at least some of the students who were most likely to be in greatest need of positive referrals were least likely to see the system as a source of positive motivation.

Monitoring cards and the reward system

The questionnaire responses showed that the system of 'monitoring cards', by which specific targets were set to support the progress of students giving cause for academic and behavioural concern, was only vaguely understood by the students themselves. The majority (64 per cent; n=207) of students indicated that the monitoring cards served a positive purpose that sometimes led to student improvement, largely in terms of academic progress and behaviour. However, a substantial minority of students (18 per cent; n=58) claimed to have no knowledge of the nature or purpose of the monitoring cards. A similar proportion of students believed that the cards served no useful purpose (15 per cent; n=49).

The students' largely positive attitudes towards the monitoring cards were reflected in their responses to questions about the reward system at the school. The overwhelming majority of students recognised that there was a fairly wide variety of rewards currently available for Ogden Nash students including:

- merits
- commendations
- good referrals
- 'unofficial Mars bars'
- certificates
- extra chips in the canteen
- trophies for sports.

In addition to these, some students expressed a desire for other concrete rewards, such as:

- money
- high street vouchers
- day off school
- music tokens
- day trips
- sweets.

This apparently mercenary position, however, should be placed in the context of the substantial minority (26 per cent; n=84) of over a quarter of students in all year groups, including Year 11, who claimed to find merit certificates a desirable form of reward. This might be interpreted as a reference to the symbolic importance of rewards, as signs of individual acknowledgement and enhancements to personal status. This interpretation is further supported by the additional status-oriented (as opposed to concrete) rewards some students (15 per cent; n=49) requested, such as for:

• letters home about good work
• more freedom and trust
• recognition.

Each of these implies a desire for personal, and possibly public acknowledgement of achievement, with the actual content of the reward being essentially symbolic, in the form of a positive reflection on the student's personal identity and public status. This was further reflected in the claims made by some students that the reward system was a source of motivation and provided a 'sense of achievement'.

The personal and symbolic importance of rewards was further illustrated in the negative responses that some students gave when describing the effects of the reward system at Ogden Nash. More than one-fifth of responding students (21 per cent; n=68) declared that the rewards served no useful purpose or were actually associated with negative outcomes. Of these, a small group (3 per cent; n=10) were clearly personally affronted by the system, seeing it as a form of 'bribery', as 'patronising' and being more appropriate for 'primary schools not upper schools'. This view of the reward system as personally demeaning alludes, in a negative way, to the same issues of personal dignity and status implied by the positive responses. The negative form of this theme is further highlighted by the sense of manipulation suggested by references to the effect of the system being to 'encourage competitiveness', and the possibility that this might lead to 'social problems' among students, through rivalry and jealousy.

Although, overall, a positive view of rewards was held by the majority of students, a large minority of students believed the rewards on offer to be ineffective or negative in effect (21 per cent; n=68) or claimed not to know what rewards were available or that there were none available (13 per cent; n=42). Taken together these two figures suggest that more than one in three of the students at Ogden Nash who responded to the questionnaire saw no benefit in the school's formal reward system: a system which had been described by the core team, at the outset of the study, as the central formal strategy for motivating students.

Factors affecting progress

Further light is shed on the factors which students found motivating in their responses to a question which required them to state which items on a list had been 'most helpful' to them during 'the past year' in relation to their 'doing well at school'. The most frequently cited factor was the 'experience of success in school work', which was identified by 77 per cent of students (n=247). This apparent tautology reminds us of the adage: 'nothing breeds success like success'. The remaining items, referring to a range of people, including Form Tutors, heads of year, other staff, other pupils and the opportunity to 'share concerns with others' were each cited as a source of positive support by between 51 per cent and 73 per cent of students. Many students (71 per cent; n=227) claimed that one or all of the formal motivational systems (i.e. the referral system, the monitoring cards and the reward system) were valuable and effective, as well as being aware of the support of school staff and/or fellow students. These findings indicate the importance, to the students, of personal relationships as a source of support for their progress at school.

It is interesting that the sizeable proportion of students (20 per cent; n=64) who claimed to see no purpose or value in the referral system, the monitoring cards or the reward system, cited school staff, other students and/or parents as making a particular contribution to a personal sense of progress in school. This suggests that the element of social support is vital for many students. Most students (85 per cent; n=273) included school staff among those who provide important support. A considerable minority of students, however, (13 per cent; n=45) claimed to have received no such support from staff. Of these, (8 per cent; n=24) cited support from fellow students and/or their parents, while 2 per cent (n=7) found support only from their own experience of success at school. Ten students (3 per cent) mentioned no persons as providing support. Finally, four students (1 per cent) not only saw no value in the referral system, the monitoring cards or the reward system, but also claimed to experience no form of social support.

These figures confirm that a sizeable minority of students at Ogden Nash are slipping through the net of formal support structures. It is clear that many students find alternative support in the social realm, while a small but troubling group of students claims to experience no support from either formal motivational systems or the social realm.

Main findings relating to the student perspective

The student data reveal much of both specific and general interest. First, at the specific level, there was clearly some confusion among students about the positive dimensions of the referral system. This was coupled with a significant thread of distrust and suspicion about the coercive, and at times manipulative and demeaning consequences of structures apparently designed to encourage and motivate students. Although these negative responses were voiced by only a minority of students, the conclusion must be that some students are not merely indifferent to, but are actively discouraged by the school's motivational systems. This is clearly a significant finding, particularly when we consider that it is, in general, the potentially disaffected minority of students who are likely to have the greatest need for encouragement and extrinsic motivation.

Second, a related, and more general, finding is the overwhelming sense, underpinning both positive and negative responses, of the importance placed by students on the personal impact of school structures on themselves as individuals. A consistent message here is that students seem to weigh up the pros and cons of these aspects of school life in terms of their consequences for their sense of self worth and personal dignity.

Teachers' perceptions: the teacher interviews

As we have seen, earlier the decision to gather staff perceptions evolved from discussions between the core team in the school and the university based researchers. The decision that this data should be gathered through one to one interviews emerged out of discussions about the nature and purpose of the research study. There were two main justifications.

First, the need was recognised for as many staff as possible to become involved directly in the research, rather than being passive objects of research or peripheral bystanders to it. Such involvement, it was decided, would engender understanding and, hopefully, commitment to the developmental aims of the research (Limerick *et al.*, 1996).

A second and more pragmatic reason was rooted in the sense, shared by members of the core team, that there were different constituencies of opinion among the staff group that had a direct bearing on the research endeavour. This was not to say that the core team was able to identify the nature of these differences. It was felt, however, that progress would have to take account of these differences. The basis for this view was the idea that staff were not simply mechanically implementing the school policy. On the contrary, their ways of construing and acting in relation to formal policies constituted the practical manifestation of policy. In effect, this meant that the way in which teachers acted actually determined policy in practice, regardless of what was written or agreed by the management team.

The need for staff to be able to speak openly and without inhibition meant that anonymity had to be ensured. The best way to achieve this anonymity, it was decided, was for the interviews to be carried out by the university researchers, rather than by colleagues of the interviewees. Furthermore, the interview schedule, while developed on the basis of interests expressed by the core team, would have to be constructed in a way that would maximise opportunities for staff to develop their individual ways of thinking about the issues involved.

All the full-time teaching staff were interviewed (n=17) with one exception. This was a teacher who, although willing to be interviewed, was not available on a mutually convenient date. The interview was open-ended and 'informant' in style (Powney and Watts, 1987). This approach to interviewing utilises only a very loose interview schedule, in the form of key issues to be explored. The main content of the interview is dictated by the interviewee, with the interviewer's role being to facilitate elaboration and exemplification of concerns that are of central importance to the interviewee (Limerick *et al.*, 1996; Cooper, 1993b). Two broad themes were made explicit by the interviewers:

• The teachers' beliefs and attitudes regarding disruptive behaviour in the school.
• The teachers' views of the ways in which the school addressed issues of pupil behaviour, in particular its success in promoting positive alternatives to school exclusion.

Interviews were carried out on school premises at times dictated largely by the availability of the interviewee. As with interviews in the other case studies, particular emphasis was placed on finding quiet, private and congenial surroundings in which the interviews could take place. All interviewees were assured that their contributions to the study would be anonymous.

Three major themes emerged from the interviews and are discussed next:

• the effects of distinctive features of the school and its intake
• teachers' personal values and practices
• the tension between formal procedures for dealing with discipline and actual practice.

The effects of distinctive features of the school and its intake

The interview data revealed what staff saw as the distinctive character of the school. As we saw in the opening section of the chapter, different staff perceived different elements of this character. What is interesting, however, is the way in which individual staff perceived these factors as, on the one hand, facilitating and, on the other, placing constraints on their ability to influence students in positive ways. Individual staff apparently felt themselves to be working within parameters which were not of their making and largely outside their personal zone of influence. Sometimes this was a positive experience and at other times it was negative.

Many teachers mentioned features of the school which affected the ways in which staff got to know about individual students. The relative smallness of the school was an advantage, and in this respect was mentioned in most interviews. For some teachers this was expressed in terms of the way in which the smallness of the school facilitated the surveillance of students:

> There are difficulties because of the size and there are advantages as well. One is that we can easily keep tabs on every single one of them. If an individual has difficulties we can pass it round very quickly.

> There is no place for them to hide. It is easy to keep track of them.

The size of the school also affected possibilities for communication among staff, as well as contributing to the creation of a cohesive community where people are known to each other as individuals both within and outwith the school:

> The bonus is knowing everybody in a year by sight and by name, even if not in the classroom.. Useful to talk to colleagues about children . . . and to know families.

> A small school is an ideal environment. Small schools have huge disadvantages in terms of finance and space available and things like that, but in terms of creating a community, I think there are different plus points.

Another important aspect of the school was the perceived character of the student intake. Several staff described a particular set of traits among Ogden Nash students which made them difficult to motivate (see earlier, p. 110).

Some teachers claimed to have learned 'the hard way' that strategies for managing students that were effective in other schools were not always successful at Ogden Nash. For example, one recalled:

> Before [when I first came to Ogden Nash] I was heavy handed, laying down the law; sometimes you got through, sometimes you didn't. For my own sanity I can't carry on doing that every day.

Other teachers put a slightly different spin on the same theme, seeing a tendency among their colleagues to over-indulge the students, sometimes to the point of being too 'soft' on them. In this way some staff found the school's apparent reluctance to use the sanction of exclusion as problematic:

> It is a small school. There should be achievement. . . we are not hard enough. Our structure could be tighter. I would like students to be more responsible and more individually driven. . . through one parent families and so on there is social disadvantage. . . the reason that they survive is that they have a lot of help. I still think we could be stricter. . . . I wonder if we are being too soft perhaps, we are not preparing them for the real world. The staff here are more inclined to give their own time, yes definitely, the staff give, give, give.

> I suspect that the kind of things that students don't get expelled for here they would have been close to exclusion in other schools. . . the way students talk to each other, their type of behaviour, the way they address staff and this sort of thing.

> There is a reluctance to exclude and steps are put in place to slow down the process. . . the problem stays with the head of department and the head of year. Teachers can be frustrated if they think there is no real action or result.

> Exclusions are seen to be avoided by a high degree of patience. . . we do have sanctions but they are not very clearly delineated. . . a long ladder of steps before we get to the end.

Other teachers saw, in the reluctance of the school to utilise the exclusion option, a reflection of another aspect of the school's character, namely its Christian ethos:

The governors feel particularly strongly that as a Catholic School we have responsibility to care for even society's least favoured children, who also tend to be the most disruptive.

That's what we do quite well, the reconciling part, even when the kids keep getting into quite a lot of trouble. They should get a fresh start free from all the former baggage. It is important to see them as individuals. It goes all the way through, forgiveness and reconciliation.

I believe the main way of avoiding exclusion has got a lot to do with accepting students as individuals . . . first being nice to them and being nasty later. Most of it depends on interaction between year head, the teacher, the head or whoever it happens to be, with students allowed to have their say.

Part of the ethos, if you like, the rationale of the school and I do think we work very hard to make sure that students who are a bit awkward to start with are got back on track. I don't think they think of excluding them. I've been here eleven years and I can't think of many pupils who have been excluded.

I like teaching here. I think a lot comes down to the size and the Christian ethos that runs through, the treatment of kids, the values. It is explicit we see the child as an individual and the child is at the centre and that is what we are working towards. It is to help each one develop . . . I think it is a little bit more here so the kids are a bit more aware of it and so respond to that. They feel a little bit more valued.

Another teacher saw Catholic schools in general, and this one in particular, as being highly successful in creating a caring and harmonious ethos:

We are small and the majority of our pupils are so nice that you do have time to notice if someone is unhappy. Children in Catholic schools are quite carefree. They come from a very caring Middle School. They have a staff they are used to talking to and by the time they leave here they are quite chatty and pally with the staff.

Not all staff, however, as we have seen, saw the emphasis on tolerance and forgiveness as without its potential pitfalls:

way to others so some might make a referral and others not. We have agonised about the system for a long time.

Interestingly, most staff seem to agree with most students in that they see referrals as essentially negative, being related to problem behaviour:

> I only write referrals if I think the situation needs to be documented *pro tem*. This record can be used to cover a teacher if later there is a situation where it is one teacher's word against another. . . It is also useful for the tutor to have an idea of how the person is doing. Often staff talk among themselves rather than filing an official referral.

Conclusions

This chapter illustrates very clearly the ways in which an investigation of different perspectives can illuminate key aspects of a school's culture. The first finding from this case study is concerned with the quality of record keeping and intra-staff communication about students with problems. The dysfunctions of the established system were starkly revealed in the course of the study, and this led to the realisation that staff were not always interacting effectively with students as whole persons, but rather tending to deal with fragmented accounts of students. This appeared to have the knock-on effect of the most sensational and negative aspects of students' lives being brought into focus and taken out of context, with disastrous effects for some students in the form of exclusion.

The theme of fragmentation is reflected elsewhere in the Ogden Nash case study. In this school we can discern a wide range of sub-groups, each defined by a different set of beliefs and understandings about the school. There are differences in the ways in which staff give accounts of the most effective ways to motivate and influence the student group. One group sees the formal motivational system as central to these processes, while another group places much stronger emphasis on the importance of relationships, and their power to influence students as persons. Another sub-group of staff presents a fatalistic view which leads them to believe that they have little or no influence on the behaviour of students. These staff tend to divide students into two main groups, those who are biddable and, therefore, amenable to teacher influence, and those who are neither of these things.

There is a powerful consensus among the staff about the fact that the school's Catholic status is significant; there are diverse accounts of the value of this spiritual influence, however. The students make no reference to the school's Christian ethos; however, they share with the staff a fragmented set of views, with some students favouring different aspects of the school's formal systems, another group favouring the power of relationships over these, and yet another small group apparently finding no source of motivation in either of these sources. Within the student group favouring relationships as a source of support there is a sub-group who finds that support only among peers or in their out of school relationships.

These findings demonstrate that the complexity of the factors underlying issues of student engagement and motivation is greater than the core team initially thought. What emerges most powerfully from this case study is the extent to which the core team underestimated the importance of relationships between staff and students and how these helped to motivate some students. It is also clear that there is considerable confusion and lack of knowledge in some quarters about the nature of the positive aspects of the referral system. Finally, the core team and students are united in their recognition of the need for individual support and personal recognition: students thrive on the experience of being positively acknowledged as persons (an insight in keeping with the findings of other case studies in this book). This fact is clearly understood by some staff, and employed in their dealings with students to good effect. Similarly, we find powerful testimony of the importance of staff experience and personal values.

The identification of these factors creates a clear basis for development at Ogden Nash, showing where the school's strengths lie. At the time of writing, staff members are engaged in a number of endeavours designed to build on these findings. First, there has been a overhaul of record-keeping procedures, so that more holistic accounts of student lives are readily accessible. Second, there is much effort being put into overhauling the referral system and ensuring a more coherent and consistent staff approach to its implementation. Finally, there is another process underway which is less consciously directed, but which appears to have been stimulated by the process of engaging in this study. This is a process of reflection and communication about some of the issues raised. Staff, it is claimed by members of the core team, are talking with each other about aspects of the school highlighted in the research. This might be taken to signify an increased emphasis on the importance of staff members' personal experience and its significance for the future development of the school.

7   William Shakespeare Upper School

Introduction

William Shakespeare upper school is a mixed comprehensive school, catering for students in the 13–18 years age range.[1] It is located in a busy town in the Greater London area, with a population of approximately 30,000, recorded at the 1991 census. This figure includes approximately 4,500 children and young people of school age. The school was founded in the mid-1950s as a grammar school. In the early 1970s it converted to comprehensive status, and in 1975 became an upper school, as a result of the LEA's move to a three-tier system of first, middle and upper schools.

At the time of the study there were 280 students on the school roll. This represents a considerable reduction compared with the 1975 roll of 758, and the 1988 figure of 388. The head teacher identifies two main reasons for this decline. First, demographic changes have led to a general decrease in the number of school age children in the town. Second, and more significant, is the fact that the school is less popular than its main rival upper school, the roll of which has not been significantly affected by demographic changes. The head does not shy away from the obvious implication that William Shakespeare is the second choice school for most local parents. He openly admits that in 1989, when he took up the headship, the school's examination results were 'mediocre' and staff morale was low. The sense of decline and despondency was worsened by what he describes as 'rumours of imminent closure', which had been fuelled by a combination of the school's decline and the fact that governors and the LEA had not treated the need to appoint a new head as a priority, when the former head teacher retired in 1988, preferring instead to appoint a deputy to an acting headship for two years.

Statistical information provided by the local authority paints an interesting picture of the social and economic characteristics of the area served by the school. It is noted, for example, that the town served by William Shakespeare has an unemployment rate of 10 per cent, while 21 per cent of households with dependent children have no wage earner. It is also shown that 19 per cent of children in the town live in accommodation that is deemed 'unsuitable' for children, such as non-self contained and non-permanent settings. While these figures may not indicate severe deprivation when considered in the national context, they do show that when within-region comparisons are made, this is one of the most deprived areas served by this LEA. Among the 300 wards within the local authority the ward served by William Shakespeare appears in the bottom 7 per cent on each of the measures mentioned earlier and in relation to other factors indicative of deprivation, including numbers of families: living in overcrowded conditions; with no car; without central heating and with a household member suffering from a long term illness.

Why this school joined the project

It was the head teacher of William Shakespeare School who first broached the idea of engaging in the PASE project to his colleagues. A 1996 OFSTED report, while praising the school for the quality of social relationships among pupils and between staff and pupils, had drawn attention to what the inspectors saw as the academic under-performance of some pupils. The head argued that the inspectors had failed to take account of the relatively high level of deprivation in the local area. He acknowledged, however, that OFSTED, even if they were wrong, have the final say in matters of school performance. Involvement in the PASE project, he reasoned, would provide a good opportunity for the school to examine its practices and possibly improve practices where improvement was found to be needed. He also felt that the perspective of outside impartial researchers might lead to the generation of new ideas. Above all, however, the head stressed the desire to 'open up' his school through a process of non-judgmental self exploration.

On the face of it, the head teacher's avowed intentions were completely in accord with those of the project, as the university team construed them. However, we were also alert to the possibility that this desire for self exploration might not be shared by the rest of the staff. As in the other schools, the first stage of our engagement with the school, therefore, was an attempt to gauge how welcome the project was, school-wide, through meeting with a larger group of staff than had been involved in the initial contacts. At this meeting the intentions of the project were presented and explored, and only after this would the final decision be taken as to whether or not the school would take part.

It is always difficult to make generalisations about whole schools. In this case, however, we were reassured from a very early stage that there was a strong interest among a substantial proportion of the staff of William Shakespeare School that being involved in the project was a good idea. This assurance stemmed from the fact that our initial negotiations with the school involved meetings with the school's senior management team (referred to as the 'steering committee' at William Shakespeare), which consisted of seven members of staff, including the head. This represented over one-third of the total William Shakespeare staff complement of eighteen full time teachers. Later we were to find interest and willingness (and in some cases eagerness) to participate in the project widespread among staff and students at the school.

Defining the focus

The business of defining the focus for the research at William Shakespeare took up something like three hours of meeting time, over two sessions, with a break of one month between the first and second meeting. Whether or not one considers this to be a short or long time for such a purpose very much depends on the perspective one is taking. What emerges from an analysis of these meetings, however, is a fairly complex and subtle process of negotiation that, in retrospect, was ultimately essential to the success of this case study. It is this process that forms the substance of this section.

It is important to stress that support for the project among staff was not always wholly unqualified. While there was unanimous support for the aims of the project there was, initially, discernible discomfort among certain staff over the apparent lack of clarity in terms of the precise focus of the research at William Shakespeare. From the researchers' point of view this was an important step in the process of encouraging school staff to take a leading role in the identification of the focus (or foci) for the research, rather than this being determined by the university researchers. The role of the university researchers in facilitating this was to strive for a non-directive, but supportive role in the focus generating process. Thus the researchers presented the steering committee with the following question:

> What measures are taken in this school to prevent children who might otherwise be at risk of exclusion from being excluded?

It would not be an exaggeration to suggest that the initial response to these questions by some members of the steering committee was that of scepticism about the value of the process that we were attempting to initiate. Several steering committee members expressed the view that what the school was doing could be improved, but felt uncertain as to the direction they might take to secure such improvement. The most difficult idea to articulate and gain a shared understanding of, was that knowledge of how to create more positive alternatives to school exclusion in a particular school is likely to be generated from within the existing knowledge and practice of members of the school community. Difficulty with this idea was sometimes articulated in terms of speculation about the need to search for externally validated solutions to perceived problems.

In retrospect a critical moment for the university based researchers came during the course of one of the initial meetings when one of the committee members raised the issue of Attention Deficit/ Hyperactivity Disorder (AD/HD) as a possible contributory factor to difficulties that the school was experiencing with a pupil. The consensus of the seminar was that this should be followed up by one of the steering committee members who would attend a forthcoming professional meeting on the topic. Coincidentally it happened to be the case that one of the university based researchers present at this meeting was at that time engaged in research into AD/HD and had published on the subject, as well as being engaged in the training of teachers on the topic. A decision was made, however, not to disclose this information to the steering committee, since this might cast the university researcher in the role of 'experts' in relation to emotional and behavioural difficulties. This might, in turn, affect the confidence of staff to uncover and explore their own, at this time largely unarticulated (in the context of this study) knowledge and practice in relation to issues of emotional and behavioural problems. The university researchers wished to stress that the expertise they were bringing to this study was in terms of research skills, rather than in the sphere of emotional and behavioural problems in schools.

Progress in finding a focus began once we established the value of identifying positive aspects of existing practice, even if at this initial stage there was uncertainty about its overall quality. The next step was to isolate particular practices. This was not as straightforward as it might first seem. For although the committee could point to formal policies and procedures the consensus was that these did not really reflect what they and their colleagues actually did when addressing the kinds of problems that might lead to exclusion. It was agreed that these practices were less tangible and lacking in formality than one might perhaps expect. A sense emerged that individual cases of students at risk of exclusion tended to be dealt with on their merits according to the particular features of the given case. The starting point for intervention it transpired, was almost always some form of dialogue or discussion between concerned parties.

An example was given of a current problem that involved a Year 10 (15 year old) boy who had arrived at the school one month into the start of Year 9 with a history of disruptive behaviour in his previous schools, and a record of fixed-term exclusions. The concern was that although the boy had gone through Year 9 showing signs of improved progress and behaviour, since being in Year 10 his behaviour was increasingly seen by staff as disruptive and unacceptable in whole class situations. Members of the steering committee were concerned that this problem was escalating to such a degree that staff were beginning to feel that they could no longer cope with the boy in normal classroom situations and that exclusion was beginning to be a realistic, though undesirable, possibility.

Brief discussion of this real situation revealed a number of important issues that began to indicate avenues for further investigation. First, the problems surrounding this boy and the possible threat of exclusion were a serious source of concern to the steering committee staff. They convinced us of their belief that their sense of upset and regret was reflected among the staff group as a whole, who shared the view that exclusion of a pupil represented a failure on the part of the school. Second, something of the upset related to this case was attributable to the fact that this boy had come to them with a history of difficulty, and that measures taken in the school had succeeded in keeping him out of the potential exclusion zone for over a year. Third, it further transpired that this boy was one of fifteen students currently on roll (5 per cent of the total school population) who had been transferred to William Shakespeare as a direct result of displaying and/or experiencing emotional and behavioural difficulties in their former school or schools.

The identification of the importance of staff attitudes, as well as the presence of an identifiable group of students with difficult histories immediately offered opportunities for detailed research, as did the case of the boy in question. It was agreed between the staff and the university researchers to focus initially on the case of the boy. The first step was to arrange for the audio-taping of the forthcoming meeting at which the boy's case was to be discussed. This tape was then transcribed and distributed among those who had attended the case meeting. A further meeting was then called at which the transcript was discussed. The following section describes the nature and outcomes of these meetings.

Emergent themes: 'trying always to be very positive'

The case meeting was attended by the head teacher, the deputy head teacher and the head of pastoral care (all members of the steering committee) and the pupil's form teacher, who was also the boy's head of year. The initial account of the problems surrounding the boy indicated that he had a long history of disruption in school prior to attending William Shakespeare. He was described as experiencing difficult family circumstances in the form of parental divorce and the presence of a father who was believed to be 'very physical' in his methods of disciplining the boy. An effect of this was believed to be that the boy sometimes used the less coercive school setting as a chance to 'ease off', behaviourally. His stepmother had shown enormous concern with the boy's difficulties at school, to the extent that she had telephoned the school on a daily basis since the most recent problems had been drawn to her attention. The boy, however, experienced deep feelings of rejection by his birth mother. The boy himself was described by the head of pastoral care:

> a likeable lad but he just can't cope in situations where there is more than one person. He must have the teacher's attention. He is desperately attention seeking. I believe he was with his mother.

The tone was unanimously one of sympathy for the boy, who was believed to be struggling with highly adverse circumstances in the family situation. There was also a sense that somewhat unsympathetic handling by his previous school had exacerbated his problems. He had been unofficially permanently excluded from his previous school, arriving at William Shakespeare with a history of 'offences' including:

> setting fire extinguishers off, damaging property with other children, being disruptive, not doing his homework.
> (Head of pastoral care)

Tellingly, however, the head of pastoral care notes that in all the documentation that came from the boy's former school there 'is not an overall thought about his behaviour.' In other words, there is little evidence of attempts by staff in his former school to look at what might lie behind the boy's behaviour, while this endeavour was clearly important to the members of this case meeting. This is not to say that William Shakespeare staff were paragons of virtue. It was the consensus of the meeting that the boy was increasingly being experienced as unmanageable in the classroom, and that the patience and tolerance of a highly committed teaching staff was being stretched to the limit. However, there was also a recognition that a staff group which could pride itself in terms of its collective ability to keep sometimes very difficult students positively engaged in schooling could also fall victim to danger of self-fulfilling prophecies. This was illustrated by the head:

> The other thing of course is that he is lumbered. Whenever something happens it's his fault. There is an incident which bears relating, I think, where he was in a situation but so was someone else. Both of them were there when the chair got thrown, pushed, or whatever, and the note said '[the boy in question] threw the chair'. He might have, but he was sorely provoked. It was two fellows just mucking about. And I think that is the other thing. There are two standards sometimes for some children and not for others. I think we work hard not to make it so, but inevitably I think it is the perception that it is him [who is usually the culprit].

It was interesting to observe the ways in which the staff in this meeting seemed to be constantly searching for understanding of the situation. There was a tacit refusal to accept that either the boy or his behaviour were irredeemable, and that to accept circumstances at face value is usually a mistake. Several times in the course of the meeting different staff showed how their understanding of the boy and his behaviour were reshaped, usually for the better, as a result of actively seeking the boy's perspective:

> Just to come back to the [the idea] that he can actually control what he is doing. You know when I said about the incident with the chair. My initial reaction was, 'Oh, all right let's let him go home for the day.'. And then I thought, 'Oh, no, that is not the answer to send him home!'. And he [the boy] said, 'Look, this happened, and this happened, and this happened. And if you listen carefully you will see it as not my fault. And I promise I'll be good.'. And he was good! I checked up on him. So he can [be good]
> (Head)

I think he actually understands to a certain extent why he behaves the way he does. We talked to him at the [behavioural] support centre. We actually said, 'Why do you do the things you do? Why do you think you do what you do in class to constantly distract?' And he said that he thought it went back to the time when he was very small, and there were lots of children. And his mother on her own, trying to cope. 'And I wanted to be noticed. So I talked and talked, and I was funny!' And I think it is absolutely true.

(Deputy head)

We removed him from an English class, because he was being completely disruptive in an English class. And I removed him, and had him sitting there with me. And I was thinking what he could do to make him feel valued. And I said, 'Do you like writing poetry?'. And he said, 'Yes.'. I said to write me a poem about school. It was funny. It rhymed, and it was very funny. We published it [in the school newspaper] and we gave him a prize for it.

(Form teacher/ head of year)

The question posed by the form teacher about what could be done 'to make him feel valued', seemed to encapsulate much of what was being said at this meeting. The deputy head stressed this, when she mentioned to the fact that the boy has recently been referred to a behaviour support centre for one day per week:

I think we're trying always to be very positive with him. Certainly the whole accent on sending him to the [behavioural support centre] was that we didn't want to lose him. Between us we should come to some sort of way of helping his problems. This was another chance to help sort it out. It's always positive for him at school, and I think he is aware that people [here] are very supportive.

The main source of anxiety expressed by staff at this meeting was the fact that the boy's allotted six weeks at the support centre was drawing to an imminent close. The loss of the respite and reflection time that his attendance at the centre provided (to both the boy and the staff) was seen to be threatening, in the light of the fact that the boy's behaviour in school had not shown significant improvement over the time of his attendance at the centre. In many respects it was unlikely that this attendance would have produced much change, given the perception shared by staff in this group, and, according to them, by the boy himself, that the boy's behavioural problems were often an expression of feelings largely rooted in his domestic circumstances. He felt unwanted by his step-mother, while at the same time, emotionally drawn to his birth mother, but confused by her contradictory responses to him. In addition he was subject to the oppressive disciplinary regime imposed by his father, against which he reacted by acting out in settings where external controls were less threatening (that is with his stepmother and at school).

The prognosis was not felt to be good for this student. Efforts would continue to be made to support his positive engagement in school, but there was a sense that existing strategies had not, ultimately, succeeded for this student. From the viewpoint of the research project (and, more importantly, the school and the student), this was a disappointing outcome:

Researcher: So how inevitable do you see it that he will have to be excluded?

Deputy head: I think it will happen, unless we can find a solution to the problem.

This equating of exclusion with the school's failure to 'find a solution' suggests that there was an aspiration to create positive alternatives to exclusion from school, though it was not, as we noted earlier, easy to articulate the precise procedures involved in promoting such positive alternatives. Towards the end of this meeting, however, the deputy head came closer to such an account than had been possible in earlier discussions:

You know it is not so rigid that there is no second chance [for pupils with difficulties at this school]. That's just the regime we have because of the personalities within the staff and because of how it has developed. And I think the other thing is that actually it has proved to be very successful. We don't have outrageous behaviour. . . but if we do [have very difficult behaviour] it's contained and it is dealt with very quickly. Children feel you are fair about it – you know . . . 'Alright, I've done it, I'll take the consequences.' And the others see that it is that way. It's not punitive in a nasty way. It's supportive, that we're all working together. We're a community that works together. We're all aiming that they have a good education and a good chance in life. We do hope that you [the student] will get something worthwhile out of it – and that's quite strong for the school; that is what it is all about. They [students] don't feel rules are silly or unnecessary. They don't really argue about that at all.

This belief that the students trust staff and the fairness of their approach to management is, according to the deputy head again, reflected in the respect and trust that the staff feel for the steering committee. She referred to the way in which sensitive information about the private lives of students is sometimes withheld from the main body of staff, to protect students' rights to privacy:

> The promise we had in years gone by [under a former head] was perhaps that when senior staff knew something confidential they did not even give the rest of the staff a hint that there were major problems. We haven't really developed a strategy. We just say, 'trust us, [a student] has got problems at home, and we genuinely mean that'. Actually we don't get any criticism from the staff because I think they have learnt to respect what we are saying to them, without going into details. We just say, 'look, there are real problems there, back off a little; give him a little bit of space; try and be as supportive as you can'.

The possibility that the boy who was the subject of this meeting might eventually be excluded by the school was a source of great regret to these staff. It is interesting, however, that this regret was rooted, in part, in a shared sense of pride that William Shakespeare school has in the past been successful in enabling students with histories of difficulty to become appropriately engaged in schooling. It was agreed, however, between the steering committee and the university researchers that the validity of the claims about the school's success in these respects would depend on more than the beliefs and observations of the steering committee. In fact, while there was unanimity among this group about the success of the school in this respect, there remained some uncertainty about the nature of student views on the topic. Further, there was significant vagueness about the precise mechanisms by which the perceived success was achieved. The consensus of the steering committee was that it would indeed be a very useful exercise to test their assumptions and explore the existing mechanisms for encouraging student engagement. This, it was felt, would form a good basis on which to plan future developments, and thus, possibly, improve their collective ability to meet the needs of vulnerable and at risk students. It was decided, therefore, that the next step of the study should involve an exploration of two key questions:

- To what extent did the wider school population of staff, students and their parents, share the views uncovered in this first stage of the study?

- If there was agreement that the school was effective in providing positive alternatives to exclusion, to what factors was this success attributable?

In order to address these questions the following data collection strategies were agreed:

- interviews with staff and students
- lesson observation
- ethnographic participant observation
- parent questionnaire.

Students' perceptions

An important source of data here is the testimony of the students (making up 5 per cent of this school's student population) who had been excluded from previous schools. An important aspect of these students' accounts proved to be the way in which they compared William Shakespeare School with other schools they had attended. It was decided that pupils would be more confident of anonymity if the university researchers conducted the interviews rather than members of the school's staff.

These interviews revealed a strong sense of satisfaction with the quality of relationships the students shared with staff. In particular the commonly expressed view was that the willingness of students to conform and co-operate with school staff was rooted in what they saw as their personal commitment to staff as individual persons rather than to the bureaucratic arrangements made by the school. This point was stressed repeatedly by different students in separate interviews, and was sometimes made on the basis of a comparison between William Shakespeare and former schools. Students who had been excluded from the rival upper school in the town often compared the mechanistic, bureaucratic and punitive discipline system at that school with the far more personal and humane regime at William Shakespeare.

The common complaint was that the discipline system at the former school was based on a tariff of escalating sanctions which were intended to reflect the quantity rather than the quality of rule breaking behaviour.[2] One pupil described the system in the following, highly detailed, terms:

> C1 is getting your name written on the board, and C2s are five minute detentions after the lesson, at break time or after school. C3

is ten minutes and C4 is written in homework diaries, so your parents see it, and sent to the head of year. And after that it goes to C5, where they write in your homework diary again, so that parents see it, and you are sent to the headmaster. And he gives you punishment which he thinks is right.

The same student went on to reflect the complaints of all the other students who referred to this system:

I don't think that is right, because there is different degrees of offences. From a C1 to a C2, what is the difference? Say like you turned around, and they didn't want you they would say, 'C1!' And then if you did the same again, it would be C2. There isn't any difference between them!

For instance, if someone was talking they got C5 and sent to the headmaster. There is a difference between someone fighting and they get sent to the headmaster!

This mechanistic indifference inherent in the system to the nature of the disciplinary offence committed, not only offended students' sense of justice, in some cases it contributed to the escalation of discipline problems and, therefore, punishment:

Well, at the beginning of the year it was all right. But then it would be getting silly when I would be getting C3s, and I would be complaining. But then they would give me a C4 for speaking back at them!

Eventually:

I was getting fed up of being told silly things like that, and, in the end, I was getting quite high levels of discipline. I would be sent to the headmaster because I was getting annoyed with why I should have to put up with [it] like if I am asking a simple question, why, I should get punishment!

This black comedy of errors was repeated in five interviews with pupils from this school. Each story ended in exclusion, sometimes formal, but usually informal, with parents/carers being invited to find an alternative school for their child. What makes this a comedy, rather than a tragedy, however, is the fact that exclusion was experienced, ultimately, as a positive experience. This is illustrated by the same student, who accounts for his improved disciplinary record at William Shakespeare in the following terms:

> No [I didn't have discipline problems when I came here], not really, because the way they do it [here] is they all speak to you about it. They don't go straight in with punishment. They will say, 'Look, stop, or I am going to have to do something.' The thing is, is that you can talk to these teachers. The teachers here are a lot more friendly, and are easier to learn off, because they are like your mates as well. As well as being like a teacher. So it really does help.

The unprompted reference to learning here, is particularly interesting. Again, it reflects accounts given by other students of the way in which the quality of staff interest in and concern about students as people engenders student commitment and engagement:

> I think it is important to have your own opinion, because if they are not going to listen to you, you are just going to rebel. And you would think, 'What the heck! They don't care!' I think these teachers [at William Shakespeare] care a lot about – not only in school but out of school – what we do. Because they take a lot of interest in what we do out of school. They would say, 'What did you do at the weekend?' or something like that. They will talk about it. Some of the teachers who talk to you about what sort of music you like – they talk about it, and football. Like outside activities. I play hockey. I can talk to my PE teacher about what I do; my achievements, and what I have done and stuff like that. And he will listen and say: 'Good!' at what I have done and carry on, sort of thing. And that really does help. You feel a lot easier, when it comes to lessons.

Other students provide examples of how the quality of teacher interest in them as persons encourages them to complete homework assignments, whereas in previous schools they had refused to do homework as a protest against individual teachers. Further to this, the quality of teacher relationships was seen to have, what might be termed, a therapeutic effect at times:

> I seemed to get on with teachers a lot quicker when I was here. I don't know why, but teachers would help you along. They would make sure, if you were upset – they will make a note of having to

see you. They won't like say, 'We will do it another time; we will leave it and see what happens.' They make sure that they start at the beginning. They will come and see you if you are distressed or upset.

This student also provided some corroboration to the deputy head's claim about the way in which confidences are maintained, and as a result, trust is engendered between students and staff:

> I like the way they keep confidence in the school. They say to you, 'I am not going to tell the other teachers. We will keep it between you and me.' I like the way they do it.

The evident trust in staff that many pupils expressed contributes to a sense of being cared for and, thus, a sense of security among many pupils:

> here the teachers: they care about you more here [than at previous school], and you can talk to them and they give you advice. Whereas at [previous school] they wouldn't give you advice. If you ask for advice they tell you, but you just don't want to ask at [previous school] . . . It's just different – they care about you more.

This student valued in particular the 'advice' she has received on a range of highly important issues:

> about drugs and stuff like that. Don't get pregnant too young, and things like that.

Like many students, she described the staff at William Shakespeare as caring, in general, but singled out a particular member of staff as especially supportive:

> I get on with my RE teacher really well.

> Here [at William Shakespeare] there's people; they've all got their own character and stuff. But at [former school] it's more like they are all robots.'

> It's like they teach and then that's it. Whereas, I dunno, teachers at William Shakespeare give you that little extra.

The dramatic effect of 'that little extra' is presented in terms of the difference between rejection of and resistance to teachers and schooling, and a commitment to and willing engagement in schooling:

> Whereas at [former school] you get more annoyed with the teachers. Whereas when you like a teacher here – and when you get close to them, you don't want to be horrible anyway. You don't want to be naughty and stuff.

It is important to stress that, on the evidence of both teachers and students, the caring regime at William Shakespeare does not mean that staff–student conflict is eradicated. The school operates a fairly conventional system of sanctions in the form of a detention system. Students often referred to this in passing, giving the impression that they, by and large, grudgingly accepted the system, and believed that it was generally applied fairly. When discussing the way in which misbehaviour was handled, however, the students, again, referred to ways in which relationships between staff and students served a regulatory function. For example:

> I won't bow down to anyone. Same as my dad. We're the same. I would just say, 'No, I'm not doing it. And once I say, No, I mean No!'. But now they [the William Shakespeare staff] don't put me in that position for me to get my back up, because they know me more. Instead of telling me to do something, like: 'Move over there!' (That's what they used to say.) – but now they say, 'Can you please move over there?' They ask me. And they show us they have got more respect. They ask instead of tell.

For this student, being known and respected as an individual, with her own feelings, values and standards of behaviour are fundamental requirements for cooperative relationships with their teachers:

> I feel that if someone cannot speak to you with respect, then why should you do what they say? If they can be polite and ask you, you in turn should be polite . . . I have always said, 'You cannot have respect [automatically], you have to earn it.' . . . And if you have a relationship with a teacher where you both respect each other, then you do work.

The example that this student went on to provide of these principles in practice gives great insight into her feelings and thought processes, and how these were influenced by the manner and approach of her teachers. Her example also involves a comparison between two teachers at William Shakespeare, indicating that, in her view, not all teachers at the school maintain the desired standard of behaviour at all times:

> I mean, my English now, with my Form Tutor. We respect each other and we work a lot better. And if I am out of line then he says so, and I stop it.
>
> Because he speaks to me as an equal. Not as a child. Some teachers, they speak to you as a child, like, 'Why haven't you done your work?' And if I say, 'I don't understand it,' she goes, 'Oh! You should ask me questions then, shouldn't you?' And my English teacher Mr [name], he'll say, 'Have you done the homework?' And I'll say, 'No, I'm sorry, I haven't. I didn't understand it. I was going to come to you but I didn't have time.' And he'll say, 'Alright then. I'd rather you stayed behind, if you can, and we'll discuss it then.' So then the vibes that he gives me is that he is understanding my situation, and he is willing to help. Whereas she gives out the vibes that I am being bad, and, the way she talks to me makes me feel like I'm so young, and that I am in the wrong. And I don't like that. And I just end up walking away.

Time and again, students reflected the view that teachers were most successful in influencing their behaviour in positive ways and encouraging engagement in learning, and other school based activities, when they related to the students as persons. This involved taking account of students' individual circumstances and feelings, showing sympathy and empathy, and being respectful of their individuality and rights as persons.

Peer interviews

In order to test the validity and generalisability of these student findings it was decided to develop a strategy for interviewing a broader range of students which would maximise the anonymity of respondents, while giving them the fullest opportunity for expressing their views about the experience of being students at William Shakespeare school. In order to achieve this a group of students were recruited and trained as peer interviewers.

The outcomes of these interviews tended to offer full support for the views expressed by the researcher-interviewed group, with a strong emphasis on the positive nature of staff–student relationships at the school. The key distinguishing feature of the peer interviews, however, was a greater tendency for students to complain about issues that included: the negative behaviour of some staff, the tendency of some lessons to be 'boring' or 'too long', and a distaste for the detention system. As one student put it:

> most people don't want to go to school, do they? I don't mind going to school. It isn't – I don't get up in the morning and think, 'Oh, I hate school!' and that. It's all right once you get there, and it doesn't – I don't hate it here. I just don't like having to get up and come here really. Once I get here it's OK.

There is a transparent candour in this account which could be taken to indicate the mild disaffection that is common among secondary school students (Keys and Fernandes, 1993; Schostak, 1983). What follows, however, shows that such a view is not incompatible with a belief in the benign quality of the school and its staff:

> Well at the moment, because I'm not very good in some subjects and . . . because I was ill before Christmas, I haven't got most of my project work. They [teachers at William Shakespeare] do help you to pass the exams that you have to do. . . So the teachers, instead of saying, 'no, you still have to do this or you will muck up all your other exams,' they help you and they say, 'Well, you can do this in that lesson then, so you can get a better mark,' instead of just making you do it.

> They treat you with respect, some teachers. You have your moments with teachers though. . . Some of the teachers can be a bit nasty and that, but most are just all right really. I get on with most of the teachers. You have your ups and downs . . .

Once again this account illustrates the way in which situations which might develop into serious conflict between students and staff tend to be handled with care, humanity and a respect for persons which in turn engenders student engagement, not only in the form of prosocial behaviour, but also in relation to the academic curriculum.

Staff perceptions and the role of pedagogy: the lesson as a 'human situation'

Fourteen staff were also interviewed. These interviews were carried out following lessons that had been observed by the interviewer, so as to create a shared source of reference between interviewer and interviewee, and thus provide a factual grounding for the interview (Cooper and McIntyre, 1996).

Findings from these interviews drew attention to the way in which teachers prevented and controlled undesirable behaviour during lessons through pedagogical rather than disciplinary means. That is, they described their thinking during and about the lessons observed very much in pedagogical terms, nearly always emphasising the efforts they made to make the content of the lesson accessible and engaging to students. Key means of achieving this often involved teachers fostering and drawing on good quality interpersonal and social relationships in the classroom, characterised by teacher flexibility:

> I like the children to be able to communicate with me; to feel free to communicate with me and ask questions. And I like for them to be able to communicate with each other, and ask questions. Obviously, a by product of this is if they are allowed to talk then some of it is going to get a bit off the straight and narrow track. And I think you've got to allow for that in any human situation.

A prime example of the way in which a lesson, with an ostensibly highly abstract content, was developed into a 'human situation' was provided by a maths lesson on probability. From the outset and throughout the lesson the teacher repeatedly employed examples which related to the class as a population. He made a series of predictions based on knowledge of the different characteristics represented in the class and invited students to generate their own examples. In this way the teacher made a distinct effort to engage the students on an affective/interpersonal level as well as on a cognitive level. His means of doing this was to allow the abstract content of the lesson to be discovered through an exploration of students' personal experience. This ensured that the new cognitive information was presented to students in a way which enabled them to relate it to the personal and affective dimensions of their existing knowledge (Bruner and Haste, 1987).

The centrality of respect and empathy to the quality of teaching at the school is exemplified in the following statement by another teacher:

> Gradually I started to recognise – You look at the way you teach; you look at the results – the more you look at the social graces; the niceties; the politeness; the manners; the friendship; the empathy with the kid who can't do it; it comes out more. And I think that

just has developed as I matured; as I have gone from being a young pup of a [subject] teacher.

Another teacher commented on the need to move beyond the concepts of discipline and control and to recognise that student compliance often follows from 'making them feel positive about what they are doing'. This concern for the individual student as a person with feelings also extends into the area of responding to student difficulties. Several teachers described the way in which punishments and sanctions were applied selectively, according to perceived appropriateness. Sometimes apparent misbehaviour was interpreted as an expression of more deep-seated problems:

> I treat different kids in different ways. I don't think that's treating them unequally, 'cos you are bearing in mind their circumstances. Some kids that I know are having a really hard time, and they are disrupting the class. I quite often let them go next door and sit there with the other teacher. [This way] I can get rid of the problem and sort it out later.

Conclusion

A number of interesting issues emerge from this case study that illuminates our understanding of positive alternatives to school exclusion.

The relationship between values, attitudes and procedures

Initial difficulties in getting this case study off the ground were related, in part at least, to a desire to find answers to the research question in formal systems, strategies and procedures. What this study indicates is that while there is clearly a place for such formal structures, the crucial factors in the positive engagement of at risk students were to be found in the informal and personal. The former experience of certain students illustrated the failure of systems of response which depend too heavily on what might be termed bureaucratic approaches to dealing with problem behaviour. The central quality that staff and students found successful in promoting positive engagement was the personal; the need to engage with individuals in terms of their own needs, circumstances and identities. The impersonal (which is the defining quality of bureaucratic approaches) was equated with indifference and disrespect, while the personal was equated with care and respect. These qualities in staff ways of relating to students were not engendered through edict, but rather, it is suggested, through enactment: the open, consultative style of management among the staff seemed to be echoed in the ways in which staff related to students.

While consistency remains a key concern of students and teachers, the most important locus of consistency is principles and values, rather than in formal rules, structure and procedures. In fact what consistently emerges from this case study is the demand for consistency in the exercise of flexibility in the application of rules and procedures. This applies not only to rules and procedures governing student behaviour, it also applies to the formal status hierarchy among teachers and patterns of communication and authority. Authority and power, it is suggested, are exercised most effectively when applied in accordance with a clear and well defined ethos.

These observations are in accordance with the observations of Fullan (1992) regarding the importance of school culture in school improvement. William Shakespeare School seems to reflect the atmosphere of collegiality among staff which has been associated by researchers such as Fullan, with effective school development.

A dialogic approach to conflict and difficulties

Obstacles to creating positive alternatives to school exclusion are often found in the form of difficulties that staff experience in attempting to balance apparently competing demands. Thus (for example) the imperative to meet individual needs is sometimes contrasted with the need to be fair and equitable in dealing with all children. Where such difficulties were perceived in this school they were approached through dialogue, with a view to seeking solutions that were agreeable to all parties. Of central concern here is the need for clear and transparent lines of communication, with opportunities for all concerned to have their views and concerns heard and respected. This applies to students as well as teachers.

This emphasis on dialogue and the importance of the quality of interpersonal relationships between teachers and students reflect themes that are well established in the research literature on student disaffection. This research suggests that student disaffection and prosocial behaviour are often functions of the quality, as perceived by students, of teacher attention to and interaction with students as persons (Cooper, 1993a; Cronk, 1987; Tattum, 1982; Rosser and Harré, 1976).

Adoption of a solution as opposed to problem focus when addressing difficulties

A striking feature of the approach taken to difficulties in this school was the common search for positive outcomes for all the students. This usually took the form of searching for ways in which teacher behaviour, school and classroom routines or other factors could be changed to better accommodate the individual circumstances of students in difficulty. This is very reminiscent of what is sometimes referred to by clinicians as a 'solution focus' to social and emotional problems (for example De Shazer, 1985).

Effective classroom management is most usefully seen as a by product of appropriate pedagogy

The conceptual separation of 'classroom management' and 'teaching' was resisted by teachers in this school. Where teachers focused on pedagogy in their approach to classroom teaching there was a tendency for staff and students to express satisfaction with both teaching/learning and management issues. In this case, however, pedagogy was seen to have at its centre a recognition of the need to involve students as persons. Students repeatedly remarked on how their engagement in lessons was motivated by their feelings of being valued and cared for by staff, not only in terms of their emotional and social well-being, but also in terms of their need for academic support.

This tendency to see teaching and learning as a complex of affective, social and cognitive processes is consistent with contemporary theories of learning as reflected in the socio-cultural theories of learning espoused by Vygotsky (1987) and Bruner (Bruner and Haste, 1987). The application of this approach to understanding the nature of learning in classrooms draws particular attention to the importance of interpersonal relationships between teacher and learner in the promotion of cognitive development. The emphasis here is on the need for relationships which foster students' sense of emotional security and self worth (Tappan, 1998; Cooper and McIntyre, 1996; Wood, 1988).

The importance of history and context

Finally, a significant aspect of this case study is the sense which emerges of a school which has created a positive and successful community in very difficult circumstances, largely out of its own, mainly human, resources. As we have already noted, this development is rooted in a set of firmly held, largely humanistic values. It is also, however, influenced by pragmatism. The development and deployment of these resources has always been made with careful reference to the real circumstances, both current and historical, in which the school, the staff and the students operate.

This is illustrated, in an unfortunate sense, by the case of the Year 10 boy with which this case study began. The boy was eventually excluded, and began attendance at a Pupil Referral Unit. The decision was made because it was felt that the boy required the small group setting which was now only available through the exclusion option, since attempts to keep the boy positively engaged at William Shakespeare were felt to be failing to the detriment of the boy's personal and educational development. In the head's account, this decision was taken with a heavy heart, though it was taken with a strong emphasis on what were perceived to be the boy's individual needs and best interests, as well as consideration for the other pupils and the already stretched resources of the staff.

The report of the 1998 OFSTED inspection indicates that William Shakespeare is an improving school, with high quality staff–student relationships and a good academic profile. The school continues to develop through the processes of self reflection and dialogue that are illustrated in this chapter.

8 Rudyard Kipling Further Education College

Building bridges: students under sixteen in further education

Further Education and students under sixteen

There was, from the start, an awareness that this element of the research was different in that it focused on provision for students who were either failing to attend school, or were at risk of exclusion, or had already been excluded from school. However, the principle of focusing on exclusion from education rather than on exclusion from school was important to the research team. For some years further education colleges have been involved in reaching out to 'young people who are poorly motivated and not engaged in formal education or training.' (Reisenberger and Crowther, 1997) – a group of students referred to by the FEDA Report as the 'disengaged' (ibid.). We were particularly interested in the school-age students rather than the whole spectrum of young people in further education colleges.

Over the last two decades there has been much work in further education with students who are outside the traditional school structures as well as with those who are technically still at school or of school age. Lovey, Docking and Evans (1993) identified the co-operation of schools and units with local colleges of education to be one of the most important strategies for keeping pupils excluded from mainstream schools within the educational system. In addition, Further Education colleges offer an alternative pathway through award bearing courses that span the 14–19 year old stage and are recognised as being a 'different environment' which can motivate students. The Dearing review of 14–19 education (1996) recognised that:

> For some students, links with the more 'adult' environment of a local further education college may also be motivating. For a school

with limited resources, this may be a practical way of opening up new learning opportunities. But such links need to be carefully structured and planned by each individual school.

(Dearing, 1996: 12.38)

Dearing felt that Further Education colleges had an important part to play in the development of a national strategy to tackle under achievement and the problems of the disengaged. He felt that this involvement should be cross-phase and that staff in FE colleges had developed considerable expertise in working with students who were demotivated. There is now considerable interest in the notion of a variety settings for the education of fourteen year olds rather than the mainstream school for all; the FEDA study is based on the idea that colleges should be encouraged to work with disengaged young people under sixteen (Reisenberger and Crowther, 1997, p. 5).

It was felt that by studying this alternative context we might learn about important factors in the school learning environment as well as understand the elements of the Further Education college setting which help to motivate students.

The College

Rudyard Kipling College is situated on two sites, one older building in the centre of town and another purpose built campus on the edge of town, making it one of the best accommodated and equipped Further Education colleges in the country. A wide range of programmes is offered, from supported learning through to Higher National Diplomas and the first years of degrees. Students can study for A levels, GCSEs and a comprehensive range of vocational qualifications. Many students are local young people aged between sixteen and twenty, but there are also large numbers of older students on both full and part time courses, following courses on campus and at a distance.

The college provides support services for students with a variety of needs. Specialist staff are available to support students who are aurally impaired, visually impaired, physically disabled or dyslexic. The college has developed its pre-sixteen link provision over the last three years to cover twelve curriculum areas for special and mainstream schools, and to meet a range of accreditation needs in consultation with feeder schools. In addition, the college acts as sole learning provider for an increasing number of under-sixteen year olds and the staff are committed to refining both support systems and curriculum areas in response to research findings.

A particular partnership: the focus of the study

This case study describes a particular partnership between Rudyard Kipling Further Education College and its local LEA Student Support Service in developing a pilot project for a small group of Year 11 students. There had been a close partnership between the Student Support Centre and the college through Link courses, Bridge courses and access to other provision for students on a part time basis. There was evidence of an increased demand for this last form of provision. There had also been a parallel identification of the need for more full-time opportunities for Year 11 students who were being provided for by the Support Service. Prior to the start of the pilot development for full time provision there was

- Agreement between the college and the support service about access arrangements through the support centre.
- A recognition that changes were needed to existing levels of support for school age students attending the FE college.
- Agreement about roles, responsibilities, referral process and costs; and funding was assured through the Student Support Service, not individual schools.
- It was also agreed that the pilot project needed to be monitored and evaluated in order to inform future development.

This was both a new initiative and a development of the role that the college had played. A selected group of students in Year 11, who were under sixteen, attended the college full time (eighteen hours a week) as part of a group retaking GCSEs. The pilot group of students were the legal and professional responsibility of the LEA Student Support Service but the Service contracted to the Further Education College to provide education for this small group of students. The Support Service identified the students after an assessment of who would be likely to benefit and be able to undertake the GCSE courses. Other factors taken into account were the ability to cope with the pressures and responsibilities of a college environment and a desire and ability to make relationships with peers and others. The college environment was seen as challenging in different ways to the school environment and students needed, with support, to be able to meet this new set of demands.

Another innovation was the creation of the role of Home Tutor, who was based at the college, was employed by the Student Support service for fifteen hours a week and was responsible for overseeing this group of students. She acted as a bridge between the students, the support service, the college and the parents. Her role was to provide extra pastoral support as well as in-class support during classes in college. She was to monitor the students and deal with any issues that emerged. As will be seen, her role was perceived by all parties as crucial to the success of the venture. In addition there was a pre-sixteen co-ordinator in the college who was also involved in overseeing this provision and working with the Home Tutor to support both students and staff. The Educational Liaison Manager oversaw the whole pilot in the college.

Each student was treated as a regular member of the college and allocated a personal tutor from among the staff teaching GCSE classes. If a subject or personal tutor was concerned about a student the issue would be referred to the pre-sixteen co-ordinator who would liaise with the Home Tutor to agree a course of action or support.

The students

Eleven students took part in this pilot scheme, although twelve were originally selected. Several of them had been persistent non attenders or 'school refusers'; one had been withdrawn from school by his parents; some had been at risk of exclusion due to behaviour that the school found unacceptable; and some had been through the formal exclusion process. All had been referred to the Student Support Service and had been offered college-based provision among other options. The students were placed on a GCSE retake course of one year. Of the eleven that set out on the course, six took their examinations and passed; two did not take the examinations but reapplied to college; one dropped out because of family illness; one completed a different course and two failed to attend and complete any course at the college. Students who did not attend or 'dropped out' of the college were then offered home tuition by the Home Tutor. In the last two cohorts approximately 75 per cent of the students have taken their GCSEs at the end of the course.

The research

We aimed to collect data that would reflect the many viewpoints of those engaged in this pilot: the students, the college lecturers, the teachers from the schools the students had attended and the key personnel in the project. The data reported here are drawn from a variety of sources, including:

- Interviews with eight students who were in the pilot scheme (six males and two females. This gender imbalance reflects the gender balance of those referred to the Student Support Service.) These interviews were undertaken by the Educational Liaison Manager at the college or the Head of the Student Support Service.

- Interviews with key personnel involved in the college provision for the pilot group. These were the Home Tutor, the co-ordinator for Under-sixteen Provision and the Educational Liaison Manager.
- Case studies of two students involved in the provision. Interviews were carried out with the students, their parents, and personnel from the schools they had previously attended.
- Questionnaires given to eleven staff at the college who taught many of the students in the pilot scheme, and follow-up interviews with three of these lecturers.

In this process the areas identified for investigation were: the factors that enabled the students to gain access to education through a Further Education college context; how the provision was perceived by staff and students; and what supported or hindered the inclusion of pre-sixteen-students.

Support and preparation

Students commented upon the importance of choosing this option from among the many that the Support Service offered. In the words of one student, 'Having options about coming was essential to me.'

Students valued being given information about their choices at the outset. For example, they mentioned discussion about where they would be based and what courses were available. With one exception, the students described the vital role of a college tutor or in-school support teacher in 'allowing them to reach a decision' and subsequently preparing them for the referral and interview process. Support and preparation at all stages of the process emerged as important, not just at the outset.

Staff, on the other hand, had mixed feelings about what informa-tion they wanted about the students. They recognised the impor-tance of allowing students to make a fresh start but did want to know about particular behavioural difficulties and students' academic achievements. It was acknowledged that there were some initial anxieties among the lecturers at the college about the nature of the student difficulties. After the lecturers had embarked on the teaching of the students in the pilot, these anxieties were allayed and students and staff did not experience the anticipated behavioural difficulties.

Being treated like an adult: a bridge to the adult world

Staff and students alike felt that the more adult environment referred to by Dearing was a motivating factor for the students. Staff commented on the ethos of the college and the expectations they had of students. Differences between the college environment and that of the school were drawn out. Examples given were that students could call staff by their first name, were free of restrictions such as being in school all day and were allowed to smoke.

Without exception students interviewed noted these increased freedoms and the 'adult' environment as the biggest asset to them and the biggest difference between college and school. One student commented, 'you have more freedom to do what you like.' Students felt that they were being treated differently as people.

> I don't feel like I'm a piece of shit when I am here.

One student noted that one lecturer 'borders on secondary school teachers, if you ask him for help, he makes you feel ignorant'. These comments contained allusions to a sense of failure as persons in their previous experience, as well as an accompanying sense of failure as learners.

However some staff also noted that some students found it difficult to cope with fewer boundaries. The freedoms of the new environment were motivating but were also demanding in a new way and had to be managed. The Home Tutor talked of the transition from school to college, from child to adult, and the need to give students freedom but also support them in managing this transition.

> They are not necessarily adults but they like to be treated in a more mature way. Teachers very often treat them as children. I think in that way it is a fresh start.

Not only was there a view that college was more adult, there was also a perception of the experience as a bridge to the adult world. Staff felt that developing the social skills of students was important and that the extra freedom they were offered was not always easy for them; so support through this transition was important. The capacity to cope with the new conditions of relative freedom was also an important consideration in the selection by the Student Support Service. Students were chosen on the basis of their readiness to deal with the social demands of college as well as the academic. The ability to keep up regular attendance in a non-compulsory setting was seen as an important factor to assess in the selection process. Not all students who wanted to attend college were assessed as ready to meet these new demands.

> Some students who have not been in school could not cope because they haven't had the socialisation process.
>
> (Home Tutor)

Others have noted the connections between attendance and issues of exclusion and inclusion (for example Blyth and Milner, 1999).

A fresh start

This more adult environment was also described as a 'fresh start' by parents, staff and students. For both the interviewed parents and the two case study students, it was important that the students could start somewhere afresh and that this new environment was not the same as that of the school. In both cases the parents viewed the need to start afresh as vital: one because the parent felt the student had been bullied and was always seen as different at school: in the other because relationships had broken down between the school staff, the student and the parents.

Academic support

The students in the pilot scheme were part of an older group retaking their GCSEs and so there was some assumption of prior knowledge on the part of the lecturers. Three students said that they felt that teaching was pitched at people who had done the work before:

> It's like you're going over stuff you've already done, you know, revising . . . and I'm lost.

> Lecturers need to remember that we haven't done this stuff before . . . I need that recognition.

For the remainder of the group this was not a problem.

However, the Home Tutor was aware of this as an issue that needed addressing. She was engaged in a good deal of liaison with all those involved with the academic and pastoral needs of the group. She met fortnightly with the GCSE co-ordinator and she also offered additional academic support to the students. She did this by getting course programmes from lecturers in advance and offering home tuition to support homework. She saw this as very important since homework was a problem area, and said 'They find it difficult and that is where I come in quite often.' She felt that this was a key element in making this initiative work.

The college offered in-class support systems to students and two students said that they had ticked boxes for extra help in Maths and English and not received it. One noted that she would have liked access to one-to-one support during lectures, particularly in Maths. Two other students did receive additional support for English and Maths. In general the students saw the lecturers as helpful. Two commented that the 'interpersonal skills' of the lecturers were different from those of teachers in school.

One student did not see the experience of college as positively as the others. She had been excluded from her school in Year 9 and yearned to be back with her peer group. She did not see the support she was offered as positive and her experience was unsatisfactory for her in a number of ways:

> They weren't organised, no-one knew what group I should be in.

> My English set was changed . . . nobody asked me . . . I was upset.

> The environment is depressing . . . in sociology you can't even see through the windows, they are so dirty.

> They don't push you enough.

> We need more field trips – I learn when it comes alive – I want to go to the theatre.

She seems to long for the structure that she left in the school, since many of her comments are related to being told or pushed. She also found the experience more impersonal.

Curriculum

All students saw the gaining of academic qualifications and the planning of appropriate 'next steps' as important to them. Of the eleven students studied, six did pass their GCSEs. This was seen as a measure of success by both staff in the college and in the Support Service, although it was not seen as the only measure of the success of the programme. Some staff did query the relevance of GCSEs to some students. They felt that in spite of the low status accorded to GNVQs by some parents and students this would be a more appropriate route for some students; indeed, this is one of the changes that have been made to the programme since the pilot project.

Teaching strategies

Although most of the staff (seven out of the eleven who taught this group) said that they had had to adopt different approaches in their teaching, eight reported difficulties in working with them and said that the students had particular needs. However, the same staff also said that they did not have staff development needs in this area.

They identified particular teaching strategies as helpful. These included; establishing clear boundaries; providing a clear structure; setting ground rules; having breaks during long stretches of time (lessons at the college were two hours long); varying activities; giving rewards; getting to know and build on students' strengths and needs; and allowing students to get to know the lecturer as a person not only as a teacher.

Pastoral support

The role of the Home Tutor

As already shown, the Home Tutor had a central support role. She was engaged in individual assessment and in monitoring the academic progress of the students through regular meetings with the college's GCSE and Pre-sixteen Provision Co-ordinators. In addition she met tutors, parents and monitored attendance. All students stressed how positive and supportive they found the support from the Home Tutor both in and out of college. For example one student said, 'She does a lot of the finding out for me.'. Another student emphasised how supportive the additional help provided in Maths had been, 'although there are days when I'm not with it!'.

There was more ambivalence about the monitoring of attendance and the home/college connection. Many did not like being phoned at home. Interestingly one student noted, 'She (the Home Tutor) is very good at chasing people up; it's really important', while three concurred with a student's view that,

> When I go home it's my own space and time. . . I don't need that additional hassle . . . it seems strange when everything else is so adult.

One student made a suggestion that may turn out to be helpful,

I'd like to have a set time in the week when she rings, but I accept that if I don't turn up, it's good that she chases me.

Some students interpreted the concept of adulthood as giving them a choice about attendance, as well as not having their privacy invaded. At the same time there was evidence that the guidance they were given was important during this period of transition. The support on offer seemed to act as a bridge between the constraints of childhood and the relative freedom of adulthood.

The Home Tutor often referred to herself as a mother, and described how she used this comparison as a guide in her work with these students.

I treat them in exactly the same way as I treat my children. I certainly think they need guidance. One student I have, we had done some English, filled in an application form and I was treating her as I do my own son, giving her orders. I was saying 'do this' and 'we need to do that' and then I said 'I am sorry, you are not my child. I should not be talking to you like this' but she said 'no, I like it. What shall I do next?' I think she was quite glad to have somebody actually telling her what to do.

This comment reflects Miller's (1982) model of the key elements in guidance. He argues that the guidance and support of individuals involves a range of activities: taking action, advising, changing the system, teaching, informing and counselling. The Home Tutor was engaged in all these activities. The students felt the inevitable tensions between these different elements at different times.

College tutorial time

Two students did not value this: 'nobody attends so they're no good', but four had found it 'very supportive'. Several students referred to how helpful their tutor was and claimed that they would go to him, her or the Home Tutor if they had problems.

Peer group

In addition two of the students commented that the peer group was a source of support 'The peer group is supportive . . . they help you to do well, not like in school . . . friends encourage you.'

Some of the students reported not having had successful peer relationships at school. The pre-sixteen students in this project were not identifiable to themselves as a group and so the peer group they refer to is the wider peer group in the college. They were in separate tutor groups for their different subjects and they did not always know who the other pre-sixteen students were. They socialised with the students outside of the pilot group and this opportunity was seen as important by the Home Tutor, who identified it as a chance to form a wider range of friendships than might have been open to them in the Student Support Centre.

Developments since the project

As a direct result of this research, changes were made to increase the likelihood of the students succeeding in the college setting. The range of courses open to the students was increased: students can now choose from the following options:

- Maths and English GCSE at Foundation or Intermediate Level.
- GNVQ Foundation level units in: Engineering, Business Studies, Art and Design or Leisure and Tourism.
- Information Technology for one hour per week with the possibility of the Royal Society for the Arts Computer Literacy and Information Technology qualification.
- A full foundation GNVQ course.
- Choice is still available from the full vocational programme.

The issue of how many GCSEs the group who opt for this route should take has been examined and this has included discussion about whether four GCSEs are too many. The conclusion is that this is a matter for individual assessment and planning.

Tutorial support has been changed and increased, so that now students have tutorials with college lecturers for half an hour four times a week instead of one hour per week; these tutorials are given by specialist personal tutors. There is now one free day per week for work experience or study which is seen as helping the students cope with the additional demands of home study. Student Support Centre support is more intense at the start of year and students' needs for additional support in Maths and English are assessed at entry.

A fresh start and a continuum of education

At the start of this case study, the concept of exclusion from education rather than exclusion from school was briefly mentioned. This small scale case study shows that for a group of carefully selected and prepared students the fresh start of a new environment was a central factor in their continuing inclusion in education. This finding confirms the key concept of giving young people a new start which underpins the FEDA study. They concluded that 'under-achievement and disaffection are not just post-16 issues; the problems and their resolution require *co-operative* planning and action with pre-sixteen compulsory education as well.' (Reisenberger and Crowther, 1997, p.13).

The parents in the study valued the option of another setting where difficult histories could be discarded and where their sons and daughters could still be seen as included within the mainstream of education.

Building and crossing bridges

Attending college was a choice for the students in the pilot scheme and that was clearly important. They also saw the college environment as different from their previous school environment. The metaphor of a bridge is useful here. The students needed a bridge to the adult world that they valued and admired from across the water. They found it motivating to be treated like an adult and yet they also needed help to cross this symbolically important bridge.

They needed a good deal of focused support to manage both the learning and the social demands of the new setting, but they seemed to respond well to the differences in the college environment. In particular they seemed to respond positively to the invitation to think for themselves as adults, although they were clearly still in transition and the amount of responsibility they were offered and could take on varied. They valued highly the choices they were given and the respect for them demonstrated by their tutors and lecturers. They confirmed the ideas formulated in the Dearing Review and found the college environment a more congenial one than the school, with one significant exception. Our case study mirrored the work of the FEDA study. Reisenberger and Crowther concluded,

> Central to most programmes are ease of access, adult treatment of students, confidence building, accessible tutors, initial diagnosis of needs, learning support, flexible content, clear rules for behaviour and work, close progress monitoring, frequent opportunities for feedback, review and assessment, key skills, vocational training and progression targets. A range of staff are involved, including college teaching and support staff, schools staff and other agencies.
> (Reisenberger and Crowther, 1997, p.12)

However, we were also interested in what we could learn about the context of school, by looking at the transition from school to college. The cultures were clearly different in that the college environment is more adult, but the concept of treating students more like adults is one that has implications for schools. The model of an ideal student was very different in the two contexts, even though the processes and concerns of those teaching them were very similar. The lecturers were concerned about behaviour and discipline but the students perceived them as more respectful and giving more choice and responsibility. It would seem that schools might benefit from examining the ideal view of students that they have and how this changes as students mature. Rudduck *et al.* concluded that:

> The conditions of learning that are common across secondary schools do not adequately take account of the social maturity of young people, nor of the tensions and pressures they feel as they struggle to reconcile the demands of their social and personal lives with the development of their identity as learners.
>
> (Rudduck *et al.*: 1996, p. 1)

The students in this study echoed those ideas. They valued being given increased responsibility with support: increased and tolerable choice was also very important indeed. These students wanted to be treated as young people who will soon become adults, and who need a gradual increase in the demands and responsibilities of their changing roles, which will enable them to learn as they go forward.

9 Using insights from the case studies
Frameworks for understanding and developing practice

Introduction

We have now looked closely at what was going on in each of the case study schools, in order to understand what they were currently doing to build more harmonious communities and engage students productively in all areas of school life. In each setting, we have tried to probe beneath the surface of particular policies and practices in order to make explicit the thinking underlying them, and to explore how this related to the particular contexts and circumstances of the individual schools. As well as describing their achievements, our accounts have also noted and explored some of the dilemmas and difficulties that beset their efforts to build positive alternatives to exclusion.

In the second part of the book, we draw on the case studies in order to explore what insights they collectively provide into the task of building positive alternatives to exclusion. Our aim is to draw out and clarify our findings in a form which will enable them to be directly usable by others to inform developmental work. These more general insights are of two kinds.

In this chapter, we identify a number of frameworks which help to shed light on the task of building positive alternatives to exclusion. Each framework was developed as a means of explaining what was going on in a particular setting; each represents a particular way of conceptualising scope for taking action to reduce and prevent exclusion. We show how these frameworks lend themselves to positive and practical use by a variety of different agencies (schools, individual teachers, LEA support teams, policy makers) committed to working to reduce and prevent exclusion.

In Chapter 10, we focus on one dominant theme that has emerged forcefully across all the case studies and that we believe should be central to future development work. We draw on the discussion in each of the six case study chapters in order to elaborate the different dimensions of this theme and to explain why we now believe that priority should be given to developing this aspect of school experience. Then, in Chapter 11, we consider what we have learnt through the project overall about partnership research. We review the methodological principles outlined in Chapter 1 in the light of the experience of both school-based partners and university researchers. We consider the advantages and disadvantages of the particular approach to the research adopted in this case from a variety of participant perspectives, and review our initial conviction that the process of partnership research is in itself a form of development.

Using the findings in other situations

One of the advantages of case study research is that it provides rich and complex detail about particular situations that practitioners can relate to, and can use as a stimulus for thinking about their own situations and concerns. We imagine that some readers of the case studies will have already found ideas and issues that are relevant to their own questions and purposes. Some practitioners may have identified particular strategies that would be worth considering or experimenting with in their own institutions.

In addition to such incidental thinking and directly transferable ideas and strategies, we believe that the case studies also offer some structured ways of thinking about aspects of the task of building positive alternatives to exclusion. In this chapter, we begin by outlining five frameworks drawn from the case studies which lend themselves to use by practitioners, individually and collectively, to support the review and development of their own work. In the second part of the chapter, we go on to illustrate how these frameworks might actually be used in practice, by taking some concrete examples and showing how practitioners in those specific situations might draw on the frameworks to support them in addressing their particular concerns.

Frameworks for positive action

At William Shakespeare school (Chapter 7), the head teacher pointed to the relationship between values and structures as having been one of the key areas in which development work had been focused over a number of years. He had made it a top priority to develop a strong framework of shared values among staff, and to clarify the relationship between these values and the systems in place (policies and strategies) for promoting pro-social behaviour and positive engagement in the curriculum.

Of crucial importance, in this setting, seemed to be the way in which a fairly rigid system of formal behaviour management strategies was embedded in a therapeutic and person-centred school ethos. Positive behaviour and engagement in school work were portrayed as being engendered largely through patterns of interaction between staff and students and among staff, which were driven by shared principles that placed primary value on the dignity of students as individuals. The classic conflict between individual freedom and the need for systemic rules seemed to be handled with remarkable success in this school through the widespread adherence to the view that rules, systems and structures are employed for meeting the needs of individuals. This means that, while rules and systems were in place, they were subject to modification according to a higher principle, the need to find the solution which would best meet the needs of all individuals concerned, within the context of the community as a whole.

Framework One: the relationship between values and structures

It seemed that this approach to the task of building a more harmonious community and reducing and preventing exclusion could be represented in the form of a particular configuration of the relationship between values and structures. In this school:

- there was a strong framework of agreed values
- structures (policies and strategies) were clear
- structures and values were tightly related

These characteristics suggested the possibility that greater success in helping to reduce and prevent exclusion might be associated with the existence of a strong framework of value and a tight relationship between values and structures; and that lesser success might be associated with situations either where there was no strong framework of value shared by a majority of staff, or where the relationship between structures and values was not clearly articulated. The relationship between values and structures might take one of three forms (see Table 9.1).

One important question to ask, then, in searching out scope for constructive action, is about the existing relationship between the espoused values and ethos of the school and the working of the systems and structures that are in place to foster positive behaviour. If no clear

Table 9.1: The relationship between values and structures

Type 1	Type 2	Type 3
Value framework strong/dominant	Value framework strong	Value framework unclear
Structures clear	Structures clear and dominant	Structures clear
Structures and value framework tightly related	Structures and value framework loosely related	Structures operating independently of value framework

framework of values exists, schools might make it a priority to work towards creating one, as happened in a second case study school (Chapter 4). If a framework of value exists but seems to be disconnected from the systems and structures, development work might be focused on how to align the systems and structures more closely with the espoused values.

However, value systems – whether those of an individual or those espoused by a whole school staff – do not necessarily translate smoothly into practice, as we saw in the case of the primary head teacher who agonised over her decision to exclude a particular child for a fixed period. The complex situations in which teachers have to exercise judgment often call forth a conflict in values which is not easily resolved. This head teacher knew that excluding the child was probably the last thing that the child needed at that point; yet she felt that the situation required a short period of exclusion for the long-term benefit of the rest of the community.

Framework Two: dilemmas of intervention

The kinds of tensions which may emerge for teachers between competing courses of action, when attempting to translate their values into practice, were highlighted in our analysis of teachers' thinking at Virginia Woolf school (Chapters 3 and 4). Tensions were identified between:

These seven dilemmas were not presented as an exhaustive list; rather they suggested a way of thinking about the complexities of the teacher's task in deciding how to respond to challenging behaviour, which could be extended and developed in response to the tensions experienced by teachers in other situations. Indeed, when the idea was

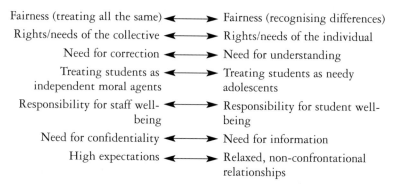

Fairness (treating all the same) ◄────► Fairness (recognising differences)

Rights/needs of the collective ◄────► Rights/needs of the individual

Need for correction ◄────► Need for understanding

Treating students as ◄────► Treating students as needy
independent moral agents   adolescents

Responsibility for staff well- ◄────► Responsibility for student well-
being   being

Need for confidentiality ◄────► Need for information

High expectations ◄────► Relaxed, non-confrontational
relationships

Figure 9.1 Dilemmas of intervention

applied in the context of our other case studies, a number of further dilemmas were identified.

At Anne Fine primary school, for example, a tension was described between the goals of obedience and autonomy. On the one hand, it was vital that teachers were in a position to command instant obedience from pupils, in order to ensure pupils' safety, for instance, in crossing the road. On the other hand, teachers were seeking to develop in pupils – both with respect to their learning and their behaviour – an ability to exercise control and decide upon courses of action for themselves. Was it possible to achieve the first goal without undermining the latter? Which was most prominent in their day to day interactions with children? Were teachers sometimes emphasising obedience where it would have been more appropriate to emphasise autonomy, or vice versa?

The analysis of thinking and practice at this school also highlighted a tension between the public and the private, the institutional and the personal: how to reconcile the demands and needs of the public and the private worlds of teachers and pupils in an institutional context. The difference between these two worlds was reflected in different kinds of entries in the 'Special Mentions' books: on the one hand for children's achievements, for example, with respect to spelling or meticulously following rules for crossing the road; and on the other hand, for acts of human kindness and sympathy to one another or to the teacher. The public world has expectations of teachers and pupils in terms of how they fulfil their institutional role. Teachers are expected to exercise authority over students and students to defer to teachers' authority. These institutional roles can be difficult to reconcile with the relationships of trust and intimate interpersonal understanding that may be prerequisites for significant learning.

A further tension was also identified in some of the secondary case studies between the need for clarity in the definition of roles and responsibilities and the need for permeability between different layers of institutional responsibility. While most schools find it helpful and necessary to clarify responsibilities and divide additional responsibilities between more senior staff, it was also found to be important that role boundaries were not adhered to rigidly. There needed to be permeability between boundaries, so that, for instance, individuals felt empowered to intervene in a situation even if it was not their specific responsibility, if they had a particularly strong relationship with an individual or class and so were likely to be successful in steering a problematic situation towards a positive outcome.

For example, at William Shakespeare school (Chapter 7), there was a clearly established hierarchy of responsibility for dealing with classroom incidents, starting with the subject teacher who was supported by the head of department, who was in turn supported by the head of year, who was backed up by the deputy head. An incident arose in a Year 10 class, when one pupil refused to co-operate with the subject teacher's request for the class to move to a different room. The teacher sent for the head of department, who was also unable to resolve the problem. Knowing that the head of year was unavailable, the head of department set off to find the deputy head. Meanwhile, a part-time, newly qualified teacher – who happened to have observed the incident as she passed the classroom – offered her support. She knew the pupil concerned and had a good relationship with him. The subject teacher escorted the class to the new room while the other teacher talked quietly to the pupil concerned. After a few moments, the boy agreed to follow the rest of the class and did so. Interviewed later, both the deputy head (who had arrived to find an empty room) and the teacher who had intervened recognised that in some schools such bending of the procedures would be frowned upon. Yet they viewed flexibility of this kind as a strength of William Shakespeare school, that was made possible by the shared understandings and priorities of staff.

The dilemmas help to highlight the values and assumptions underlying different responses to disruptive behaviour, and to explain why the task of deciding how to respond is by no means straightforward. They also illustrate, at the level of individual teacher judgment, the thesis that what teachers do makes a difference. How teachers resolve the dilemmas on a day-to-day basis in their interactions with students affects their subsequent relationships with students and their students' attitudes towards them, towards learning and towards school. It affects the learning opportunities they make available, as well as students' willingness to take up these opportunities. For some secondary students interviewed, for example (Chapter 7), how teachers resolve the tension between the institutional and the personal roles was of critical importance to how the students behaved and responded to lessons. If they felt themselves to be trusted and respected as people, they were less inclined to engage in resistance or disruptive behaviour.

Once we have recognised the importance, yet uncertainty and inherent complexity, of teacher judgment in responding to disruptive behaviour, the issue of how such dilemmas are resolved by teachers individually and collectively can become a focus for inquiry and development work at a number of different levels. We have already discussed how the dilemmas were used, at Virginia Woolf school, to support the introduction of the newly agreed mission statement. It was hoped that the dilemmas would stimulate discussion of the challenges and tensions that staff were likely to find themselves facing in their attempts to realise the aims embodied in the statement; that they would offer a shared language for discussing these tensions and how to resolve them in specific cases, and help staff and management identify the support needed in order to achieve the closest possible match between values and practice.

The dilemmas could be used by individual teachers (on their own initiative or as part of planned staff development activities) to explore the circumstances which lead them to resolve the dilemmas in particular ways. In relation to concerns about particular pupils, teachers could examine instances of interaction or conflict, and consider how they resolved the dilemmas that the situation presented and how they justified the particular course of action chosen. They might experiment by trying a different course of action on the next occasion, to see if this made a difference; or with colleagues search out creative ways of resolving the dilemmas that might provide the breakthrough they have been seeking.

The layout of the dilemmas may also contribute to an understanding of variations in levels of exclusion, and the problems that may beset schools in moving forward constructively. If a majority of teachers in a school routinely resolve the dilemmas in a way which favours the considerations found in the left-hand column of Table 9.2, then it would seem likely that their approach would be associated with a higher level of exclusion. This is not to imply, however, that one way to help reduce exclusions would simply be to shift policy and practice in favour of the considerations lined up on the right hand side. As experience at Virginia Woolf illustrates, where initiatives to prevent or reduce exclusion tend to emphasise right-hand resolutions, these are in turn likely to create tensions for staff, because it will seem that equally important considerations are being neglected.

If initiatives are to win the support and commitment of staff, the most effective approach may be to choose strategies for their transformative potential, that is to develop strategies which transcend the dilemmas by addressing both sides simultaneously. The introduction of Circle Time at Virginia Woolf, for example, could be seen as one such strategy, justifiable both for its contribution to the development of positive, non-confrontational relationships and for its contribution to enhancing pupils' academic achievements (through enhanced self-esteem and more active, confident participation in the curriculum).

Framework Three: the dynamics of feeling

At Virginia Woolf school, the dilemmas were also intended to address a need to provide more opportunities for dialogue: for people to talk about their experiences, to have their views listened to and taken seriously. They were not simply a rational tool to assist with a complex decision-making task. They were also developed in the light of a growing recognition that part of the task of building positive alternatives to exclusion involved addressing the emotional needs and experience of teachers as well as students.

Challenging behaviour can powerfully undermine teachers' sense of professional identity and worthiness. Traditional cultures of teaching place such a high premium upon teachers' ability to keep order that teachers are often loath to discuss difficulties openly and seek support from colleagues. Preservation of the 'self' can be achieved by locating 'the problem' in an external source; but this also leaves teachers feeling powerless to take action that is likely to have a positive impact on behaviour within the immediate situation (Seligman, 1992, p. xvii).

The alternative is to change the school culture, so that teachers feel supported, are able to seek advice from colleagues, and do not fear repercussions if they admit to experiencing problems. This may be an important area for development work in some schools. In Chapter 4, we noted, drawing on the work of Salzberger-Wittenberg (1996), that learning is impossible for teachers or pupils if their minds are taken up with the feelings they are experiencing. We explored possible parallels between students' emotional experiences and those of teachers, and arrived at two contrasting ways of representing the emotional dynamics of teaching and learning (see p. 83). One attempted to represent the conditions that lock teachers and students into a static, self-perpetuating cycle; the other identified conditions that foster growth and learning.

Our idea, in presenting this framework, was to suggest the kinds of intervention that might be helpful in schools to help create conditions in which both teachers and students feel supported and empowered as learners. If teachers are to be able to take a learning stance towards their practice and towards the challenges presented by disruptive behaviour, they need to feel respected, supported, listened to and understood. The contrasting dynamics represented in these two diagrams also have implications for how schools organise meetings and professional training in such a way as to contribute to genuine dialogue and to a climate of learning and experimentation with regard to students' behaviour.

Depending upon how we understand learning, it could be argued that experiences of support and constructive dialogue are not simply essential pre-requisites but also the means by which learning (for teachers or students) occurs. Learning has to connect with and build on the learner's existing knowledge, understanding and ways of seeing the world. Although other teachers' experience can be a very helpful resource for stimulating ideas and suggesting possibilities, it cannot provide instant solutions. Teachers have to make connections between new ideas and their existing understandings and practices, and reconstruct existing understandings and practices in order to take new ideas into account. Just as with pupils' learning (Vygotsky, 1978; Bruner ,1985), forms of scaffolding are needed to support teachers' professional development. Mutual sharing and dialogue are important means by which such development is achieved.

Framework Four: three-dimensional support

Applied to the learning of students, the idea of 'scaffolding' was also found to be useful in establishing what was genuinely preventative about the 'individual monitoring' strategy used at Virginia Woolf school for supporting excluded pupils on re-entry. It was suggested that the strategy was specifically operating to alter the balance of pressures and resources in such a way as to make it possible for pupils to succeed in doing what they could not yet do on their own (Chapter 3). Again, dialogue was the principal medium through which such changes were brought about.

We realised that the contribution to the task of reducing and preventing exclusion of other initiatives being developed in the school could also be construed in these terms. They were all, in different ways, helping to create conditions that would enable pupils to engage more constructively in school life, either by helping to reduce pressures and/or build students' inner resources. Pursuing this idea as one possible way of understanding the task of building positive alternatives to exclusion, we found a further important dimension of supportive change reflected in the data: developments designed to extend opportunities to experience a sense of personal satisfaction and belonging.

This three-dimensional approach can be used to identify the kinds of changes that it may be most useful to pursue in particular circumstances, based on their potential to:

• Reduce pressures, so that success in coping with them becomes more likely.
• Build inner resources so that students have more resources to draw on to cope successfully with the pressures on them.
• Opportunities for feeling a sense of personal satisfaction and belonging.

There is an interesting parallel here between this three-dimensional approach and a set of curriculum guidelines for early childhood education recently published in New Zealand, known as *Te Whāriki*. This is a bilingual document, named after the Maori word for a woven floormat, and the metaphor of weaving is one of the key ideas in the framework. The document sets out four guiding principles and five over-arching aims for early childhood education; each early years setting or centre (and there are a great variety of these) weaves its own detailed curriculum or programme. The five aims or goals include three that closely resemble the three elements of support described in Framework Four, that is

• well-being
• contributing
• belonging.

Early childhood educators in New Zealand are using the *Te Whāriki* document, not just to plan and implement their daily/weekly/year long programmes, but also as an evaluative tool, rigorously examining the quality of their work within each of the strands of the 'woven' curriculum. The focus of this evaluation work is not the individual child, or groups of children, but the role of the adult (which is characterised as constructing responsive, reciprocal and respectful relationships) and the dynamics of the particular contexts in which young children find themselves.

In the specific context of development work to reduce and prevent exclusion, the three-dimensional approach provides a positive support for the essential belief underlying constructive action: that change is

possible, that no individual is 'irredeemable', while providing a particular view of what teachers can constructively do to bring about worthwhile and lasting change in their work with individuals, within the
curriculum and within the school as a whole.

Framework Five: alternative narratives

The importance of maintaining a belief that change is possible was
also underlined in the case study of Ogden Nash school where the
research began by tape recording staff discussions of individual pupils
at risk of exclusion. The process of assembling all that was known
about one individual (from existing documentation and perceptions
of staff who knew him) left staff with a strong sense of how things
might have turned out differently if this had been done at an earlier
stage. They had, of course, provided support and encouragement for
the student at every opportunity. However, in discussion, the teachers
began to use the idea of a narrative to talk about this individual's
student's school career in terms of chapters, plots and possible
endings. Developing the metaphor, they realised that none of the staff
had had access to the whole story; it was as if different people had
been reading different chapters at different times, not necessarily in
the same order. Twists and turns in the plot went unidentified
because of the fragmentation of the story as a whole. Possibilities for
intervening to change the plot, or bring about a happier ending, had
perhaps been missed.

With hindsight, the staff group could see that there had been critical
moments when action could have been taken that might have significantly altered the course of events that had led this individual to the
brink of exclusion. The experience brought home to them that teachers'
powers to make a difference depend, in part, on the quality of information available to them and the opportunity to form an informed, collective view about action to be taken. This is admittedly difficult to
organise because of the many pressures on teachers' time. It is particularly difficult in a secondary context where so many staff need to be
involved. Yet it is in secondary contexts where it is most important to
gather together all the evidence and agree on a collective plan of action,
since pieces of the jigsaw or chapters of the story are held in so many
different hands.

Studying the experience of individuals across the various case studies
also drew attention to the way that the structures designed to secure
and maintain discipline can also, paradoxically, be powerful influences
inhibiting teachers and students from altering the onward trajectory

towards exclusion. The system of escalating sanctions that most schools operate in some form tends to limit the possibility of interpreting and responding to challenging behaviour in ways other than those laid down by the system. The system itself becomes a force for exclusion, since each new instance of unacceptable behaviour calls forth a yet more serious sanction until available options run out. Exclusion then seems justifiable, if regrettable, as the 'only alternative'.

In such situations, the possibility of intervening to change the course of events for one individual depends upon a preparedness to reconsider the effects of the operation of the system as a whole. One way of counteracting these effects, as described in Chapter 7 is by emphasising the underlying values and principles which the system was intended to serve, and appealing to these rather than requiring rigid adherence to the rules and procedures of the system *per se*. The consistency sought was in the exercise of flexibility in the application of rules, thus creating space to take individual needs and circumstances into account.

How might this way of thinking about the trajectory of individual pupils lives in school be helpful in building positive alternatives to exclusion? At Ogden Nash, the teachers were deeply affected by the sense that maybe things could have been different for the individual if only alternative possibilities had been recognised and exploited earlier. Perhaps the most important general message is that, no matter how difficult things currently seem, there are always other ways of thinking and being to be found and tried which could fundamentally alter the path of an individual pupil's subsequent development. What is certain is that finding them depends upon teachers' attitudes and actions. It depends upon teachers' compassion, commitment and belief that alternatives can be found, coupled with their close knowledge of the situation and of the dynamics affecting children's responses to school learning.

Using the frameworks for reflection and development

These various different frameworks offer different ways of understanding the approaches to the task of developing 'positive alternatives to exclusion' reflected in the work of the schools that we studied. We now move on to consider in a more concrete way how they might also be used as tools by teachers, schools and other agencies to support their own processes of reflection and development. We will take three imaginary scenarios and examine each in turn to illustrate possible ways of using the frameworks.

We would emphasise that the frameworks lend themselves to many different uses at different levels: by individual teachers, groups of teachers, management teams, whole-school staffs, work with parents, governors and communities, by LEA officers and support services and by policy makers at national level. Which frameworks are used will depend not just on who uses them and for what purpose, but on specific features of the context in which the work is to be carried out.

Scenario one

> *Staff at a primary school in a metropolitan area (recently amalgamated from an infant and junior school) are concerned about an increasing number of pupils who find it difficult to adhere to the school's expectations and guidelines for appropriate behaviour. The behaviour of some is so challenging that fixed-term exclusion has already been resorted to on more than one occasion. Staff are keen to take steps to prevent further exclusion but are not sure what might be the best way of setting about this.*

Given that this is a newly amalgamated staff group, it is likely that there will not yet have been time for staff to discuss and negotiate a common framework of values. There may well be some important work to be done (supported by Framework One) in examining the existing relationship between overall school ethos and values on the one hand, and the systems currently in place for promoting positive engagement with the curriculum on the other. What are the values that staff share? Are they reflected in the systems in place? Does the system serve the values or operate independently of them?

As a first step, opportunities may well need to be provided for staff to get to know one another better, to build trust, to overcome tensions that may be left over from the amalgamation process. The set of dilemmas reflected in Framework Two could provide a useful tool for staff to begin to explore and reflect on their values and practices in a way which encourages discussion and avoids polarisation of views. Since the assumption is that individual teachers will feel some sympathy for, and pull towards, both poles of each dilemma, it should be possible to create enough common ground for constructive dialogue. Approaching staff discussion in this way would help to acknowledge the challenging nature of the task and the fact that there are never simple and straightforward answers. It would help, therefore, to lay the foundations of emotional support needed to create the emotional space for learning (Framework Three).

In the course of these discussions, staff may look more closely at how they resolve the dilemmas with respect to particular individuals whose behaviour is giving most cause for concern. They may find that they respond in different ways to these individuals than to others; and this may in turn suggest that they might try changing their patterns of responses in order to see if this has any impact on the children's behaviour. Alternatively, they might realise that they are routinely emphasising some values more than others that they hold to be equally important. This might lead them to think up and pursue some transformative strategies, that is strategies chosen for their potential to address both sides of the dilemma simultaneously. The introduction of Circle Time discussed earlier might indeed be a very positive focus for development work (if the school was not already using it), or highlighted as an area for further evaluation and development if it was already in use.

Additionally or alternatively, staff discussion might focus on the three-dimensional approach to support (Framework Four) as a means of recognising the kinds of support currently in place, and considering what might be further done to change the current balance of pressures, resources and opportunities in a way that was likely to be enabling for the children. If there is enough flexibility, teachers might carry out shadow observations of individual children and use the information to reflect on what aspects of the environment seem to be causing them difficulty, and on what might be done to reduce these pressures (for example, by making printed texts more accessible or by introducing structured play activities at dinnertime), to develop inner resources (for example, through judicious feedback about work and acknowledgement of the child as an individual) and to extend opportunities for the child to achieve a sense of personal satisfaction (for example, through offering choices and opportunities for children to pursue personal interests through the curriculum). Such information need not lead only to ideas for adjustments to current provision at an individual level. It could equally well prompt ideas for the development of practice for the potential benefit of all children.

Such work would, by its very nature, help to reinforce teachers' belief that no matter what the difficulties presented by individual children, it may be possible to influence and enable children to respond differently if conditions change in ways which support and foster such positive developments (Framework Five).

In this first example, we have examined a school with features and circumstances that are reasonably similar to those of the schools from which the frameworks were originally derived. But how helpful and applicable are the frameworks likely to be to those working in or with schools which are markedly different from our case study settings?

Scenario two

> *An LEA advisor and local behaviour support team are meeting to discuss how they can support schools in meeting their targets for reducing exclusions over the next three years. The LEA serves a culturally, socially and linguistically diverse community. Exclusion rates overall are four times higher than they were a decade before, and there is some evidence that the familiar pattern of over-representation of particular minority ethnic groups is reflected in these figures. There are considerable variations between schools in terms of their rates of exclusion. The group wants to develop a strategy that will use available resources to support schools in the most positive and effective way possible.*

Since none of our case study schools served communities as diverse as those represented in this LEA, practitioners in this setting might well question if there is anything to be learnt from them that is of direct relevance to their own particular context. Certainly, there are many issues to do with the ways that schools respond to social, cultural, linguistic and religious diversity that we have not been able to address directly through our case studies. Nevertheless, we believe that the frameworks derived from the case study settings do have a wider application and that they could indeed have a contribution to make to this group of practitioners in pursuing their urgent, local agenda.

As part of the groundwork for developing a successful support strategy, the group would no doubt be seeking to understand what lay behind the different rates of exclusion in schools with similar intakes. Frameworks One and Two both offer ways of understanding such differences which could contribute to their analysis. Is the difference between high and low excluding schools one which reflects the various relationships between values and systems suggested by Framework One? Do the high excluding schools have an ethos where staff tend to resolve the dilemmas of Framework Two most frequently by emphasising the considerations on the left hand side of Figure 9.1 (p.170)? If either of these frameworks does seem to shed useful light on the differences in exclusion rates between schools, then this understanding would also provide a focus for positive development work.

An important part of the LEA team's overall approach might also be to create opportunities for teachers to share ideas and successful strategies within and between schools. The three-dimensional support framework could be helpful here, in structuring the process of identifying strategies and explaining their contribution to the task of reducing and preventing exclusion. Applied in schools which do serve diverse communities, this framework could be a powerful tool for exploring, from the perspective of particular groups of students, what the school could do that would make a difference. It would provide a structured stimulus for re-examining existing practices, which could lead schools towards the kinds of positive strategies identified by Blair and Bourne (1998), in their study of successful multi-ethnic schools, as helping to raise achievement and counter disaffection among particular groups of students.

The dimension concerned with '*reducing pressures*' might lead to a consideration of the particular pressures experienced, for example, by students who are new to English, who are refugees or whose cultural, linguistic or religious background differs significantly from the majority of staff and/or students in the school. It could focus attention on issues of racial harassment or social exclusion and what schools can do that would make a difference. According to Blair and Bourne (1998), an important characteristic of successful schools lies in the recognition by staff of the pressures faced by students both in and outside school, in staff's preparedness to take those pressures into account, to see them from the students' point of view and to take active steps to mitigate their influence.

In a multi-ethnic context, the framework's second focus on how to support students in 'building inner resources' might also open up many areas beyond those considered in the original case study. Blair and Bourne (1998) point to the positive efforts made by some schools to reinforce the confidence, motivation and self-esteem of students of very diverse backgrounds, for example by incorporating the specific cultural, class, religious and language identities of students into curriculum activities; by developing mentoring schemes involving older pupils or members of the local community, and other specific support provision to meet the needs (both academic and pastoral) of refugees, asylum seekers and other late arriving students new to English.

The third dimension, concerned with extending opportunities for students to experience personal satisfaction and belonging within the school community, could – within a multi-ethnic context – also lead to significant developments tailored to the needs of particular groups.

Developments might include, for example, extending opportunities within the school curriculum for students whose first language is not English to learn in their first language as well as in English; or exploring ways of creating an overall school ethos which is more inclusive of Gypsy traveller children.

Blair and Bourne emphasise the importance of the ongoing process of questioning existing practices and deciding what can be done that will make a difference, in the light of information gleaned from listening to students and from careful differential analysis of the achievements of different groups of students. The framework provides a structure which can support this process, helping to ensure that development work is broadly conceived and suggesting some key areas to consider as schools search out constructive ways forward.

As well as supporting significant whole-school development initiatives, we hope that the various frameworks will also have something to offer readers as individual teachers seeking to find constructive ways of addressing challenging situations arising in their own teaching, as our third example seeks to explore.

Scenario three

> *Frances, a newly appointed head of History in an urban comprehensive school, is dismayed to find that the expertise in establishing positive relationships with her classes that she took for granted in her old school does not seem to have transferred into her new situation. In one Year 9 group, in particular, there is a student (Tom) who continually challenges her authority by refusing to work or to abide by basic rules of classroom behaviour. She doesn't want to publicise her difficulties by asking for help, just when she is trying to establish herself with a new group of colleagues. However, it is obvious that her existing repertoire isn't working, and she is not sure what else to do to address the problem constructively.*

Conscious of the heightened emotional pressure that this student's behaviour is creating for her, Frances might be drawn, first and foremost, to examine and analyse her situation using Framework Three, concerned with the dynamics of feeling. This framework would provide her with a resource for thinking through the dynamics of her own relationship with Tom, and help her to appreciate what kinds of changes might need to be made if both of them were to be freed from what seemed to be becoming a self-perpetuating cycle.

The framework might help to crystallise for Frances awareness of the part that her own fear of failure was playing in the situation: inhibiting her from taking steps that could both provide her with collegial support and with additional information that might help her to understand Tom's perspective and build a more positive relationship with him. At the same time, the parallels drawn between teachers' and pupils' experience could help Frances to decentre, to think about the meaning of Tom's behaviour – not simply from her own point of view as a threat to her professional identity – but from Tom's point of view, as a possible expression of his feelings of failure, alienation or powerlessness. This shift could be significant in itself if, as a result, she is able to empathise more with where Tom might be coming from, and manages to communicate this empathy to Tom in her interactions with him. Recognition that no situation is irredeemable, that change is always possible, might help to restore and reinforce Frances' feelings of efficacy, her sense of her own power to influence the situation for the better – feelings that are essential prerequisites for further progress.

She might decide that, as a first step, she must try to talk to Tom privately, away from the gaze of other students, and try to break down the barrier of hostility that has been growing between them. She might hope to conduct this conversation, not as a 'teacher' trying to exhort a pupil into good behaviour, but in a person-to-person way that communicates genuine respect and willingness to listen. Recognising, though, that change depends upon creating conditions in which teachers as well as pupils feel accepted, cared for and listened to, she might decide also to seek the support of a carefully selected colleague or colleagues to discuss what was happening and explore possible options. Finding out more about Tom's background and progress more generally would help to establish if this was simply an isolated problem or one which many teachers experienced. In either case, once the issue had been broached with a colleague, there would be scope for drawing on other colleagues' successful (and unsuccessful) experiences in order to work out a way of trying to get through to Tom and engage him more positively in classroom learning.

Frances might thus also draw on the Alternative Narratives framework (Framework Five) in order to develop her positive strategy. If the problem with Tom was indeed being experienced by teachers more generally, then Frances's initiative might provide the catalyst needed to build up a fuller picture and to decide on action that might be taken to help Tom find an alternative, more constructive way of living out his life in school.

A particular orientation towards problems

As these various examples have illustrated, the function of the five frameworks is not to provide answers but to support practitioners in doing the kinds of thinking that will enable them to define their own strategies and directions for positive change adapted to the particular needs and circumstances of their own contexts. What they illustrate is a particular orientation towards challenging situations arising in schools: a willingness to approach problems in a spirit of enquiry, to listen to and learn from pupils, and to develop practices in the light of developing understandings, in the belief and expectation that what teachers and schools do can and will make a difference.

Like Blair and Bourne (1998), we do not believe that there is any simple formula, or any one 'right way' for schools to work at developing positive alternatives to exclusion. The frameworks described in this chapter are simply intended as tools to be used judiciously in conjunction with all the other important resources that practitioners bring, from experience and research, to contribute to the development task. They reflect our understandings of the particular approaches being pursued in the case study schools; from our experience so far, it seems that other practitioners also find them useful to think about their own work. Together they offer one particular kind of answer to our original question 'What can schools do to prevent and reduce exclusion?'

As well as these various frameworks, however, the case studies also drew attention to one key area as a priority for further research and development work in schools. This key concept of 'personal experience' is examined in the next chapter.

10 Making human sense
The importance of personal experience

Introduction

In this chapter we discuss how the concept of personal experience, which emerged as a significant feature of all the case studies, plays a central part in the dynamics of inclusion and exclusion. We argue that a focus on personal experience is a priority area for development work in schools committed to building positive alternatives to exclusion. We suggest some ways in which the key idea of personal experience could be developed systematically in schools and colleges, in the conviction that such developments could radically transform the social and pedagogical relationships at the heart of schooling.

Making personal meaning: the impact of institutional life

The notion of personal experience is bound up with the continuous acts of meaning making that teachers and students engage in throughout the school day. Day after day, and week after week, every member of the school community is actively processing numerous vivid and various experiences of institutional life, constructing meanings of enormous significance. It is these acts of meaning making that shape, for good or ill, the feelings, actions and interactions of staff and students alike. Staff and students, in the daily exercise of their institutionalised roles, are doing more than playing a part within the systems of the school; they are also actively constructing their individual biographies, daily adding to their accumulating personal histories, to a history of feeling, thinking, doing, responding, deciding, accepting or refusing, despairing or surviving.

At early meetings of the research team, when the case studies were getting underway, we often reminded one another of one of our key questions: what makes a difference in the dynamics of inclusion or exclusion? As the case study work progressed, we began to understand how particular strategies and systems in each of the case study institutions were contributing to positive alternatives to exclusion, and we have presented full accounts of this emerging understanding in the seven chapters in the first part of this book. But looking back over the case study record as a whole, we can now see that our question was insufficiently focused. What makes a difference? *Everything* makes a difference. Every act of meaning making, as students and staff process their school experience, contributes in some way to how they respond to that experience. Institutional life impacts on every individual self within the institution: the self who learns and the self who teaches, the self who is a member of the peer group and the self in the staff group. The impact of school experience on the self is daily manifested in classrooms, corridors, playgrounds and staffrooms. The visible records of life in school are also records of 'what makes a difference'.

Our case studies provide a rich source of insight into those acts of meaning making that make a difference to the dynamic of inclusion, as staff and students make personal sense of what is happening to them in ways that contribute to their commitment to the purposes of their shared enterprise in school. There are examples of these throughout the case study chapters, and some of them are revisited below. There are also telling examples of staff and students who respond to the demands made upon them in the course of a school day in ways that contribute to a sense of alienation, disaffection, rejection. There is evidence that some members of our case study schools come to understand the institution as a place where they experience unbearable pressures. But these people (students or staff) were in a minority. When the institutions we studied were functioning most effectively, the significance of personal experience was manifested in a number of different and positive ways, some of which are briefly reviewed below.

Making sense: students' and teachers' experiences

There were moving examples in the case studies of moments of genuine communication and empathy, when meanings were shared across the student/teacher divide, when teachers and students reached mutual understanding of each other's positions. In interview after interview the students were warm in their praise for the teachers who made these empathetic moves, who tried to see things from their perspective:

(the) teachers would help you along. They would make sure, if you were upset – they will make a note of having to see you . . . They will come and see you if you are distressed or upset.

(William Shakespeare)

She just like understands how I feel . . . and she'll say something, like, that'll mean something.

The teachers believing me is the most important sort of help I could have.

(Virginia Woolf)

There were many examples in the teacher interviews, too, of how staff try to understand and enter into their pupils' personal experiences. As they made these efforts towards empathy, they were sometimes met halfway, as it were, by the pupils themselves, who were engaged in their own work of trying to understand. For example, the head and deputy at William Shakespeare both commented on the capacity for self-knowledge of a Year 10 boy seen as in danger of exclusion.

I think he actually understands to a certain extent why he behaves the way he does . . . We actually said 'Why do you do the things you do?'. . . . And he said he thought it went back to the time when he was very small [explanation continues] . . . and I think it is absolutely true.

[The incident with the chair]. . . . And he [the boy] said 'Look this happened and this happened and this happened. And if you listen carefully, you will see it as not my fault.'

The disposition to try to understand that we see in this example is clearly a contributing factor to the process by which the pupil was not, in fact, excluded, but remained within the community. Another example from the same school reinforces the connection between the process of inclusion and the act of trying to understand. In reviewing the case of a boy excluded from another school, the head of pastoral care noted with some concern the previous school's apparent indifference to the boy in question: 'Not an overall thought about his behaviour. . .'. This comment suggests that it is only by taking thought, by looking for explanations and underlying causes, that a staff group can learn how to include the most challenging pupils.

At a more practical level, the behaviour policy at Anne Fine, by incorporating elements contributed by the pupils themselves ('playing lurgy games', 'putting notes in people's trays'), gave formal recognition to the importance of the pupils' ways of seeing. If the behaviour policy was to prevent bullying, the reasoning goes, it must prevent bullying behaviour as the children define it; their experiences are central to the school's definition of what is and what is not acceptable. The pupils' perspective contributed both to the teachers' understanding of their pupils' lives, and to the process by which the incidence of bullying was reduced, making the pupils' experience of school more rewarding and sustaining.

However, in some of the case study schools there was evidence of what can happen when there is a lack of congruence between the teachers' and students' understanding of one another's purposes. At Ogden Nash, for example, the students' questionnaire revealed that there was a substantial mismatch between the expressed purposes of the system of rewards and referrals, and the students' understanding of it. It was not that the students did *not* understand the system, but that they made sense of it in ways that were at odds with the aspirations of those who had constructed it. To see the school's reward system as 'patronising' or as 'bribery', as some students did, is not to fail to understand; it is to make sense of school in a way that is damaging both to the self and to the possibility of an inclusive and harmonious student group. These students' views, and others like them, however unwelcome they may at first have been to their teachers, are, under closer scrutiny, crucial evidence of the ways in which the accumulating sense of frustration, of lack of engagement, of unmanageable pressures, contribute to some pupils' personal experiences of school. There is no possibility of improving these pupils' experiences by denying them, or ignoring them. Rather, as Salmon (1995) eloquently argues in a powerful account of the relationship between knowledge, understanding and personal meaning, teachers must find ways of meeting their pupils' constructions. They need the

> willingness and capacity to step into another person's shoes, to begin to see the world as that person sees it, to adopt, for the moment, the terms and dimensions of meaning through which that person makes sense of things.
>
> (Salmon, 1995, p. 36)

In short, teachers must listen, not to the sound of their own voices, but to what their students hear. Much of the time, in most of the schools, there was evidence that teachers could and did commit themselves to just such respectful and attentive listening; this commitment was one of the factors that made a crucial difference to the quality of the students' lives and their commitment to their school.

Another manifestation of how the intersection of teacher and pupil perspective can have beneficial effects on the life of the institution is seen in the ways in which teachers recognise and acknowledge individual differences. Indeed the whole pilot project at Rudyard Kipling college was predicated on the assumption that for a small group of students with particular characteristics a different kind of provision was appropriate. As we have seen, the students responded very positively to being treated differently, as people, (as they saw it) rather than as part of the homogenous student population of their secondary school.

At T. S. Eliot, the classroom observation and interview data show individual teachers who have recognised, with sympathy, some particular differences between pupils. When the teachers act upon this recognition, they seem to make a significant contribution to creating a positive learning environment. 'Tracey shouts', commented one teacher, when asked about a particular pupil's behaviour. Without condoning the behaviour ('I just keep griping away at it'), this teacher was able to contain it, and doing so, she was confident, made a difference to Tracey; and, we may assume, to other relationships in the classroom.

At Ogden Nash, where the Year 11 group was perceived as being 'difficult', members of the pastoral team hypothesised about the causes of this disaffection, demonstrating their openness to understanding the relationship between the students' previous experiences, and their current lack of motivation and sense of insecurity. In these examples, we see teachers trying to understand and acknowledge difference, making meaning of it in a way that emphasises the need to accept and include, rather than stigmatise and reject.

The process of trying to understand another's perspective, which we have been illustrating here, is an intensely personal one, in which the teacher, acting as a person, looks for the person within the student, rather than confining either party to an institutional role. There was widespread satisfaction, across the case study schools, when students saw their teachers acting in this way, and expressing value for them as persons. At Rudyard Kipling, one student graphically compared his treatment with his previous experience:

I don't feel like I'm a piece of shit when I am here.

At the other end of the system, a pupil at Anne Fine defined a good teacher as one who will 'push you into believing that you can do it,' suggesting that the high value a teacher sets on a pupil's potential can be a positive and motivating force in the pupil's life. The head teacher at Anne Fine was explicit about her practice of expressing the value she sets on individual pupils, including those exhibiting the most challenging behaviour. In describing her approach to individual disciplinary interviews with children, she commented:

> it helps me to say 'I care about you very much as a human being and I want to do my best by you, and I want this school to be somewhere that you want to be, and to achieve in.'

At Ogden Nash the staff were equally clear:

> It is explicit we see the child as an individual and the child is at the centre and that is what we are working towards . . .

And at Virginia Woolf, a student described her feelings about her Personal Tutor's work on her behalf:

> That's the good thing about it, because I know that she's always checking up on me. That tells me that she's actually trying to help me, so I should pay her back in some way.

This student is well aware of the extent of her tutor's commitment to the relationship between them. At Ogden Nash, where such a commitment was strongly, if not universally, expressed, there was also an awareness that such relationships are time-consuming, demanding, difficult, requiring conscious efforts and, sometimes, in need of re-negotiation and repair. The work of the Home Tutor at the FE college, who was described by one student as 'very good at chasing people up – it's really important', is another example of the way in which the personal relationships that teachers worked hard to build paid dividends in terms of co-operation, loyalty, a sense of solidarity and inclusion. At their best, these relationships remind us of the recommendation made by Cronk (1987), in her illuminating study of how teacher–pupil conflict might be transformed by an approach rooted in respect for persons. It is necessary, she writes,

> for teachers not merely (to) understand their pupils. They should give their pupils the opportunity to understand them.
>
> (Cronk, 1987, p. 209)

Within these strong and supportive relationships, both teachers and students recognised the need for there to be space and time for reflection, sometimes away from the immediate pressures of classroom life. A teacher at Anne Fine commented on the considerable amount of time that this aspect of her work could take, but was completely convinced that it was time well spent. At Virginia Woolf, the extra support offered to excluded pupils on re-entry included the opportunity for frequent meetings between the pupils and the co-ordinator of the scheme, at regular intervals throughout the day. The analysis of pupil perceptions of this scheme (Chapter 3) demonstrated how these moments of relative calm, when co-operative dialogue could take place, contributed both to reducing pressures on the pupils and to building their inner resources.

The concept of dialogue emerged as important in a number of the case studies. At Ogden Nash there was an explicit emphasis on the importance of dialogue, of finding a way of keeping effective communication going, drawing on strengths and insights from the school community as a whole ('The only way is to talk' Ogden Nash, p. 127). At William Shakespeare, pupils who had attended other schools, with a more bureaucratic and mechanistic approach to discipline, were emphatic about the value of dialogue, and the benefits of this particular kind of talk with teachers, which demonstrably enhanced student commitment and engagement.

> No (I didn't have discipline problems when I came here) not really, because the way they do it (here) is they speak to you about it. They don't go straight in with the punishment . . . The thing is, that you can talk to these teachers. The teachers here are a lot more friendly, and are easier to learn off, because they are like your mates as well. As well as being like a teacher. So it really does help.

A teacher at Virginia Woolf was explicit about the purposes of the dialogue she engaged in with individual students. She saw the overall goal as being

> for them to be strong enough to have their own morality, and own guidelines within themselves . . . not being swayed by the family or by the peer situation – to know inside themselves that this is me.
> (Virginia Woolf, p. 59)

The work of Cronk is, once again, relevant. Her first-hand report of an 'educational approach' to classroom conflict concludes that the practice of dialogue is essential to the creation of the harmonious classroom. The outcomes of such an approach are seen as highly desirable:

> Classrooms would become places where people stopped fighting one

another, and discussed ideas, where they co-operated. . . to find ways in which their contradictory evaluations and insights could be made to cohere.

(Cronk, 1987, p. 6)

And in the concluding sentences of the book Cronk summarises the ways in which her approach could have far-reaching benefits for teachers and students alike:

> If teachers merely choose to relate to pupils as persons, conflict may indeed be avoided. If they then use the space which the reduction in disruptive behaviour provides to introduce and discuss important ideas, their teaching role will be fulfilled. They will be instrumental in increasing their pupils' liberty.

(Cronk, 1987, p. 211)

Some of the case study schools have gone further than others in formalising the times and places in which the work of dialogue, negotiation and engagement can be carried out. But in all six case studies there is evidence that there are structures, systems, policies and practices in place that – at least some of the time – make a difference to both teachers' and students' sense of emotional and psychological security and well-being, to their capacities to persevere. At their most effective, these structures and systems support the 'person within the teacher' and the 'person within the student'. They energise and encourage teachers and students alike to commit themselves as persons to the community they build together day by day, week by week.

But it is not just the systems and structures in the public domain that contribute to a sense of community within a particular institution. There is a private and internal dimension to the process: the individual's awareness of the significance of personal experience. Individual students and teachers are, in every school and college, continuously engaged in making sense of their experiences. But in these inclusive and including case study schools, they were doing more. The teachers did not dismiss their personal understanding and insight as insignificant or irrelevant; they were aware of its importance, and they acted on it. They used their awareness to intervene in classroom processes in ways that were, as we have seen, respectful of their students as persons, and that tended towards solidarity, commitment and inclusion. Their awareness of the significance of personal experience was the light by which they acted in generating positive and inclusive experiences for all their pupils.

Moving on: possibilities for development

In the final section of this chapter we consider ways in which the key idea of personal experience could be developed, in schools and colleges: our argument for doing so is that however far a staff group has gone in developing a harmonious and inclusive school community, attending to the concept of personal experience can make a qualitative difference to the lives of both students and teachers. We see this particular focus for development as a priority; the discussion that follows is not offered as a prescription or programme for staff groups to follow, but as a way of suggesting starting points for continuing work on constructing positive alternatives to exclusion.

The concept of personal experience, as we have come to understand it through the analysis of the case studies, is a complex one, built up moment by moment in a cumulative dynamic that can work for good or ill in people's lives. When schools and classrooms are most effectively working towards inclusion, teachers' and students' personal experience includes

- a sense of being valued as a person
- a sense of belonging and involvement
- a sense of personal satisfaction and achievement
- a sense of being accepted and listened to
- a sense of congruence between personal and institutional values
- a sense of the personal meaningfulness of the tasks of teaching and learning
- a sense of efficacy, of power to influence things for the better.

An awareness of these structures of feeling, we have argued, is a crucial dimension in the dynamic of inclusion.

Developing an awareness of the key concept of personal experience, and then acting on it, is a school development project that could take many forms, by focusing on any one (or more) of various aspects of schooling: on discipline and organisation, for example, or on curriculum, pedagogy or assessment. A focus on discipline might entail teachers and students working together to consider how different their lives might be if the importance of personal experience were brought to the forefront in disciplinary encounters. Development work here would be able to build on the useful distinction made more than once by Galton (1989, 1995) between those pupil behaviours governed by the teacher's instruction 'do as you think best' and those by the teacher's commandment 'do as I say'. In elaborating this distinction, Galton discusses the possibility that a teacher can convey to a class of pupils that anti-social actions or other unacceptable behaviours occur as a result of human weaknesses, rather than because of serious character defects; they do not therefore signal the irretrievable end of good relationships (Galton, 1995, pp. 120–2).

Galton speculates that negotiated rules for behaviour as well as for learning could eliminate the ambiguity he has detected, but his account clearly prioritises the teacher, rather than the dialogue that teachers and pupils might have together, in the course of building approaches to discipline that are respectful of all participants as persons, making personal meaning of their encounters. Classroom organisation and routines would be another fruitful ground for development through teacher/student dialogue. Fielding's innovative work with students as co-researchers (1999) for example, suggests that students' experience and understanding of some of the routine practices that affect their daily lives – seating and grouping arrangements are one such area of expertise – have a very great deal to contribute to teachers' understanding of the same practices.

There are several examples in the case studies of the enhanced engagement of students when the curriculum they experience is made personally meaningful to them. A mathematics lesson on probability, at William Shakespeare, was described as a 'human situation' because of the way the teacher allowed 'the abstract content of the lesson to be discovered through an exploration of students' personal experience' (p. 148). There are enormously exciting possibilities to consider here: what might happen if a whole subject area, or even the curriculum as a whole, could be threaded through with personal meaning? What part might students play in the construction of such a curriculum? And the same sorts of questions and possibilities would open up if we were to consider assessment practices across a school as a site on which to develop person-centred approaches. The recent comprehensive review of research evidence by Black and Wiliam (1998) is a source of encouragement here, particularly in its emphasis on the relationship between formative assessment by the teacher and self-assessment by pupils.

> This link . . . is not an accident – it is indeed inevitable . . . Self-assessment by pupils, far from being a luxury, is in fact an essential component of formative assessment.
>
> (Black and Wiliam, 1998, pp. 9–10)

Black and Wiliam's review holds out the promise of improved teaching and learning in all classrooms where dialogue replaces question and answer routines and where teachers and learners together create

> a classroom culture of questioning and deep thinking in which

pupils will learn from shared discussions with teachers and from one another.

(Black and Wiliam, 1998, p. 13)

The concept of personal experience has, we believe, an important part to play in the construction of such a learning community. In sketching these possibilities for development, we are inviting teachers to re-consider and reconstruct what counts as legitimate knowledge and information on which to act in the thousands of decisions that are made day by day in schools and classrooms. We are arguing that teachers who use their knowledge of students' personal experiences, and of their own, will have an enriched understanding. The insights gained by recognising the 'person within the student', and the 'person within the teacher', strengthen the individual's capacity to act in the best interest of those persons, to draw on the professional values of solidarity and commitment and to make humane and empathetic responses to the demands of institutional life.

Conclusion

Throughout the fieldwork period, when researchers, students and teachers had many opportunities to discuss and debate their experiences and aspirations, it was clear that everyone involved in the project could articulate, to a greater or lesser extent, his or her vision of the school as an inclusive community. What became even more apparent over that same period, and during the time taken for thinking and analysis within the university team, was that these visions were unrealised, these schools were uninhabited. The schools and classrooms we had visited and observed exist in the real world, not in visionary imaginings. They are the constructs of living, fallible people, who are committed to improving them. So the findings of the research project must be applicable to the continuing, co-construction work that teachers and students are already doing, in the everyday world in which they teach and learn, rather than being read as an endorsement of the visions that motivate them to persevere in their undertakings.

The truly inclusive school, where exclusion has become a redundant option, is not to be achieved by perfecting the specification of a vision, but by a particular kind of work – the construction of personal meaning, the making of human sense – the work that is undertaken by teachers and students together. In this chapter we have tried to identify the key characteristics of the work that we saw in progress in the case study institutions, and to suggest ways in which it could be developed in the future.

11 Research as development

Introduction

In this chapter the focus shifts to reflection on the research process, with particular emphasis being given to the experience of being a participant in the PASE research project. It is here that we revisit some of the aspirations which guided the early development of the project and attempt to draw out the lessons from this experience that can guide future work. To what extent have we succeeded in living up to our aspirations? What, if any, were the benefits to the participating schools? What problems have arisen that might be avoided in the future if we, or others, undertake similar studies? We are reporting largely on the teachers' perspectives but also include the perspective of the university-based researchers in a separate section at the end.

The bulk of this chapter is devoted to the analysis of data gathered through a focus group held in the late spring of 1999, well after the work reported in this book was completed. The focus group was conducted by two members of the university research team and was attended by representatives from three of the institutions that took part in the study. The focus group was a free-flowing discussion loosely structured around five major questions:

- how has the project affected what has happened in the schools?
- how effective was the project in terms of its aspirations for collaboration and partnership?
- to what extent did the project live up to people's expectations?
- which aspects of the project were experienced as 'successful' and which aspects 'unsatisfactory'?
- what do participants see as likely and desirable ways to build on and extend the project in the future?

Some reference is also made in this chapter to issues that emerged from another meeting with the university research team attended by representatives from three schools, in the summer of 1999. Overall, this chapter draws upon data from four of the project institutions. It is an incomplete account, but we believe that the two meetings raised many issues of interest to the theme of research partnerships with schools.

In many ways this analysis of the research process echoes and reinforces findings of the study itself, by highlighting the ways in which the private and personal aspects of engagement relate to the wider public and formal aspects of school life. In particular, this chapter will show how the benefits to individuals from engaging in the research process were not necessarily matched by benefits to the school as a whole. In order to define and elaborate on this and other insights, this chapter will present an analysis of the accounts given by this small group of staff of the costs and benefits of their involvement with the project. This will be undertaken within the context of consideration of the intentions underpinning the project.

Before reporting on this data, it is necessary to digress briefly in order to remind readers of some of the key ideas underpinning our approach to the research.

What we wanted to avoid: the researcher as hunter

It is salutary to consider the extent to which social research can be seen as similar to the act of hunting. For educational researcher-hunters, teachers, students and schools can be seen as the game. Sometimes, the hunters will be satisfied with the meat of statistical tables, or other already processed information; at other times the researchers are committed to the 'capture' of data from schools and classrooms *in vivo*. Members of the school community are attracted to the project by claims that it will benefit them in some way. The school then admits the researchers, who hunt for data before departing, sometimes leaving behind them a bewildered set of victims. Staff groups may even feel diminished by the process, and exploited.

We wanted to avoid the excesses of this caricature, not least because we wanted participation in the research project to be enriching for the schools.

An alternative approach: the researcher as agriculturist

The research methodology, it will be recalled, was conceived as a device for both identifying and promoting positive alternatives to school exclusion. It emphasised the importance of partnership as the defining characteristic of the relationship between the outside (university based) researchers and the staff in the fieldwork institutions. This differs from the traditional roles of researcher and subject. In a partnership, it is argued, the specific roles adopted by the parties involved are not pre-formed, but are negotiated. For example, in the project reported here, in some instances the data gathering was undertaken by members of the university team, at other times by staff and pupils in the fieldwork institutions. In this way our approach also differs from traditional teacher-led action research, which tends to involve school staff alone in researching their own practice. Our study engaged us in a limited form of partnership in that many aspects of the project were pre-formed, before the schools and college were recruited and negotiation with the staff group took place. The university researchers initiated the research project itself, the finance and the broad themes of the enquiry.

In rejecting the hunting metaphor, we are drawn towards a more agricultural perspective to describe our approach. Rather than being preoccupied with the capture of data we were driven by a desire to cultivate and nurture, intending to leave the institutions with which we worked enriched by the experience and in a position to further promote their own growth.

The chief characteristics of this approach, it has been shown, lie in the way in which the research agenda is dictated both by the on-the-spot concerns and needs of the school-based participants, as well as the broader, sometimes theoretical, concerns of external researchers. The intention behind such an approach is to ensure that the project is 'owned' equally by the two parties and, therefore, is developed and shaped by their sometimes different concerns. This maximises the utility of the research by closely associating it with key professional concerns and needs; it, therefore, combines high relevance with practical problem solving.

In the following sections of this chapter we explore the extent to which the project lived up to these aspirations.

Research is difficult

Making time for research

It has been recently suggested that British professional educational researchers are an expensive luxury; that their functions could be carried out, more effectively, by practising teachers in schools and the inspectors employed by the Office for Standards in Education (OFSTED) (Woodhead, 1998). The teachers who participated in this study did not share this view. For them the presence of the university research team served an enabling function, without which the research would never have become a reality. One teacher, when asked the question 'what helped or hindered the research process for you?' replied, laconically: 'Teaching hindered it.'

Behind this response is the widely shared view that while many staff in schools felt a commitment to the aims of the research, and even a desire to engage with it, the day to day practicalities of carrying out research in addition to all their existing professional functions created considerable difficulties. The project did allocate funds to release staff from teaching duties, and this was seen by some teachers to be essential: '[We] couldn't have done without it.' For some teachers, however, the allowance for supply cover did not meet their needs. For one teacher, it would have been preferable to have the services of an administrative helper.

Differences in the use of supply cover might be accounted for in terms of variety of circumstances in the schools, the roles of individual staff and the precise nature of their involvement in the research. For example, the provision of supply cover is likely to be of less value to a teacher whose duties are mainly managerial and administrative than it is for teachers who spend most of their time teaching. Also, the availability of appropriately qualified supply staff may vary from school to school. Furthermore, in our study, schools differed not only in terms of the precise form that the research took, but also in terms of the involvement of staff in data gathering, leading to some staff in some schools having a higher time commitment to the project than staff in other schools.

The result was that the take up of supply cover was erratic, with one school taking advantage of their full entitlement of fifteen teacher days over the year, while other schools did not use all the supply cover allocated. This reflects the difference between the ways in which primary and secondary schools work and the different roles of the teachers involved. Providing this particular form of support did not turn out to be as useful for some as for others and so affected the roles the different partners adopted in data collection. The mode of partnership was largely dictated by what was possible in the day to day life of that school rather than by a theoretical model.

Expertise

Although some of the school personnel involved in the project were themselves enthusiastic and skilled researchers, there was also a sense that the members of the university team provided an important resource in terms of research expertise. One school-based participant put it this way:

> I am not sure that teachers ever make good researchers. I don't know a teacher who would actually know how to set it out: doing a piece of research. And I cannot imagine that we as a school could have come up with the systematic approach that you [the university based researchers] brought.

Another gave the following response:

> You [university researchers] bring in a wealth of experience and expertise . . . and what I think we all value, and me in particular . . . was the incisiveness of the perceptions that you [university researchers] . . . to what was going on. And it helped us see the wood through the trees. And without that collaboration, and without your understanding of what was going on, that wouldn't have happened.

This expertise was utilised in different ways in different settings, with university staff often taking a lead in developing ideas about what ought to be researched into feasible research plans. This sometimes involved the development of questionnaires, or the design and carrying out of interviews with staff and students. In some cases quite innovative methods were employed, such as the compilation of a video diary and the development of a programme of student interviews conducted by the students themselves. Where university staff carried out interviews, schools benefited in two ways. First, it saved time for members of the school based team, and, second, it helped to reassure interviewees that their contribution would be anonymous.

It was also felt that the involvement of experienced university researchers, through their research expertise, gave additional credibility and support to staff in schools seeking to address the group of problems which were the focus of the project:

> because it was the School of Education, it wasn't just me or somebody else wanting to implement change . . . it was someone out there who was there to help us through it who perhaps had more of an advantage than I had by academic authority, and, therefore, it was going to give it some credibility really. Helping us through it, instead of just mainly swimming around and not knowing where we were going to go.

Impetus

As we have already noted, having the will and interest to carry out research in schools is one thing; having the time is another. Some of the time, in some schools, the research project became yet another burdensome task in what for all participating staff was an already overcrowded work schedule. Having said this, it is clear that the research was seen as an important task in the long term, which made the short term inconvenience worthwhile. The problem in schools seems to be that long-term objectives are often overshadowed by more immediate imperatives. For staff involved in the PASE project, being part of a larger initiative, and, therefore, subject, to a degree, to a broader timetable and accountability structure that went beyond the school, meant that the project was given added status, and thus could become a priority:

> We need that impetus from outside to get us focused on it . . . We did find it very helpful when X and Y came in, because it said we've got to get this ready for them . . .

> It was good to have you [the university researchers] there because . . . [I don't know] how much we would have got on with it et cetera, et cetera – [we would probably have] left it on the back burner a bit longer. It was helpful having you there to help you [that is us] through it.

In some cases the external deadlines were seen as providing support to school staff who wished to make the project a high priority:

> Having people coming [from the university] was very, very helpful. To be focused. A bit of support.

Unfortunately, there is a down side to relying on external stimuli for impetus: once the stimulus is removed the impetus slows. This was a particular problem for some participants:

> I just feel we need a bit of help from outside to be able to do that [carry on meeting with other members of the project team], because we can always find excuses not to meet, and quite genuine excuses.

This sense of slowing down is related to a sense of dissatisfaction with the way in which the project as a whole seemed, from some teachers' perspectives, simply to fade from view, without any sense of closure:

That's one thing people in my school keep saying to me: 'what's happening to it?' [the project]. . . It's just that we've lost a bit of impetus now, because we were waiting to get going again, and I think some of the staff feel, well, we did this, and we got some good stuff out of it; we've done this, that and the other, but we haven't ever seen an overview or had any feedback really; just left in limbo a little.

Here there is a further indication of the university team's failure to live up to its aspirations. This can be interpreted, partly at least, in terms of the dissonance which inevitably exists between the work rhythms of schools and universities. The processes of analysis and writing up, which were largely appropriated by the university staff, required them to be absent from the research settings for what, to some school-based colleagues, seemed an inordinate amount of time. The eagerness of some school-based colleagues to maintain the impetus of the project and to move immediately on to further developments, was sometimes undermined by the absence of their source of impetus. The university staff, meanwhile, were working hard to complete the analytical phase of the project while also trying to secure further funding to continue the project. Again, it seems as if there was insufficient communication between the university and school-based members of the team about these issues.

Research is messy

It is tempting to think of research as a sequential, linear and above all a rational process, in which plans are made, data gathered, and analysed, then findings acted upon to the benefit of all. While broadly speaking this is a fair reflection of the ideal research process, the reality is usually altogether muddier, untidier and more unpredictable. This is illustrated by the candid responses we received to the question: 'Did the project meet your expectations?' One teacher responded:

I don't know, because to be honest, I don't know what my expectations were. I jumped on the bandwagon because I thought, 'we need to look at this issue.'. But I don't know what expectations I had about it.

A teacher from another school stated:

I would say that my expectations were met, and I'd share your view [i.e. the previous quotation]. [I'm] not sure what they were, but I would say they were met during the first term of the project, and then they were exceeded as things went on. As you picked things up and we could respond to them, I can remember thinking, 'yeah! This is really good and I am really getting stuck in here,' Whereas at first it was a little routine.

This point is further emphasised by a third teacher:

I think they [expectations] were discovered at the first conference [that is after the project had been running for several months].

The idea that participants retrospectively 'discovered' their expectations of the project seems, at first, counter-intuitive, but in many respects is an accurate representation of what happened during the course of the project. A way of interpreting this might be to consider the complexity of the research task from its inception, and to recognise that it was only through participation in the project that its potential for opening up new possibilities in relation to the problem of exclusion could be realised. By its very nature, there were many important aspects of the project that, at the planning stage, we were unable to specify, such as: who would be involved; which institutions would be involved (other than the university school of education); what would be the foci of research in those institutions; what research methods would be used. Although the university team spent many hours, over many meetings, developing the research framework, which was eventually presented in a whole day conference attended by representatives of all but one of the participating institutions, it is clear that the decision by teachers to volunteer their involvement was often motivated by first, the desire to look at the issue of exclusion and its prevention in their professional settings, and secondly, an unstated, but apparent trust in the possibility that working with the university team might prove to be fruitful.

It would be refreshingly simple to be able to report that the university team recruited research partners in schools and an FE college who were wholly committed to the research proposal that we had developed and that they shared a full and informed understanding of the kind of research enterprise which they were joining. The truth about (and behind) research, however, is rarely this simple. This is because the truth is usually different for different people.

From the earliest stages in the development of the project, the proposers of the research (that is the university team) debated the aims and methods that were to be pursued. Inevitably, the nature of group process being what it is, the final agreed outline of the project was probably perceived slightly differently by different members of the team. In turn, these differences of view were bound to interact with the different perceptions and motives that led staff in the fieldwork institutions to volunteer.

The outcome of this was the distinctive quality of each case study, a feature that suggests to us that the project developed through a genuine process of collaboration. This also means, however, that in reconstructing the experience of working on this project in the focus groups, and in the process of writing this book, the benefit of hindsight causes us to emphasise certain things and to diminish the importance of other things that may have seemed significant at the time. One of the participating teachers highlighted this point, in expressing regret that opportunities for sharing thinking and ideas between the different case study schools had not arisen more frequently during the project:

> It was only later that we discovered commonalities [between the case studies]. I think we are now in a position where we can engage in meaningful dialogue with each other, because those commonalities are now on the table. But in hindsight, it might not have been beneficial to meet in the way that we are thinking of [for the future] at the time.

In the remaining sections of this chapter we turn our attention to some of the positive and negative outcomes experienced by staff in the fieldwork institutions. We must bear in mind, however, that these were generated with the benefit of hindsight.

Some benefits from the research process

The feedback from the staff in the fieldwork institutions who participated directly in the study was by and large highly positive. They valued the experience both personally and, often, in terms of its outcomes for their institutions as a whole. It should be noted, however, that benefits to particular individuals did not always equate with benefits to other individuals or whole institutions.

Research as a resource to support progress

A strong theme to emerge from the focus group was the value that participating staff placed on the research project as a resource to be drawn on in various ways. The data and findings from the project were valued most often in terms of what they offered as a basis for further development. The forging of links with other institutions was seen as particularly valuable in this respect, although participants would have liked this aspect to have been more significant:

> It was a pity perhaps that certainly as far as I am aware we haven't been able to have a kind of opportunity to actually preview, if you like, what other people's experiences were before today. It would have been quite nice had there been some sort of arrangement whereby we would have met – even if it was for just half a day – just to have various bits and pieces on the table.

> I just have a nagging feeling that a half-day session – morning or afternoon – here, might have been quite pleasant for those participating schools. Where we could have sat down and just discussed how we all felt about how it was going. I would have loved to have known as it progressed precisely what was being done there [at other schools] and heard, 'and really, we are doing this!'

Underpinning these comments is a sense of the extent to which the project provided a valuable resource. Others agreed that there was enormous value in this form of interchange, and acknowledged that while it had not taken place as often as some would have liked, or in the form suggested above, such interactions had gone on. They cited the day conference at which interim findings from the project had been presented in the form of workshops led by members of the fieldwork research teams:

> That particular day [that is the research conference] I found it particularly important, because it was the one input that schools participating in it gave for each other. And I thought it was a very interesting day ... Yours [to one of the representatives] was on school records, wasn't it? Which, you know – that's a classic I think. All school records look like that.

This sharing and comparing of experiences and findings was seen by some to provide insights into how to approach certain school-based problems, as well as a kind of moral support, both in term of the project and in terms of the fact that others shared similar difficulties in their schools:

> I think that each little project that each school raised in actual fact was one of the elements about which we had a particular concern. And it was interesting to share them with each other and to have

come away and said, 'we thought we were the only ones struggling with that!' It was good to hear that someone else was [too] and [to hear about] the way they were trying to approach it.

For some participants the book of the project was expected to provide a focus for future developments, both in their own schools, and jointly with other institutions involved in the PASE project.

On a slightly different note, one participant referred to the way in which the school's involvement in the PASE project had contributed to the account the school gave of itself during an OFSTED inspection:

> What was very interesting – we just had an OFSTED inspection in October, and they [the OFSTED team] were fascinated by this [the school's involvement in the PASE project]. It kept them going for hours.

This benefit was not without its price, however:

> I thought, 'God! I've got to keep it going now, because of next time [i.e. the next OFSTED inspection].' To show that we had taken it forward.

There are several interesting points suggested by these comments. First, the fact that the school continued to be engaged with the project throughout the stresses and strains of an OFSTED inspection indicates the seriousness and importance with which the project was treated by staff in this school. Second, the sharing of the school's experience on the project with the OFSTED team suggests that the project was seen as providing a promising way forward in relation to school development. Finally, the intention to continue with the developments inspired by the project confirms the sense of value attached to the project by this participant.

Reflexivity

An important way in which the research project appears to have contributed to the process of development is through its effect of stimulating analytical thought among school staff. This in turn seems to have led to the generation of new perspectives on important issues. An important aspect of this process is the development of a critical awareness of the ways in which one approaches problems; in certain cases, this leads to an adjustment in the perspective taken. This active and critical consciousness of perspective can be summarised by the term 'reflexivity'. Below we explore some of the ways in which participants claimed the research process contributed to the development of a reflexive approach.

At a basic level, participation in the project was associated with the opening up of new possibilities in the search for positive alternatives to school exclusion. In some schools the new possibilities arose from interaction between staff from the different fieldwork settings. The idea that such a 'network' of project schools should continue to meet after the project was over was greeted with great enthusiasm:

> It [the continuation of the network] would be [of interest] to us. . . because it would help us focus, and help us to move forward. Cos I feel there are sort of possibilities – not solutions. But [we would] come up with some more positive strategies and [engage in] testing out [new ideas] really.

The conscious resistance to the idea that the study might produce 'solutions' is interesting here. Unfortunately, there is no explanation in the focus group data for this objection to the term 'solutions'. However, the shared understanding of the university based researchers in relation to this perception is that the notion of 'solution' implies the unrealistic possibility of reaching a point of closure on the issue of exclusion, to the extent that a once-and-for-all strategy could be identified that, when applied, would effectively, put an end to the practice. When we define exclusion in the broad terms chosen by the originators of the current study, this view is clearly inadequate. In this respect the 'solution' to the problem of exclusion resides in the processes by which situations that might, in some circumstances, result in exclusion are handled. Of course, an alternative interpretation might be that the fervour of the university-based researchers had resulted in the outlawing of the word 'solution'!

Central to the process of reflexivity is the need to be self-critical. This requires the ability to distance oneself from the issues under examination. The project appears to have aided the process of gaining distance, partly through the fact that participation in it required extended reflection, as opposed to rushing to take action. Another factor which was seen to have helped was the involvement of outside researchers, which entailed further discussion and exploration than would normally take place in the school setting:

> We didn't jump into something too big and say, 'well, this is it – we are not giving it too much thought beforehand.' I think [the project] has forced us to think of the issues; but the issues we thought were the issues, weren't the issues. And I think maybe a lot of the other

staff who are in school, you know [would benefit] from a bit more of this collaboration [with outside researchers], and you might go down the right line, rather than going down a cul-de-sac that you think is the issue, but actually isn't the issue. I think that was very important for us. I think we would have wasted a lot of time reorganising, or maybe doing things in school that we would not have necessarily benefited from. . . It helps us take a step back and look at it.

A teacher from another school added to this that participation in the project enabled some staff to: 'summarise, [engage in] reflection and view things as a cohesive whole, rather than bits and pieces.'

Another way in which the research contributed to reflexivity was by creating access to views and perspectives that were sometimes neglected. These included the views of a wide range of colleagues as well as those of students. It was the consideration of these wider perspectives that sometimes led research participants to review the ways in which they framed a particular problem. The process of reflection also helped some participants to feel more comfortable with the limits of their endeavours.

Staff in school, particularly in senior management are aware and are comfortable with understanding what our own limits are. We now know when we are taking on too much.

Change

The central purpose of the study was to generate understanding and practice that would contribute to positive change in schools. There was a powerful sense among the focus group members that participation in the project had contributed to positive changes in their schools. In some cases these changes were seen to have had a direct impact on the exclusion process:

Every member of staff has been involved in it [the project] and we have had quite a few changes that are there and appear to be working. And they work to a greater or lesser extent because the staff are making them work. And while some of them are saying 'get rid of him!' or 'have we set him up to get rid of him?' I mean, it is still the fact that they are making systems work that we actually changed as a consequence.

This teacher is referring to the way in which the staff revised their record keeping system in the light of the research, and began to place an emphasis on the individual life histories of students, rather than simply reacting to staff indignation about students' misdemeanours. She went on to state:

> There are still staff who, when there are difficult students, want you to get rid of them as soon as possible. Unless it's an absolute major incident. . . we say, 'well. . . we must look at ways of keeping them in. And if you look at the files, there is not the evidence to exclude that child.' . . . As we look at the files, there's nothing on that student. Nothing's been reported. Or there are only three in six months. That's no reason to chuck anybody out at all. Whereas before, without a file, it would be very difficult to say.

> [as a result of these changes we are] excluding less.

> There is more evidence base now therefore, it's throwing it back to a member of staff who is saying, 'get rid of them!' Where is the evidence that this child is so disruptive?

A teacher from another school described an increase in the flexibility with which students at risk of exclusion are handled by the school. He illustrated this with reference to two strategies:

> I'm using, with two Year 11 boys at the moment, distance learning. Where I have been able to persuade parents to keep them at home, and we will exchange work regularly on a Friday . . . So I suppose, if I were to state that we do not exclude, we do in that way, because we actually persuade parents.

The second approach concerns a Year 10 boy who had been subject to a fixed term exclusion and was at risk of permanent exclusion. Staff had detected a pattern in the boy's disruptive behaviour, noting that it tended to occur at the beginnings and ends of days. These times also often coincided with a particular subject on the boy's timetable which seemed to be particularly problematic for the boy. The teacher went on to describe the strategy that the school has adopted, in consultation with the boy's parents, to prevent these difficulties leading to permanent exclusion:

> The arrangement is, he goes to our [the heads of year] office if he doesn't arrive at registration time [where he waits until the end of lesson one] . . . and he goes directly to lesson two . . . and then, when he has finished his sessions, he goes home again. And that has worked.

And to be perfectly honest, I didn't expect it to. I actually gave him twenty-four hours . . . He's exceeded everyone's expectations.

Although, on the face of it, it might be argued that these are examples of 'informal exclusion', they are, in fact, presented as genuine alternatives to exclusion. It is clear from the teacher's testimony that it would not be difficult for the school to justify excluding the boy. What emerges from the second story is the idea that these strategies can be seen in a developmental light, in that they are part of an continuing process, the ultimate aim of which is to return the boy to full participation in the life of the school. The effect of the current intervention has been to reverse the decline in the boy's behaviour and to replace the conflictual relationship which had developed between the boy and staff with one characterised by co-operation. This appears to have had a desirable effect on the boy's view of himself and his motivation to behave well:

> He actually is a kid – whatever you said to that kid, he would not have followed [that is before the current strategy was identified]. He was given specific targets, when he came back in. And it was simple things, like actually sitting on a chair, and actually putting his hand up instead of calling out. And he has actually kept to those targets for weeks. I was really amazed. And he comes and shows me his [homework] diary, [saying] 'look, I've got these [positive teacher] comments written in my diary!' And he was so pleased for someone to see them. But before he wouldn't have taken any notice. He wouldn't have bothered to get staff to write things down.

The sense that the school has hit upon a successful strategy for dealing with this boy, and the delight that this teacher shows in having his negative expectations of the boy confounded, is palpable in these quotations.

A further change being contemplated by staff at this school is a restructuring of the school day in order to reduce the period of delay between registration and the first lesson of the day, caused by a whole school assembly. The intention is to replace this assembly with year group assemblies later in the day. This illustrates the way in which a reflexive approach to problems affecting individuals can lead to the identification of wider-scale problems, in this case across the institution as a whole.

Another positive outcome was related to the quality of communication within the pastoral team. They reported that the style of reflexive working that the project had demanded had been adopted by the team in their routine work:

I think it [the PASE project] has affected the way we, as a pastoral team, work. Because we do [now] talk about life histories. And we say, 'hang on!' before we decide what to do with a student. We need to check what's gone on before, and which strategies have been used et cetera. We do talk about students, which we didn't do before.

This theme of staff behaviour changing in ways that reflect the reflexive approach was mentioned a great deal by one teacher; the important issue was the extent to which other staff had taken on the desired approach.

Valuing human activities

Another important reported effect of participation in the project was how human activities were given value. This effect can be clearly seen in some of the positive outcomes already reported; however, there were two specific, and clearly very important, aspects of school experience that were seen to have been given value through the project. First it was clear that staff felt valued and listened to during the project, both as researchers and researched.

Teachers sometimes feel that nobody listens to them . . . I think they were pleased to have that time with someone [that is when they were interviewed].

It was suggested that the presence of an outside research team was beneficial in this respect:

Just having a research team in and around the school. Teacher colleagues actually appreciating [that]. . . someone has come to listen to their point of view and it is going to be represented somewhere.

Another teacher referred to the intellectual stimulation that staff in the school experienced through the project saying: 'It is not often that teachers get the opportunity to be intellectually stimulated in the way that they have been.'

The second major area where values were perceived to be affirmed was in relation to pupils. The focus of the search for positive alternatives to school exclusion inevitably brought thinking and talking about individual pupils to the fore:

I think the other thing is that it helped re-focus on the child . . . the needs of the child. It comes back to my life history thing. What are the needs of that child and how do we meet them?

The word 're-focus' is significant here. Teachers in this study did not need a research project to introduce them to the idea that pupils are important. However, as we have already noted, the complexity, multiplicity and weight of the everyday demands on teachers and schools sometimes makes it difficult to maintain one's priorities. One effect of the project, therefore, was to give staff in schools a reason and structure for rediscovering individual pupils as priorities, and to examine the extent to which pupils themselves can contribute to the process of inclusion.

Some difficulties in the research process

The process of research in schools is regrettably not always as straightforward or positive as the outcomes just described would suggest, although there is a dearth of literature dealing with this subject. An exception to this is the collection of papers edited by Walford (1991). Of these, Mac an Ghaill's account of carrying out research in multiracial educational settings is the most pertinent to our intention in this chapter. An important aspect of Mac an Ghaill's paper is his concern with the collaborative quality of the research relationship he developed with the teachers in his study, and how, according to their own verbatim accounts, this motivated staff to co-operate with the research. Their accounts compare their willing co-operation with Mac an Ghaill and their hostility towards a previous researcher whose presence they had found intrusive. As a result they had 'made things up' in answer to her questions, which they felt, were inquiring into things that were 'none of her business' (Mac an Ghaill, 1991, p. 115). Mac an Ghaill goes on to report that the two 'key participants' who aided his work:

> informed me that my anti-racist stance within Connolly College was of primary significance in their deciding to participate in the ethnography.
>
> (Mac an Ghaill, 1991, p. 115)

This reference to the importance of shared value positions resonates with aspects of the PASE project in interesting ways, as the following section demonstrates.

Research and differences of viewpoint: polarisation

As the preceding sections of this chapter illustrate, there was a strong sense among focus group members that the project had had a positive effect on their schools. However the process of research also caused some difficulties for both the school and the university partners. One representative in the focus group voiced some of these. This teacher was clearly highly committed to the aims and values of the project, and gave every indication of having found the experience of participation highly enriching from a personal point of view. He was also able to report that some of his colleagues had also found the project rewarding. However, a major theme of his account was the extent to which the research process had highlighted divisions between different members of the school staff:

> I think there's a feeling that lessons were learnt, and effective practice was seen. . . [but] positive action didn't necessarily follow that, not because impetus ran out, but [for] number of reasons. There are staff who say, 'we'd like to try to do this.' And there are staff who said, 'well, we tried that'. . . . So the differences are becoming much more obvious.

Though he is clear to stress that these differences in viewpoint were present before the research project, he also claims that the project has led to these differences becoming more visible. This was an important ethical issue for the research team. How does one deal constructively with differences becoming very visible between colleagues, when previously these colleagues had co-existed knowing there were differences but were content to leave them shadowy or unspoken? From his well-informed perspective on the process of change in the context of school development, Fullan describes a similar process:

> The difficulties in the relationship between external and internal groups are central to the problem and process of meaning. Not only is meaning hard to come by when two different worlds have limited interaction but misinterpretation, attribution of motives, feelings of being misunderstood and disillusionment on both sides are almost guaranteed.
>
> (Fullan, 1982, p. 74)

Fullan describes the differences that emerge when internal and external groups try to work together; the participant in the PASE project is saying that these same processes operate between sub divisions of the internal group. The feelings of being misunderstood and the attribution of motive referred to by Fullan can also be seen in the following quotation from the same teacher:

> It's difficult to say how – whether things would have been polarised anyway. But the fact that there is a core staff who can see that the way that we were working was effective, and now we are not able to work in that way for a number of reasons. You've got the somewhat more cynical sort of teachers who are always blaming the kids. [They] are becoming more and more vociferous, so that the people who were committed to this project feel that they've lost some sort of interest and credibility to push their point of view.

Research and anxiety

Another issue raised was the potential for the research project to create anxiety within the whole staff group.

> I was very struck. . . after the first conference here, when you [the university research team] asked for interest from any schools. And I went back to my school and said, 'I volunteered [us for] this.' I was very struck by the fact that there were some people – key people – who felt intimidated by the fact that we were actually going to work with people from here [that is the university school of education].

In a climate of accountability there is bound to be anxiety about the scrutiny that will result from inquiring into practice and displaying the findings, even when one has chosen to take part in such a process. In addition, the speaker seems to be suggesting that there are issues of power and status in joint working with a university: the university group here is accorded a status that is seen as intimidating by some staff.

Disappointment

There was also, regrettably, a sense of disappointment felt by some staff, in some of the participating schools. It is clear that in spite of our best intentions there were those who felt that the research process had been exploitative.

> Some staff felt the research dragged on. . . [and they are saying:] 'So what. They [the university researchers] have got what they wanted, and now, what is going to happen?' And although I explained the

fact that they were waiting [to receive funding] for the second phase
. . . that, for some staff, wasn't really enough. Because, after all, 'they
have got what they wanted, and that's the data, and with a book
coming out. Who is going to benefit, but them?'

In some ways these emotional responses are well justified and compre-
hensible. The involvement of university staff in research activity in the
fieldwork settings had come to an end as soon as the financial support
had ended. Although the staff directly involved in the project were aware
that this would happen, they had also been told that the university team
was confident of achieving further funding. In other ways there is
evidence that some of the expectations held by school staff of the research
process were unrealistic.

Finally, it is important to mention briefly the role of school students
in this research. Although they were an explicit focus of the research from
the outset, it has to be admitted that in some schools they remained
largely the objects of the research. There were schools in which students
did participate as data collectors; however we neglected to offer students
the opportunity to comment on their perceptions of the research process.
No students' representatives were invited to the focus group meeting.
Future studies of this kind should make provision to correct this
deficiency.

The university team perspective

This section raises some issues related to partnership work from the
perspective of the university-based research team. Many of the issues
raised by the participants resonated with us: the fear of making things
worse; the desire to make the research less messy; the struggle with ethical
issues; and the awareness that the reality of different rhythms and work
demands weakened the collaboration we aspired to. However, as outsiders
to the schools, there were also certain aspects that we were aware of which
may not have been so significant for those working on the inside.

Teachers under pressure

At times we were very aware that the collaborative model we had
designed made heavy demands on teachers already under pressure.
Meetings with the university team were often held at the end of the
school day and were in addition to teachers' already busy schedules. Our
concerns to negotiate the detail and ethics of the research process were
often in tension with the desire not to overload our colleagues in the

schools. At times, debating the finer points of research methods felt like a luxury and had to be foregone. We wanted to foster ownership, but, at the same time, we wanted to offer our services as data collectors so that the demands on the teachers were not too heavy. As has already been shown, offering time in the form of money for supply cover is not a simple answer to this dilemma. The relationship between the pressure the teachers were under and our desire to be helpful by taking responsibility for different aspects of the work, had unanticipated effects on the partnership relationship, as some of the participants recognised.

Different voices, different messages

There were many different voices contributing to this research project: the voices of students, staff in the research groups in the schools, as well as those not in the group, and the university research team. There were many different messages being received since different colleagues had different concerns and there were sometimes tensions between these messages. Senior managers were sometimes appropriately preoccupied with running a tight ship; other staff were preoccupied with expressing feelings during a confidential interview that they felt unable to express in the form of the staff meeting or staff room discussion. Teachers seemed to experience a range of feelings over the different stages of the process. They felt relief at being listened to, but also at times showed concern about being overheard or at expressing dissenting points of view. One young teacher exemplified this position, concluding a long interview very solemnly and quietly with the words: 'Well I don't know if it's right, but it's what I really think.'

There seemed to be an understandable desire in some teachers to be on their best behaviour, to present a good view of their work and to get it 'right'.

The university team was the conduit for all these voices and so we heard more than other people engaged in the project. In listening to these different voices, usually in private rather than in public, we had to try to fulfil our responsibilities to partners in the research in ways that would not make life more difficult for our partners in schools when we left. We had joined a community and so had responsibilities to the ongoing life of that community, as well as to the democracy of the research process. We had also committed ourselves to the principle of the research project being developmental. While much case study research aims to be representational, we aimed to facilitate the staff in their development of positive alternatives to exclusion from school.

Fulfilling these responsibilities created a number of dilemmas for the research team. For example, anonymity was harder to sustain since we were working so closely with our partners. There was some data, particularly on students, which we chose not to use since the students would have been easily identifiable. We also had to wrestle with the presentation of data that could have amplified conflict rather than fostered a constructive engagement with the emerging themes (the discussion of the dilemmas in Chapter 3 is a good example of this). Engaging in research as development meant that data was not the only priority. Our involvement also raised expectations. Both staff and students told us about matters on which they hoped to see action. Our role as researchers rather than actors meant that we were inevitably going to disappoint some expectations.

Living with loose ends: withdrawal and ending

It could be said that endings are always less neat and tidy than most people would hope for. The university team found the issues around withdrawal and ending difficult, not least because of the their financial implications. We had hoped to secure funding for a second phase of the research almost immediately and this meant that the official ending of our work was delayed, while we were in constant hope of a new beginning. Consequently, our withdrawal was more confused than we had anticipated. We had to accept being good-enough researchers and collaborators, which entailed living with loose ends, and leaving unfinished business behind us in some of the schools.

Conclusion

In revisiting the aspirations that we declared at the beginning of our study, we have to admit that they have not been entirely met. There are, however, in all the case study schools many indications that the project was an extremely worthwhile experience. Our concern is that future studies should build on these both positive and negative evaluations to create increasingly more effective and rewarding collaborations between university and school based researchers. As others have written, we have to live with the messiness of real world research (Robson, 1993) but we end with the hope that our collaborative venture, for all its short comings, has still been good enough to move the discussion and practice of partnership research. In particular we hope that future research, conducted by ourselves and others, will help to refine and elaborate the model of research as development that we have explored in this project.

Endnote
Looking forward

When we embarked on the research described in this book, our intention was that there should be a second phase to the work. In the first phase, our principal objective was to document the thinking that underpinned the work that schools were already doing to build positive alternatives to exclusion. We also planned to draw on this data, and the creative insights of our partners in the schools, to identify further scope for constructive action to help reduce and prevent exclusion. Our expectation was that, in phase two, the research would then focus upon how schools could actively use the ideas arising from phase one to develop their inclusive practices.

In Chapter 9 and Chapter 10, we have summarised the main findings arising from phase one, including some possibilities for further constructive action which these findings have helped us to identify. In Chapter 9 we outlined a set of frameworks that can be used by teachers and other educators to help identify their own priorities for development work in their particular professional contexts. These frameworks provide a resource for review and reflection, which can support on-going inquiry and development work. In Chapter 10, we identified one key area – personal experience – which our case studies, taken together, strongly suggest should be a major focus for further development work.

Pursuing this key concept of personal experience, we are now at the stage of seeking funding for phase two of the research in which we hope in particular to explore, with staff in schools, what happens when teachers and pupils make a conscious effort to focus on their own and one another's personal experience in learning and teaching, and take active steps to enhance that experience, individually and collectively. Our working hypothesis is that, in the development of an inclusive and harmonious school community, a conscious focus on personal experience will make a qualitative difference in the lives of all involved. The second phase of the project will be designed to build on and develop the insights gained so far with respect to the importance of personal experience.

We have already discussed, in Chapter 10, some possible ways in which schools might choose to take up and pursue a focus on personal experience, by developing innovatory practice in, for example, classroom organisation, discipline, curriculum, pedagogy or assessment. It would not be not appropriate here to go into more detail about our plans for the next phase of the research. Our purpose is simply to highlight the need for – and reiterate our commitment to – making research work for practice. This means taking steps to ensure that 'findings' of projects such as ours are fed back into the structures of education at a number of different levels, so that they can be of direct and immediate benefit to staff and pupils. We believe that a second, explicitly developmental phase is a necessary follow-up to the research we have already done. Only in this way can we bridge the traditional divide between research and practice; only if this is done, in the context of our own topic, can we ensure that research serves practice by contributing to the on-going task of building schools as harmonious communities in which exclusion can increasingly become a redundant option.

Notes

7 William Shakespeare upper school

1 Much of the background information on this school is taken from a document entitled 'Head teacher's statement' which was prepared by the current head teacher for the OFSTED inspection which took place in 1996.

2 The consistency of the reports suggests that this is a form of 'Assertive Discipline', a behaviouristic approach to discipline developed by Lee Canter (Canter and Canter, 1976).

References

Ball, S. (1993) 'Education Policy, Power Relations and Teachers' Work'; *British Journal of Educational Studies,* 41, 2, pp. 106–21.

Berlak, H. and Berlak, A. (1980) *Dilemmas of Schooling*, London: Macmillan.

Black, P. and Wiliam, D. (1998) *Inside the Black Box. Raising Standards through Classroom Assessment*, School of Education: Kings College London.

Blair, M. and Bourne, J. (1998) *Making the Difference: Teaching and Learning Strategies in Successful Multi-ethnic Schools*, Sudbury: DfEE.

Blau, G. and Gullotta, T. (1996) *Adolescent Dysfunctional Behavior*, Thousand Oaks, Calif./New Dehli/London: Sage.

Blyth, E. and Milner J. (1996) *Exclusion from School:Interprofessional Issues for Policy and Practice*, London: Routledge.

Blyth, E. and Milner, J. (eds) (1999) *Improving School Attendance*, London: Routledge.

Booth, T. (1996) 'Stories of Exclusion: Natural and Un-natural Selection' in Blyth, E. and Milner, J. (eds), *Exclusion From School*, London: Routledge.

Booth, T. and Ainscow, M. (1998) *From Them to Us*, London: Routledge.

Bourne, J. *et al* (1994) *Outcast England: How Schools Exclude Black Children*, London: Institute of Race Relations.

Bruner, J. (1985) 'Vygotsky: A Historical and Conceptual Perspective' in J. V. Wertsch (ed), *Culture, Communication and Cognition: Vygotskyan Perspectives*, Cambridge: Cambridge University Press.

Bruner, J. and Haste, H. (eds) (1987) *Making Sense*, London: Routledge.

Canter, L. and Canter, M. (1976) *Assertive Discipline: A Take-charge Approach for Today's Education,* Seal Beach, Calif.: Canter and Associates.

Carr, D. (1991) *Educating the Virtues*, London: Routledge.

Castle, F. and Parsons, C. (1997) 'Disruptive Behaviour and Exclusions from Schools: Redefining and Responding to the Problem', *Emotional and Behavioural Difficulties* 2, 3, pp. 4–11.

Cooper, P. (1993a) *Effective Schools for Disaffected Students*, London: Routledge.

Cooper, P. (1993b) 'Field Relations and the Problem of Authenticity in Researching Participants' Perceptions of Teaching and Learning in Classrooms', *British Educational Research Journal* 19, 4, pp. 323-38.

Cooper, P. and McIntyre, D. (1996) *Effective Teaching and Learning: Teachers' and Students'*

Perceptions, Buckingham: Open University.

Cronk, K. A. (1987) *Teacher-Pupil Conflict in Secondary Schools: An Educational Approach*, London: Falmer.

Daniels, H., Visser, J., Cole, T. and Reybekill, N (1999) *Emotional and Behavioural Difficulties in Mainstream Schools*, London: DFEE.

Dearing, R. (1996) *Review of Qualifications for 16-19 Year Olds*, Middlesex: SCAA.

De Shazer, S. (1985) *Keys to Solution*, New York: Norton.

DFE (1995) *Final Report to the Department for Education : National Survey of Local Authorities' Policies and Procedures for the Identification of, and Provision for, Children who are out of School by Reason of Exclusion or Otherwise*, Canterbury: Christ Church College.

DFEE (1997) *Excellence for All*, London: Stationery Office.

DFEE (1999) *Draft Guidance: Social Inclusion: Pupil Support*, London: DFEE.

Farrington, P. (1990) 'Implications for Criminal Career Research for the Prevention of Offending,' *Journal of Adolescence* 13, pp. 93–113.

Fielding, M. (1999) 'Target Setting, Policy, Pathology and Student Perspectives: Learning to Labour in New Times', *Cambridge Journal of Education,* 29, 2, pp. 277–87.

Fisher, D. C. (1913) *A Montessori Mother*, London: Constable.

Fromm, E. (1956) *The Sane Society*, London: Routledge and Kegan Paul.

Fullan, M. (1982) *The Meaning of Educational Change*, New York: Teachers College Press.

Fullan, M. (1992) *Successful School Improvement*, Buckingham: Open University.

Galton, M. (1989) *Teaching in the Primary School*, London: David Fulton.

Galton, M. (1995) *Crisis in the Primary Classroom*, London: David Fulton.

Gilligan, J. (1976) 'Beyond Morality: Psychoanalytic Reflections on Shame, Guilt and Love' in Lickona, T. (ed), *Moral Development and Behaviour*, New York: Holt Rinehart and Winston.

Gittings, R. (1966) *Selected Letters and Poems of Keats*, London: Heinemann.

Golding, W. (1954) *Lord of the Flies*, London: Faber and Faber.

Grumet, M. (1988) *Bitter Milk*, Amherst: University of Massachusetts Press.

Hargreaves, A. (1998) 'The Emotional Politics of Teaching and Teacher Development: With Implications for Educational Leadership', *International Journal of Leadership in Education*, 1, 4, pp. 315–36.

Hayden, C. (1997a) 'Exclusion from Primary School: Children in 'Need' and Children with 'Special Educational Needs', *Emotional and Behavioural Difficulties* 2, 3, pp. 36-44.

Hayden, C. (1997b) *Children Excluded From Primary School: Debates, Evidence, Responses,* Buckingham: Open University Press.

Holmes, E. (1911) *What Is and What Might Be*, London: Constable.

Isaacs, S. (1932) *The Children We Teach*, London: University of London Press.

Keys, W. and Fernandes, C. (1993) *What Do Students Think About School?*, Slough, National Foundation for Educational Research.

Kinder, K., Kendall, S., Downing, D., Atkinson, M., and Hogarth, S. (1999a) *Raising Behaviour 2. Nil Exclusion? Policy and Practice*, Slough: National Foundation for Educational Research.

Kinder, K., Kendall, S., Halsey, K., and Atkinson, M. (1999b) *Disaffection Talks: A Report for the Merseyside Learning Partnership. Interagency Development Programme.*, Slough: National Foundation for Educational Research.

Limerick, B., Burgess-Limerick, T. and Grace, M. (1996) 'The Politics of Interviewing: Power Relations and Accepting the Gift,' *Qualitative Studies in Education* 9, 4, pp. 449–60.

Lovey, J., Docking, J. and Evans, M. (1993) *Exclusion from School: Provision for Disaffection at Key Stage 4*, London: David Fulton.

Mac an Ghiall, M. (1991) 'Young, Gifted and Black: Methodological Reflections of a Teacher/Researcher', in Walford, G. (ed) *Doing Educational Research*, London: Routledge.

Martin, J. R. (1992) *The School Home: Rethinking Schools for Changing Families*, Cambridge, Mass.: Harvard University Press.

Miller, J. C. (1982) *Training in Individual Guidance and Support*, London: Manpower Services Commission.

Munton, A., Silvester, J., Stratton, P. and Hanks, H. (1999) *Attributions in Action: A Practical Approach to Coding Qualitative Data*, Chichester: Wiley.

Nobel, A. (1991) *Educating through Art: The Steiner School Approach*, Edinburgh: Floris Books.

Noddings, N. (1992) *The Challenge to Care in Schools: An Alternative Approach to Education*, London: Teachers College Press.

Oliver, M. (1990) 'Post-Positivism, Paradigms and Power: Disabling Research or Researching Disability', Paper presented at the International Symposium, Normalisation and then? Social research about disability – setting the agenda for the 1990s, Stockholm.

Parsons, C. and Howlett, K. (1996) 'Permanent Exclusion from School: A Case where Society is Failing its Children' *Support for Learning* 11, 3.

Parsons, C. (1999) *Education, Exclusion and Citizenship*, London/New York: Routledge.

Pollard, A. (1987) *Reflective Teaching*, 3rd edn, London: Cassell.

Powney, C. and Watts, J. (1987) *Interviewing in Educational Research*, London: Routledge.

Pye, J. (1988) *Invisible Children: Who are the Real Losers at School?*, Oxford: Oxford University Press.

Reisenberger, A. and Crowther, R. (1997) *Further Education: Giving Young People a Newstart*, Bristol: Further Education Unit.

Rogers, B. (1990) *You know the Fair Rule: Strategies for Making the Hard Job of Discipline in School Easier*, London: Longman.

Robson, C. (1993) *Real World Research*, Oxford: Blackwell.

Rosser, E. and Harré, R. (1976) 'The Meaning of Trouble', in Hammersley, M. and Woods, P. (eds), *The Process of Schooling*, Milton Keynes: Open University.

Rudduck, J., Chaplain, R. and Wallace, G. (eds) (1996) School Improvement – What Can Pupils Tell us? London: David Fulton.

Rutter, M. and Giller, H. (1983) *Juvenile Delinquency: Trends and Perspectives*, Harmondsworth: Penguin.

Rutter, M. and Smith, D. (eds) (1995) *Psychosocial Disorders in Young People*, Chichester: Wiley.

Salmon, P. (1995) *Psychology in the Classroom: Reconstructing Teachers and Learners*, London: Cassell.

Salzberger-Wittenberg, I. (1996) 'The Emotional Climate in the Classroom' in Alfred, G. and Fleming, M. (eds) *Priorities in Education*, Durham: Fieldhouse Press/ University of Durham.

Schostak, J. (1983) *Maladjusted Schooling*, Lewes: Falmer Press.

Seligman, M. E. P. (1992) *Helplessness: On Development, Depression and Death* (2nd edn), New York: W. H. Freeman.

Smail, D. (1996) 'The Experience of School – Empowerment or Oppression?' in Alfred, G. and Fleming, M. (eds). *Priorities in Education*, Durham: Fieldhouse Press/ University of Durham.

Stirling, M. (1992) 'How Many Pupils are Being Excluded?' *British Journal of Special Education* 19, 4, pp. 128–30.

Stirling, M. (1996) 'Government Policy and Disadvantaged Children' in Blyth, E. and Milner, J. (eds), *Exclusion From School, Inter-Professional Issues For Policy and Practice*, London: Routledge.

Tannock, R. (1998) 'ADHD: Advances in Cognitive, Neurobiological and Genetic Research,' *Journal of Child Psychology and Psychiatry* 39, 1, pp. 65–99.

Tappan, M. (1998) 'Sociocultural Psychology and Caring Pedagogy,' *Educational Psychologist* 33, 1, pp. 1–22.

Tattum, D. (1982) *Disruptive Pupils in Schools and Units*, Chichester: Wiley.

Thornton, G. (1986) *Language, Ignorance and Education*, London: Edward Arnold.

Vygotsky, L. S. (1978) *Mind in Society*, London: Harvard University Press.

Vygotsky, L. (1987) *Collected Works*, London: Pellum.

Walford, G. (ed) (1991) 'Reflexive Accounts of Doing Educational Research', in Walford, G. (ed), *Doing Educational Research*, London: Routledge.

Watkins, C. and Wagner, P. (1987) *School Discipline: A Whole School Approach*, Oxford: Blackwell.

Willes, M. (1983) *Children into Pupils*, London: Routledge and Kegan Paul.

Winter, R. (1982) 'Dilemma Analysis: A Contribution to Methodology for Action Research,' *Cambridge Journal of Education* 12, 3, pp. 161–74.

Wood, D. (1988) *How Children Think and Learn*, Oxford: Blackwell.

Woodhead, C. (1998) 'Woodhead Attacks School Research.' *The Independent*, 23 July.

Young Minds (1999) Fact Sheet no.1, London: Young Minds.

Index